CELIBACY IN CRISIS

CELIBACY IN CRISIS

A Secret World Revisited

BY

A. W. RICHARD SIPE

FOREWORD BY RICHARD P. McBRIEN

Brunner-Routledge
NEW YORK AND HOVE

2/04

Published in 2003 by
Brunner-Routledge
29 West 35th Street
New York, NY 10001
www.brunner-routledge.com

Published in Great Britain by
Brunner-Routledge
27 Church Road
Hove, East Sussex
BN3 2FA
www.brunner-routledge.co.uk

Brunner-Routledge is an imprint of the Taylor & Francis Group.
Printed in the United States of America on acid-free paper.

Cover design: Scott Russo
Cover photo: Andre Burian/Corbis

10 9 8 7 6 5 4 3 2 1

Library of Congress Cataloging-in-Publication Data

Sipe, A. W. Richard, 1932–
    Celibacy in crisis : a secret world revisited / by A. W. Richard Sipe ;
foreword by Richard McBrien.
        p.   cm.
Includes bibliographical references and index.
    ISBN 0-415-94472-4 (cloth : alk. paper) — ISBN 0-415-94473-2 (pbk. :
alk. paper)
    1. Catholic Church—Clergy—Sexual behavior.   2. Celibacy—Catholic
Church.   I. Title.
    BX1912.9.S565   2003
    253'.252—dc21
                                                    2003009530

For
Father Frank O'Connor, S. J.
Who lives in Light and Truth
and
Jeffrey Anderson
Who goads other priests to do the same

CONTENTS

FOREWORD

For centuries the "secret world" of clerical sexuality has been securely closed off from public scrutiny, both within and beyond the Roman Catholic Church. If lapses from the code of celibate conduct came occasionally to public notice, church officials quickly dismissed them as aberrations, the priests in question were quietly reassigned, and the civil authorities (if they had an interest in the matter) were effectively neutralized. The secrecy came to an abrupt end in early January, 2002, when *The Boston Globe* exposed the first of many cases of sexual abuse by priests of that archdiocese—cases that were as much about the malfeasance of the local cardinal, archbishop and his top aides as they were about the predatory behavior of the priests.

In this revised and updated edition of his earlier, deservedly praised work, *A Secret World*, Richard Sipe does the Roman Catholic Church, its hierarchy, its many thousands of priests worldwide, and its increasingly well-educated and well-informed laity a real and distinct service. Now that the celibate cat is out of the bag, so to speak, there is a deep and pressing need for the kind of professional expertise and wisdom that Richard Sipe can provide—expertise and wisdom born not only of study and reflection, but also of years of experience as a priest and psychotherapist. Because of the efforts of persons like himself, there is hope that the "secret world" of clerical celibacy and sexuality will eventually be transformed into what he calls a "better world."

Until recently, clerical celibacy has not been studied in a sufficiently thorough and objective fashion. If the subject was broached at all in the past, the discussion was rarely, if ever, free of particular theological justifications. The literature on celibacy, Sipe points out, was almost exclusively inspirational and idealistic. In other words, of little or no practical value to priests, seminarians, or the church at large.

If Sipe is correct (and other social scientists as well as thousands of priests probably have more than a hunch that he is), celibacy simply does not work—at least not in the way that the Church believes and hopes it to work. The author concludes, on the basis of hundreds of interviews over many years with priests, sexual partners, and victims of sexual abuse, that at any one time, one-half of the priest population involve themselves with sexual activity of some sort. Competent reviewers of this book may legitimately challenge the author's method of arriving at this statistic and others like it, but none can credibly assert that the system of clerical celibacy is alive and well in the Roman Catholic Church, and functioning just as it was originally intended to a millennium ago.

One of the most important points that Richard Sipe makes in this book is that there are so-called ecclesiogenic factors that account for sexual abuse in the priesthood and that influence the practice of clerical celibacy across the board. Those factors prominently include the Catholic Church's official teaching and pastoral practice regarding human sexuality itself.

There is also, Sipe insists, an "ecclesiogenic neurosis" that regards sexuality and eroticism as taboo subjects and that bans all discussion of them. The Church's teaching is that every sexual thought, word, desire, and action outside of marriage (and some within, as, for example, the use of contraception) are gravely sinful and deserving of eternal punishment in Hell if the sin is not properly confessed and absolved before death. Although this moral doctrine is less and less credible for a growing number of Catholics, celibate priests are expected not only to teach and defend it, but also to adhere to it in their own lives—indeed, for *all* of their lives.

The most striking finding of *Celibacy in Crisis,* however, is also its most sobering. Basing his conclusion on years of close observation and clinical practice, Sipe proposes that only a tiny minority of Roman Catholic priests actually "achieve" celibacy and fully integrate it into their personalities and priestly lives. He estimates that at any one time only 2 percent of celibate clergy—some in religious vows, others in the diocesan clergy—can be said to have truly achieved celibacy, that is, they have successfully negotiated each developmental stage in their lives as human persons and as priests so that their celibate state can be described, for all intents and purposes, as "irreversible." Such priests, Sipe points out, are persons of "unusual inner resourcefulness," who possess "an independence of spirit . . . not overly dependent upon institutional props."

There is another 6 to 8 percent, he suggests, for whom the practice of celibacy is "firmly established" to the extent that it can be said that they have been gifted with the "clear charism of celibacy." These priests have "consolidated" the practice of celibacy to such a degree that it approaches the ideal achieved by the 2 percent, but includes "some missteps, fumblings, and even reversals in the past." It requires no mathematical dexterity to see that for the great majority of priests, celibacy either does not work at all or is vulnerable to frequent compromises of one sort or another.

Many might ask whether seminaries have been asleep at the switch. Is it not their responsibility to prepare young men not only for a life of priestly ministry but also for a life of total abstinence from sexual activity of any kind? Richard Sipe concludes that there is no correlation between sexual abstinence maintained during the years of seminary training and the individual priest's later celibate achievement. In fact, the seminary system "has not proved to be particularly successful in inculcating lifelong celibacy." It fails in three ways: by avoiding direct and open discussion of sexuality, by cloaking sex and celibacy in secrecy, and by providing no personal, explicit witness to celibacy, its struggles and its achievements, within seminary faculties and staffs.

But the author does not leave us without hope or a compelling ideal to pursue. That ideal, however, does not pertain to celibacy alone. It is a matter instead of human wholeness, of health and well-being, of psychic as well as sexual integration. Successful celibates are persons who have a noble cause to which they are strongly committed, effective bonds with a supportive community, vital intellectual and social interests, and a prayer-life that grows out of their personality and ministry rather than one imposed artificially, and in some traditionally stylized form, from the outside.

Such celibates have not only internalized but also de-sexualized their ties with ecclesiastical authorities. They refuse to look upon their bishops and religious superiors as father figures, nor upon themselves as their "sons." The successful celibate priest, in other words, has become his own man, in spite of a system that reinforces and rewards the opposite type of consciousness and behavior.

Those who read through to the end of this instructive and challenging work will know that its author carries no brief for the elimination of a celibacy that is freely chosen. Indeed, the themes found in the final chapter are of the sort that priests might hear at a well-structured and thoughtfully presented retreat. But other readers will lay that otherwise inspiring material alongside the data and conclusions sprinkled throughout the rest of the book, namely, that obligatory clerical celibacy is "achieved" or "consolidated" by about 10 percent of the clergy at most. What pertains to the rest has, until recently, been hidden from view, behind the veil of the "secret world" that was so abruptly torn open by the revelations of widespread sexual abuse within the Roman Catholic priesthood and of cover-ups by their bishops.

Richard Sipe properly eschews the role of an advocate in this important book. He has no wish to make the argument, on the basis of his many years of research, observation, and clinical practice, that the Roman Catholic Church should no longer require lifelong celibacy for its priests and that it should return now to the practice of the church throughout most of the first Christian millennium, when there were not only married priests but married popes and bishops as well. This practice remains in force today in the many non-Roman, but *Catholic*, churches of the East.

Sipe's self-imposed restraint, however, does not bind the author of this foreword. Obligatory celibacy and the church's official teaching on human sexuality are at the root of the worst crisis the Catholic Church has faced since the time of the Reformation. If the church is to resolve and transcend that crisis, it must address such issues as these in an objective and straightforward manner. Only then will this corrosive "secret world" give way to the "better world" toward which Richard Sipe and so many others in the church direct their labors and their hopes.

—Rev. Richard P. McBrien
Notre Dame University

ACKNOWLEDGMENTS

This book would never have materialized without the inspiration provided by the courageous work of the investigative Spotlight Team of *The Boston Globe*. Their work broke through the fortress of clerical denial that protected sexual abusers. It exposed the horror inflicted on unnumbered innocent minors and their families. Their service is lasting. No research studies could have generated the education they have provided to a nation that cares for its youth. Their challenge to moral leadership has inspired us all to rededicate our efforts to explaining the corruptibility of a culture—celibacy—that is capable of such tremendous good.

The sustaining friendship of a number of people who fight for the integrity of the celibate system, by holding its members accountable, has been indispensable to my spirit: Kelly Clark, John Manly, Sylvia Demarest, Lynn Cadigan and Kim Williamson along with Mike Rezendes are among those I owe the biggest debt of gratitude.

The editorial staff of Brunner-Routledge—George Zimmar and Shannon Vargo—along with Associate Publicist, Tooraj Kavoussi, have given me sound advice and warm support. I hope that the tone of the book reflects their spirit. Mick Spillane and T.J.Mancini are the best production team I have ever worked with. Marge Nelson has supplied the index for this book as she has for every other I have written.

All of the above deserve thanks. I reserve to myself any deficiencies the book might contain.

PART I
BACKGROUND AND CONTEXT

1

WHY STUDY CELIBACY?

His great subject was the relation of corruptible action to absolute principle; of worldly means to transcendent ends; of historical commitment to personal desire.

—Irving Howe

When a man kneels before the Pope, in the process of becoming a cardinal, he takes this vow in Latin:

> I, [name], cardinal of the Holy Roman Church, promise and swear to remain, from this moment and for as long as I live, faithful to Christ and to his gospel, constantly obedient to the Holy Apostolic Roman Church, to the Blessed Peter in the person of the Supreme Pontiff John Paul II and of his successors canonically elected; to preserve always in word and deed communion with the Catholic Church; *never to reveal to anyone whatever has been confided in me to keep secret and the revelation of which could cause damage or dishonor to the Holy Church*; to carry out with great diligence and fidelity to tasks to which I am called in my service to the Church, according to the norms of law. So help me Almighty God. (emphasis added)

> (Vatican Ritual; English translation by Baltimore Sun, Dec. 1994)

I was a monk for 18 years—a priest for 11 of them. When I began my initial studies for that career at age 13, I had no idea that I was entering into a secret world.

More surprising than that—shocking to me, in fact, as I look back at the age of 70—is the fact that it took more than half a lifetime to realize the depth and breadth of that secret world, and the tremendous implications it has for millions of lives.

I, along with many others, could not distinguish between *secrecy* and *confidentiality*. Confessional "secrecy" seemed to be the noblest

3

treasury of the church where sinful thoughts and acts could be stored for safekeeping.

Many have not yet solved the confusion between confidentiality and secrecy. Secrecy must be distinguished from confidentiality. "Confidentiality is a private personal and privileged communication that must be protected at great sacrifice (not only out of professional duty) because it is in the service of (and necessary for) personal transformation and growth. It may also be necessary to protect due process. Secrecy is a stance that reserves access to knowledge in the service of power, control, or manipulation." Secrecy is rationalized as the only way to avoid scandal.

Sex—and more precisely, celibacy—is at the core of the secret world.

One canon lawyer points out how essential celibacy is to the power system of the church:

> Celibacy holds the central role in the Roman rite regarding governance, ecclesiastical office, and authority. A person must be a *celibate* for the bishop to appoint or install him in a role of essential governance, an ecclesiastical office, or a position exercising principle authority. Negatively, once a man is released from the obligation of celibacy (laicized), canonically he is incapacitated to hold any office, function, or delegated authority. The bottom line is: celibacy is essential—key—for a man to hold a position of power and authority in the Western Rite of the Roman Catholic Church, validly and licitly (Patrick Wall, personal communication, 2002).

The value of this study lies in the questions that it addresses:

- What is celibacy?
- How is it really practiced by those who profess it?
- What is the process of celibacy?
- What is the structure of celibate achievement?

These questions are dangerous. Even examining them seriously threatens the stability of the secret system. They have a potential to disrupt—to cause chaos in any system dependent on secrecy for its image and power. The final two questions, however, address the inherent power in lived celibacy, and one avenue to strength and integrity.

In short, this is a search for a structural and dynamic model of an ancient practice that crosses cultural and religious boundaries. Although this study is limited to Catholic priests in the United States, the questions are meaningful to the understanding of celibate practice universally, including the Buddhist and Hindu traditions.

Any efforts to address questions about celibacy were greatly reinforced on January 6, 2002. Four Catholic journalists working for *The Boston Globe*—Walter Robinson, Matt Carroll, Sacha Pfeiffer, and Michael Rezendes—shattered the locks barring the doors to the secret world of the Roman Catholic priesthood that concealed the sexual abuse of minors by priests. The battering ram they used was not merely the report of individual sexual abusers, but documents that clearly demonstrated the operation of a *system* of support, concealment, denial, and deception that fostered abuse and intimidated victims (*Betrayal*, 2002).

Later Stephen Kurkjian and other writers joined the effort that resulted in seismic consequences with national and international consequences for the Catholic Church and beyond. Within six months the pope summoned all the American cardinals to Rome, and the United States bishops held a meeting devoted solely to addressing the problem of clergy sexual abuse. They set a policy of "zero tolerance" and began to reveal the names of known abusers to civil authorities. Lay people began demanding—to an unprecedented degree—accountability and transparency. Some bishops resigned when their past sexual activity was exposed.

The Vatican resisted the move toward American independence and civil justice. It countered with a set of guidelines that placed secret procedures, clerical control of investigations, and Vatican defense of the rights of clergy above any other considerations.

The initial focus of investigation and revelation had been Boston and the sexual abuse of minors. But the inevitable consequence of a peek into the secret world of Catholic clergy was uncontrollable. The tangle of questions about sex and celibacy had been raised. "What really, does celibacy mean?"

The dictionary definition of a *celibate* is simply an unmarried or single person. Religious celibacy implies complete sexual abstinence.

Those assumptions, although incomplete, will be sufficient to sustain the reader for initial consideration. A more precise definition will amplify and challenge incomplete notions.

In spite of the fact that celibacy has not been a constant tradition even in the Roman Catholic Church, there is a common *psychic presumption* of a "virginal" clergy that is reinforced even in the Jewish rabbinate. More than one psychologically sophisticated rabbi has told me that they are aware of this phenomenon among members of their congregations. This is especially evident in the celebration of any sacred service or in the recitation of sacred texts. Clerical acts and words need to be separated in the minds of the faithful from the sexuality of the minister, much as children must separate their parents from any sexual "contamination."

Questions about celibacy are not commonly asked, nor do they very often stir great interest. Some justification may help the reader understand why anyone would pursue such questions systematically for 40 years, and why the subject of celibacy should merit a reader's time and interest.

SEX/CELIBACY: BREAKING THE TABOO

My initial research spanned the quarter-century—1960 to 1985— that marked the "sexual revolution." We have all learned a great deal about and from sexual nature, expression, and sexual indulgence in those 25 years. However, there is also much to be learned about sexuality from sexual restraint and abstinence. C. S. Lewis noted that you learn more about an army by resisting it than by surrendering to it.

What better examples of sexual control are there than those who publicly profess a life full of meaning but devoid of sex—Roman Catholic priests? Yet information that would seem so easily accessible from every priest by the simple question—*What is your celibate/sexual adjustment?*—is shrouded in secrecy, denial, and mystery.

"Before the 1960s, celibates were presumed to have no sexuality. Any priest who showed signs of sexuality was considered at least strange," said a priest participant in a dialogue on the sexual maturing of celibates (Tetlow, 1985). Asking a priest about his celibacy is like asking a banker about his honesty—if one questions closely guarded and highly defended assumptions, insult, confusion, rage, and even chaos can result.

Carl Eifert, a lay spokesman for the National Conference of Catholic Bishops, asserted in an interview that statements by U.S. bishops on the issue of celibacy are "based on the assumption that priests are consistent in their adherence to their vows" (Niebuhr, 1989).

A priest spokesman for the same agency was typically defensive about the claim that "a substantial proportion of professed celibates do have a sexual life." He said, "Priests are humans and have feelings; but the great, great majority of priests that I know are faithful to their vows. I know hundreds and hundreds of priests—it's certainly not true." (Niebuhr, 1989).

That is not a passing assumption propagated by the church. In February 2000, Sr. Mary Ann Walsh, the current spokesperson for the United States Bishops Conference asserted on ABC TV that she believed that "Ninety-nine and 44/100s percent of priests keep their celibacy." When the interviewer asked her if she really believed that she reassured him and the national audience that she did.

My study looks for facts beyond all the assumptions—both positive and negative—about celibacy. There are equally unfair contrary suppositions surrounding celibacy, and not only among secular non-believers. One middle-aged priest, a poetic cynic, said, "Celibacy is like the unicorn—a perfect and absolutely noble animal. . . . I have read eloquent descriptions of it and have seen it glorified in art. I have wanted desperately to believe in its existence, but alas, I have never been able to find it on the hoof."

Priests who know "hundreds and hundreds of priests" often do not "know" the celibate/sexual adjustment of their closest friends because they do not want to. Attitudes of denial rule. Sexual adjustment is mostly secret, but an "open" secret, since a priest knows the truth, on some level, about himself *and* some others. A priest's celibate/sexual life becomes public through a scandal in which a pregnancy, a lawsuit, or an allegation comes to public attention.

Priests share the secret of their celibate achievement or compromise in the confessional. However, many priest informants revealed that they do not consistently confess what might be, at least technically, termed a transgression of the promise of celibacy, for example, masturbation.

Whereas confession *can be* accomplished in the dark and anonymously, spiritual direction and psychotherapy are two arenas where a priest can reveal his intimate lifestyle and deal openly, and yet in a privileged manner, with issues of sexuality. During the period of our study, priests increasingly talked more openly to friends or in small groups about their sexual struggles.

This shifting socio-sexual attitude made my study of celibacy possible. Psychiatry was the first legitimate and effective incursion into the secret celibate world in centuries. Men attempting to practice celibacy increasingly turned to the psychological sciences for help and understanding. Bishops and superiors did too. Individual revelations and collections of data penetrated the veil of secrecy. It was useful to those who wanted to understand sexuality better, and those who wished to live celibacy effectively. This shift provided the first window into the secret world of the celibate.

The sexual abuse crisis has kindled unprecedented public awareness of the sexuality of some priests and has cast a spotlight on the system of celibacy. The nature of the criminal and civil cases against priests and bishops has added a dimension of public scrutiny and measurability.

The ideal of celibacy has been gloriously extolled throughout history, just as it has been ingloriously ridiculed. However, it has never been examined in a way open to scientific research. This study helps open the door to more research.

There is no unseemliness in attempting to examine the secrets of celibate practice and achievement. In fact, Pope John Paul II, in speaking to journalists said, "The Church endeavors and will always endeavor more to be a house of glass, where all can see what happens and how it fulfills a mission" (*Baltimore Sun*, Jan. 28, 1984). He was speaking in a general sense, and not specifically about celibacy, but how could he exclude an element so vitally entwined with the priesthood? Personal celibacy is a public stance. Religious leaders and their own personal standards contribute significantly to the understanding of sexuality and sexual morality among their flocks. Certainly, the public witness and teaching of the clergy cannot be separated from their personal attitudes towards sexuality and the observance of their vow.

THE BROADER CONTEXT

Henry C. Lea wrote a classic 19th-century study of sacerdotal celibacy. He hoped that his study would be of interest to the general reader. ". . . not only on account of the influence which ecclesiastical celibacy has exerted, directly and indirectly, on the progress of civilization, but also from the occasional glimpse into the interior life of past ages afforded in reviewing the effect upon society of the policy of the church as respects the relations of the sexes" (Lea, 1884).

However, where Lea focused on the interior life of past ages, I focus on the current picture, but hold the same hope that he did. I invoke the broader context of celibacy and historical connections wherever I think they help the reader understand the aspects of celibate practice being discussed or wherever they might be of interest. Unlike Lea, I do believe that celibacy has *one* origin in the apostolic community, but I am well aware that it was not then nor in the first Christian millennium a universal requirement for the priesthood.

Celibacy should be viewed in its historical context to understand its relationship to ministry, and to delineate clearly what is a charism (spiritual grace) versus the discipline (church law). What is essential, what optional? Furthermore the current situation can be judged more accurately—even in the midst of its chaos—and guided to a sound resolution. Because sexual abuse of minors by priests is not the only element fomenting the celibate crisis.

In 1960, there were 53,796 Catholic priests in the United States and about 8,000 men in the final 4 years of their preparation for ordination. In 1985, 57,317 priests were recorded as active, with 4,063 men studying (Hoge, 1987, p. 229). If one looks at the priest population in 1934 (30,000), one cannot help but be struck by the steady progress in numbers between 1935 and 1965 (65,000) in glaring contrast to the plateau and decrease in total numbers between 1965 and

2002 (45,000). The leveling of the total priest population is another factor that made this study possible. The concomitant decrease in candidates for the priesthood, from 9,000 to 3,000, is at least in part due to a decline in the understanding and appeal of celibacy (Hoge, 1987, 2002).

THE STUDY: WHAT IT IS
AND WHAT IT IS NOT

There is currently a hot debate in clerical circles about a married clergy versus a celibate priesthood. I do not defend either position. The facts and analysis that follow can be used to support either view. They challenge partisans of both camps to a deeper understanding and clarification of their arguments (cf. Luhmann, 2002; Jaki, 1997; McGovern, 1998).

My work is based upon interviews with and reports from people who have firsthand knowledge of the celibate/sexual adjustment of priests. First of all, I consider priests who were in some form of psychotherapy either during inpatient or outpatient treatment. The clinical setting provides a tremendous advantage in gathering personal information because of the depth and duration of the observation. It is not merely the sexual behavior or the celibate ideal that is revealed or recorded, but the person—the history, development, and context of a life that can be observed and analyzed. Brief evaluations and longer treatment modalities have both contributed to the insights garnered for this study.

A word of caution is necessary for those who are unaware of psychotherapy or who have a bias against persons who enter it. To see those who use psychotherapy as "sick" and thereby dismiss them and their observations is like denigrating anyone who uses confession as merely a "sinner" who has nothing to teach us about values and virtue. Also, one who is sexually active, even if vowed to celibacy, may indeed be beset by a conflict of values but may be "healthy" sexually.

Other informants were priests but not patients. They shared information in interviews, consultations and meetings, both individually and in small groups. The secular cultural upheaval of recent decades and the results of the Second Vatican Council (1962–65) made priests more self-aware, open, and self-searching, especially during retreats, workshops, and in training programs. Each man knew his own celibate/sexual history and had some observation, experience, or knowledge of the celibate/sexual experience of the group with whom he lived or worked.

As a confessor, religious superior, or confidant of others, he brought a perspective to the subject that no outsider could expect to master alone or through a mere attitudinal survey. A number of men from this group kept contact with this study from 3 to 10 years, and a handful endured most of the 25 years, and some beyond.

Other informants were especially valuable in validating and corroborating the priests' observations and conclusions because they had a perspective on priests who themselves would not have reported on their celibate/sexual adjustment. This group had firsthand information on the priests' behavior because they were their lovers, sexual partners, victims, or otherwise direct observers of it. This group included men and women—married and single—nuns, seminarians, and men who had left the priesthood. The first data were recorded from this group in 1960 but increased as the study progressed, especially in the years from 1975 to 1985 and supplemented through 2002.

Additionally we asked informants to estimate the sexual/celibate practice among their group or area. Vested interests were taken into account. For instance, a bishop or religious superior would sometimes present a case or series of cases for consultation while stating defensively that this was the "only one" such instance. Active homosexual priests who knew of other active homosexual priests tended to make relatively high estimates of gay priests. Persons with a relatively long association with the study or who had broad past experience within clerical circles offered estimates remarkably close to our figures. Older participants tended to have higher rather than lower estimates; however, there were startling exceptions to that rule also.

Priests have at their disposal an important tool enabling them to be in touch with the "sexual truth"—confession. Michel Foucault (1978), in *The History of Sexuality*, points out the broadest implications of this vehicle of knowledge and power in the secret world:

Since the Middle Ages at least, Western societies have established the confession as one of the main rituals we rely on for the production of truth: the codification of the sacrament of penance by the Lateran Council in 1215, with the resulting development of confessional techniques, the declining importance of accusatory procedures in criminal justice, the abandonment of tests of guilt (sworn statements, duels, judgments of God), and the development of methods of interrogation and inquest, the increased participation of the royal administration in the prosecution of infractions at the expense of proceedings leading to private settlements, the setting up of tribunals of Inquisition: all this helped to give the confession a central role in the order of civil and religious powers. (p. 58)

A confessor has a different approach from a therapist. A priest is trained to "forgive sins" as an agent of God. The slate is wiped clean upon the acknowledgment of an act, its repentance, and a firm resolve not to repeat it in the future. Other observers cannot be quite so segmented in evaluating the celibate/sexual behavior of a person. For instance, a priest may be sexually involved with another person only four times a year for a period of a few years. According to the former calculation, this man can be judged to be celibate with some periodic lapses due to human frailty. The student of celibacy who cannot relegate the behavior merely to the category of sin will not necessarily see the sexual behavior as unrelated sexual acts or as behavior divorced from the man's celibate/sexual orientation or adjustment. Of these four annual "lapses," one lay informant said, "That's as much sexual activity as some married folks have."

This work is not a survey. It did not select a representative sample of priests and ask each of them the same standardized questions during a structured interview. I doubt that the informants in this study could have been gathered by any survey. As Sarah Boxer writes, "Sex surveyors are bedeviled scientists. Beyond the problems of hearing the respondents correctly and not making imaginative suggestions themselves, they face a number of obstacles. People lie about sex. Those who don't lie often say inaccurate things. And most sex researchers aren't exactly neutral" (*New York Times*, July 22, 2000).

This work is not a sociological study (cf. Sobo & Bell, 2001). Harvard population geneticist, Richard Lewontin, points out that even in the most careful sociological research, investigators don't know how many people lie. He cautions investigators "to be less ambitious and stop trying to make sociology into a natural science. There are some things in the world that we will never know and many that we will never know exactly" (*New York Review of Books*, 2000).

This long-term ethnographic search gets at facts useful for subsequent research. It is distinct from surveys and polls. The value of this study is in its ability to disregard assumptions and to proceed to asking questions and collecting data without a set hypothesis. It is not bound by the constraints of surveys and certainly suffers from the limitations of informal design. But its conclusions can be verified and duplicated. The facts, estimates, conclusions, and analysis presented here invite challenge and verification.

Of course, there is always a societal context to sexuality, and sexuality is important in every known culture (Marshall & Suggs, 1971). No culture is indifferent to sexuality because physical pleasure and self-disclosure are the building blocks of all human relationships. Ira Reiss (1986) worked extensively to develop a comprehensive sociological theory of human sexuality. His perspective has profound implications for the understanding of celibacy, which, like sexuality, has deep societal implications—certainly in terms of ecclesiastical societies.

Celibacy is learned and maintained within the church structure. Since the priesthood exists in many cultures, the cross-cultural comprehension that Reiss advocates is open to those who would study celibacy in its broader context. The current development of the Catholic Church in Africa—a culture with distinct sexual traditions compared with those of Europe—will challenge the coming decades (Otene, 1982).

Celibacy has economic implications and special links to authoritarian structures and power; these important considerations are not within the scope of this study. (Cf. Sipe, 1995.) Likewise gender roles and biological determinants of celibacy are only introduced. Both areas need more study.

REASONS FOR THIS STUDY

The reader may well ask, "How did this study come about?" "Who is responsible for it?" and "What motivated it?" These are fair questions, and reasonable challenges to any serious exploration. The limitations of any scientific study are practical, theoretical, and ethical. Among the practical limitations is the notorious human proclivity toward bias. Even if causes could be linked to effects with certainty, scientists would still have to reckon with the fact that, while experiments may be objectively carried out, they are never objectively set up. Michel Foucault, in *The Archaeology of Knowledge* (1972, pp. 50–53), argued that any description should include what behavior is observed. Where does such behavior emerge (meaning, in the case of human behavior, the workplace, the family, the church, etc.)? Who made the observation (for instance, doctor, employer, or priest)? What was the vantage point of the observer, and which "grids of specification" pinpoint these observations? By considering these questions, Foucault asserted, scientific description can be corrected for bias.

There is *no* existing science of celibacy. Few self-reporting surveys and polls of priests have been undertaken around the question of *celibate practice*. It may surprise some that celibacy—so long revered in several religious traditions—has never been studied free of particular theological justifications. No study about the essentials of individual practice and structure exists. My work and questions form a basis for further explorations, because any scientific endeavor begins with careful observation. Questions lead to ever more specific and testable theses and more detailed understandings.

As a search, my work was directed as much by providence as by design. That is its strength. This information could not have been amassed if it had been sought for its own sake and not genuinely in the service of practical understanding and intervention. Similarly, its limitations, of design and primary structure, in the end are the means by which I was able to extrapolate many rich implications. Yet the simplicity of its pastoral intent remains intact.

My work has always been geared to those who would like to understand more about the mystery of celibacy, its nature, and its practice, and its achievement.

The man who first inspired me to search more deeply for the dynamic of celibacy was the Very Reverend Ulric C. Beste. I was a student in Rome at the time that he was a professor of canon law and on the staff in the Vatican's Holy Office. I had chosen him as my confessor and made my weekly confession to him. He was 75 years old. A foot injury incapacitated him during the summer of 1956, and I served his mass each morning and delivered his supper tray each evening.

After supper, we would sit on the upper courtyard of the Collegio. He would talk about his work in the Vatican Curia. He had been in Rome since 1939 under Pope Pius XII and was privy to the workings of the Vatican. He reminisced about his early development in a small Minnesota farming community and his life in the monastery. He also revealed his own sexual development and his celibacy as easily as he had spoken about all the rest. "He has truly achieved celibacy," I thought to myself. Of course, that revelation also brought about my awareness that not everyone had.

Father Ulric had a quirk that also proved decisive for me. He kept numerical count of all of the confessions he had ever heard and of the masses he had said. He had done this since his ordination. After I was ordained, this factor inspired me to keep data I thought would be useful in understanding and helping others.

As a Benedictine monk and ordained Roman Catholic priest, my interest in celibacy was spurred by my desire to understand its meaning, to live it, and eventually to teach it. I quickly discovered that, while there were an abundance of theological and/or inspirational treatises and a few historical studies of celibacy, there were no practical studies about how celibacy was really lived in daily life. Nor were there any based on a comprehensive understanding of sexual nature beyond spiritual ideals.

Immediately after ordination to the priesthood in 1959, I was sent on a temporary summer parish assignment in a Midwestern state. There I learned of two exemplary and productive pastors who had long-standing, intimate relationships with a partner. They were both well accepted by fellow priests who knew their living circumstances.

In the fall of that year I assumed an assignment to a four-priest rural parish and area high school. Two priests left the parish simultaneously with my arrival. One of the priests was reassigned as a chaplain to a convent of nuns some distance away. A number of parents and students informed me he had been reported several times to his superiors for being "over familiar" with some of the high school girls. As the year progressed, I heard several firsthand accounts from victims of his abuse. This same priest previously had been a principal of a boy's school. Complaints about him "switching" boys, sometimes with their pants down, were among the reasons for a former reassignment. The other priest who left the parish had been involved with several women in a number of different pastoral settings. He left abruptly; he literally "ran off" with a young woman.

I learned about priests who approached young boys for sex, even in the setting of the confessional. I did not know then that my own novice master and his assistant were alleged abusers of minors or that one of the Abbots of my monastery admitted sexually abusing young candidates for the priesthood in his role as spiritual director. I could not have imagined in 1960 that in 2002, 15 of the 200 members of my community would be restricted because of serious sexual boundary violations.

Nonetheless, I began to observe closely how men who profess celibacy actually lived it out. I intensified my observations and increased my opportunities for learning in the work and study I pursued. And even in 1960, it was obvious that there was *not* a commonly held definition of celibacy available for study.

Two groups of priests inspired and sustained my early interest in the practical psychology and sociology of celibacy. The first was a small group of local clergy (seven, including me) who met regularly to share clerical, pastoral, and personal concerns. One of the members was a mature pastor who later volunteered and served as a missionary to South America for 25 years. Father James Rausch was a teacher at a local high school. Subsequently he received a doctorate in social work from Catholic University and became secretary of the National Conference of Catholic Bishops. He was consecrated a bishop. In 2002 allegations surfaced that he sexually abused a minor.

Another young priest was a member of the John Birch Society; currently he remains active in the priesthood as a chaplain for conservative Catholics in his diocese. One of his classmates was an assistant pastor, and became a monsignor and rector of his diocesan seminary. The other three resigned from the active priesthood 10 years later and married. I retain contact with some of this group.

In 1960 I had my initial contact with a second group of priests who influenced me profoundly. During the summer a group of 120 men—

from all parts of the United States in the first 2 years of their priesthood—gathered at Conception at Abbey in Missouri for 6 weeks of study and discussion of pastoral and personal concerns. I have remained in contact with a number of these men. These groups fostered an open exchange about personal growth and developmental experiences, including celibate/sexual struggles and revelations about celibate culture.

I had unique opportunities to observe and record data at St. John's University Institute for Mental Health—where I was executive director for 4 years—at the Menninger Foundation, and during a 2-year residency in the counseling of religious at the Seton Psychiatric Institute of Baltimore. I remained on its staff for 3 years. The data collected from all these sources would have remained merely anecdotal were it not for the opportunity provided by Dr. Leo H. Bartemeier and the Institute to establish contacts from every section of the United States. I focused the material and my questions, and built a consultation system that could estimate celibate/sexual practice and achievement within typical groups of priests.

My teaching in major seminaries from 1967 through 1996 kept me in close contact with the clerical atmosphere.

Some brief conversations with Margaret Mead in 1966 had a decisive impact on the direction of my study. She issued challenges to some of my assumptions about sexual behavior and its origins that took me a good 10 years to absorb and apply to my thinking about celibacy. Her influence was critical in making this study ethnographic.

Ethnography is the description of a culture with conclusions based on observations of a participant-observer. It is distinguished from ethnology which compares two or more cultures. There are some valuable and elegant examples of ethnography (i.e., Erik Erikson, Claude Levi-Strauss, Irving Goffman, and Robert Stoller). Study of celibacy as it is practiced provides data that is observable—and reportable. My study seeks to describe real activities, practical circumstances and apply clear reasoning about topics ordinarily not examined—sex and celibacy among priests. I have had the opportunity to explore the most commonplace activities of daily clerical life with the attention usually accorded extraordinary events, seeking to learn about celibacy as phenomena in its own right.

Celibacy truly is a *culture apart* from the average person's understanding. Like sexuality, really little is known about it. It is difficult to formulate the right research questions. The participant-observer and the interested outsider can team up—as so many anthropologists and psychiatrists have done since the 1930s—to understand culture and personality. I grasped the melding of anthropology and psychiatry as Edward Sapir described it. "The true locus of culture is in the interactions of specific individuals and on the subjective side, in the world of meanings which each one of these individuals may unconsciously abstract for himself from his participation in these interactions" (Wittkower & Dubreuil, 1971, p. 6).

Celibacy, from the celibate's point of view, is hardly separable from the religious tradition, community, and beliefs that give it form and sustain it. My own interest in religion and psychiatry were compatible with a broadly anthropological approach. Iago Galdston explained, "Anthropology is the study of the extended history of mankind; psychiatry, that of the short-range behavioral history of man. The former is the matrix of the latter and affects it profoundly" (1971, p. ix).

My studies of celibacy are not medical. They do not focus on degrees of health or illness. They simply record celibate/sexual practice and process in a *group* of men that profess non-marriage and perfect chastity. The fact that I was an ordained priest and a member of a monastic community for 18 years and trained as a counselor-psychotherapist increased and enhanced my opportunities for observation and description. I have avoided psychiatric classifications and moral judgments. I favor simple accounts of life stories.

To study human nature is to be confronted constantly with ambiguity and deviance as well as with purposefulness and ideals. I hope this book's simple account of celibate histories and analysis of the process will open up the subject of celibacy—a variant of one's sexual capacity—to further dialogue.

Practical inquiries or autobiographical reports can be validated. Reported civil cases—in the hundreds—against priests and bishops for sexual abuse of minors is one avenue for comparing estimates of one behavior. Common sense helps too. Analysis depends on making disguised facts *evident* from reports of abuse, fragments, proverbs, literature, history, and novels, from passing remarks, rumors, and partial descriptions from codified but vague catalogues.

What are the motives for such a prolonged and lonely search? Motivation is both simpler and more complex than can be speculated about, but my study is part of a life search. I am inspired and maintained by the nobility of service and self-sacrifice that I have witnessed in the lives of priests. I have benefited from it. I am conditioned by empathy for good people struggling, in Paul Ricoeur's (1964) words, "In a dynamic equilibrium of intersubjectivity where [agape] is achieving the integration and spiritualization of Eros" (p. 162). Certainly my work is sustained by a need to set the record straight and to do my part to seek the Truth that sets men and women free.

My personal psychoanalysis and marriage have added dimensions of richness and a perspective to the project that could not have been achieved without them, but they have not altered the goal. The core of my motivation—pursuing the understanding of celibacy—remains constant.

2

WHAT IS IT?

No word and no gesture can be more persuasive than the life and, if necessary, the death of a man who strives to be free, loyal, just, sincere, disinterested. A man who shows what a man can be.

—Ignazio Silone

I hold that a life of perfect continence in thought, speech and action is necessary for reaching spiritual perfection. And a nation that does not possess such men is poorer for the want.

—Gandhi

Priests striving for celibacy live, move, and have their being in a distinctly sexually aware and sexually active world. This has been highlighted in the last half-century.

Multiple elements influence the perception of celibacy and condition the framework of understanding celibate practice. Public awareness of clergy sexual abuse has set the stage for the current crisis of celibacy. But it is not the only problem contributing to the chaos around the question, *What exactly is celibacy?* That question must be addressed in the total context of our time.

FACTORS OF THE CRISIS

A MARRIED PRIESTHOOD—Should priests be married or single? is not a new question. The battle over celibacy—its relationship to church power and ministry—is centuries, actually millennia, old. Some historians (Cochini and Cholij) claim that celibacy and the priesthood are intrinsically bound together, and the discipline has been unalterably dictated from the time of the apostles. Pope John Paul II has taken this position repeatedly during his pontificate. He

21

has gone so far as to declare that it is not within his power to change the church law that requires priests to be celibate.

Theory aside, incontrovertible evidence demonstrates that many priests, bishops, and popes were married—legitimately—until 1139, when a papal decree rendered any marriage by a cleric invalid and required any candidate for major orders to be single. That 12th-century legislation did not alter the legitimacy of a past married-priesthood, nor did it ensure the practice of celibacy—perpetual and perfect chastity (cf. Sipe, Chap. 3, 1990).

Every discussion of a celibate versus a married priesthood throughout the centuries—regardless of the theological grounds propounded—has, in fact, included three eminently practical elements: *progeny, property, and power*. Sociologically and economically men are more easily controlled if single. A single-sex power system has proven to have cultural durability whether or not men practice celibacy.

The sexual corruptibility of the celibate system has repeatedly been a cause of concern over centuries. And today, the spotlight on priest abuse of minors has exposed areas of celibate conflict beyond the illegal. The perennial debate over the wisdom, advisability, and necessity of an unmarried priesthood—and even the exclusion of women from ordination—has risen to an unprecedented level of public concern. The question of a married priesthood causes chaos in the hierarchy, and consternation among lay people and many clergy. It remains a crisis conundrum to be met and solved.

LOSS OF MORAL CREDIBILITY—When, in 1994, the American bishops issued their first public report on abuse of minors they called it *Restoring Trust*. The report failed to accomplish that. In fact, the *loss of credibility* in church authority has plummeted since that time. What was once considered Protestant distrust of Catholic hierarchy is rampant among the faithful—and among some clergy as well.

Currently the hierarchy has lost credibility to an unprecedented degree. Documentation from church files, and depositions from trials have painted a picture of church officials as "liars." Words of apology belatedly wrung from pursed episcopal lips by an angry public outcry, rang hollow. Loss of confidence in the moral authority of the bishops has crippled them almost beyond repair. It has not only harmed *their* image, but that of every priest.

Exposure of bishops' complicity in protecting abusers has been underlined by their excuses: "I didn't know." "Psychiatrists said there was no danger." "Lawyers have to take care of settling with victims." The moral leadership of bishops appears bankrupt. Eugene Kennedy claims that bishops have been purveyors of chaos through their reliance on public relations and legal tactics, quick fixes and semantics. (*Chicago Tribune*, 1, 27, 2003) The questions on everybody's lips remain: "When did bishops learn that sexual abuse of a minor is against the law?" "When did bishops realize that sexual activity with a minor is a serious violation of celibacy?"

FINANCIAL ACCOUNTABILITY—The compensatory payments to abuse victims, and the correlative expenses for lawyers, psychological treatment of offenders and victims total well over 1 billion dollars by 2003. Some lay people now *demand* a financial *accountability* from the bishops. The Catholic Church in America has never before been faced with the strong demands that lay groups like *Voice of the Faithful* are making. Philanthropic organizations are also questioning bishops about their use of funds.

TATTERED IMAGE—An *image* of clergy as weak and ineffectual, duplicitous and self-serving, dangerous and hypocritical has unfairly engulfed all priests. Every priest has suffered because of the sexual abuse crisis, because every priest is besmirched by sidelong glances that ask, "Are you one?" Some priests are reluctant to wear their clerical collar outside the safe confines of their parish church. This scrutiny makes priests defensive about their whole celibate adjustment, not just abuse of minors. Church authorities initially refused to acknowledge that some clergy *do* have a problem with sexual attraction for minors. If they had tried to determine the extent of the problem—which is possible—they could have saved everybody a lot of grief and enhanced their credibility.

SEXUAL CLIMATE—We live in a *sexually aware and sexually explicit* world. Alfred Kinsey, William Masters, and Hugh Hefner have led the popular quest for the scientific study of sexuality and behavior. Their directness in approaching human sexuality was not confined to the classroom, clinic, or a specialized segment of popular publishing. Every aspect of sexual life has been exposed and questioned. Celibacy is no longer immune from scrutiny. A celibate warrior's torch—once considered a light in the darkness—dims before the glamorous glare of modern sex crusaders' spotlights.

Popularly accepted explicitness of sexuality, in music, magazines, movies, and television, challenges the secret world—the denial of sexuality—that many celibates use to keep their practice in place. That challenge to the celibate structure is not entirely hostile or negative. Explicitness can be an invitation to truth, nonsecrecy, and accountability—delicate areas, to be sure, for religion.

WOMEN'S RIGHTS—The majority of lay Catholics and many priests reject church teaching on *contraceptives*. Women's *rights* is also as much a cause of interest and support to Catholics as it is to members of other mainline churches. It does not get equal backing from the hierarchy, in spite of some politically correct statements.

GAY RIGHTS—The *gay movement* utterly confounds the church. Vatican teaching labels homosexual men and women sick—afflicted with an "intrinsic disorder." The sex abuse crisis has led some Vatican spokesmen to preposterously equate pedophilia with homosexual orientation. Distortion grew to the point where some church officials questioned whether the ordination of homosexual men was valid. Officials have reasserted the directive that homosexually oriented men can not be admitted to seminaries. This element is particularly chaotic for the church since a large proportion of the clergy are themselves gay—some of them sexually active.

Church teaching is held up to ridicule when it insists that condoms cannot be used to avoid transmitting the AIDS virus. Church officials feel justified when they use this argument in regard to homosexual acts, because they define such behavior as intrinsically evil. But the church holds to its ban even between married couples where one partner is infected. Meanwhile Catholic college students (70%) condone stable relationships between same sex partners.

CHURCH REFORM—The Second *Vatican Council* (1962–65) was also an event with major implications for religion and ministry. Sex and celibacy were not discussed at the council, but conservative voices stridently assert that the liberal reforms of the council have created the atmosphere of sexual indulgence and abuse.

VOCATIONS—The *decline in numbers* of priests, the hundreds of parishes without resident pastors, increased workloads, the growth of the Catholic population, also conspire to lower priestly morale and challenge Catholics' dedication and allegiance to church teaching (D'Antonio, Davidson, Hoge, & Meyer, 2001).

This is the crisis context in which we have to examine the question *What is celibacy*[2]. The crisis of sexual abuse by priests has focused monumental attention on that question. The scrutiny is good. It motivates everyone who claims an interest in celibacy to examine closely its practical essence.

THE MEANINGS OF CELIBACY

What is celibacy? One might think that definitions of celibacy are easy to come by—"ask any priest." This is not the case. In the mid 1980s, four bishops from different dioceses were asked that question during depositions each had to give regarding the sexual behavior of a priest. It was clear, that there simply is no clear operational definition of celibacy. One said that masturbation was a violation of celibacy, another said it was not.

A priest who was arrested in 2002 on a sex charge claimed that he was celibate since he had never married and only had sexual relations with "four women and ten men" since his ordination. He asserted that these acts were simply "sins" against chastity and did not violate his celibate vow. This patent rationalization is not uncommon. It reflects the attitude that bishops have registered in cases of offending priests.

There is a growing consciousness of the need for *celibate definition*. The emphasis, however, has been primarily on the negatives—what to avoid—rather than on the positive—how you do it.

Donald Goergen, himself a vowed celibate, wrote *The Sexual Celibate* in 1974. He took as his starting point human sexuality instead of abstinence. He treated celibacy from the vantage point of the psychology. The book is admirable—revolutionary in its directness—and includes concrete suggestions for living a chaste life. One priest evaluated and endorsed Goergen's work: "For too long we were celibates because we had to be and no reflection was needed beyond the repetition of bromides and clichés. . . . Many of us sense that our commitment to celibacy was neither irrelevant nor adolescent, but the Church lacked the theory to propound the vision of the celibate life in terms that made sense to our contemporaries. Goergen has made a major step forward toward developing a new theory of celibacy."

As I taught successive classes of seminarians, I became fascinated with this glaring lack of precise definition. Seminarians were fascinated too, and articulated the question succinctly—almost demanding—"What really *is* celibacy?" "Is it merely abstinence?" "Or is it only an ideal, like perfect beauty, to which many aspire but few if any attain?" "How do we live it?"

Older priests confirmed that these were not questions asked or answered in their education. One priest said, "The extent of my formal training about celibacy in the seminary was a statement by the rector: 'Celibacy means *no* sex, hetero, homo, auto, *basta così.*'"

Over the years various clergy responded defensively at the suggestion that there might be a deficiency in seminary training. A bishop, who had been the rector of a seminary, defended the system: "I can attest that such training takes place in many ways and in many contexts. It is simply not true that 'very little attention is paid to direct training for celibacy.' . . . Celibacy is a whole way of life and is a fundamental component in priestly spirituality. It is not something which is learned in an exclusively academic setting." Of course, no one suggested that celibacy be taught in an exclusively academic setting, only that it be given equal importance as biblical or dogmatic courses.

Another bishop said, "Most seminaries have a workshop or lectures on the subject of celibacy. But it is true that they do not have full semester courses (or six semesters as I had recommended) on the subject. Given its importance in the life of the priest and religious, one might expect a more extended treatment."

The majority of priests in our study felt that their education for celibacy and about sexuality was inadequate. When asked how their questions about sexual concerns were handled in the seminary, the most frequent replies were: "Pray about it"; "Don't think about it"; "Play sports"; "Just accept it (meaning lapses), it's human nature."

The focus is not on a "course" for the training of celibacy but rather on the need for an open and adequate arena wherein the full and honest discovery of the structure and practice of celibacy can be debated and considered. The ideal and the law of celibacy need critical and practical examination before mastery can be expected. We require no less of any other area of vital intellectual and practical interest.

I am convinced that training could be done much more effectively if emotional and sexual concerns were addressed in a direct way. The fairest evaluation I know was given by Dr. Bartemeier: "We take promising young men from thirteen to twenty-five years of age, feed them well, educate them diligently, and eight to twelve years later we ordain them, healthy, bright, emotional thirteen-year-olds." The acceptance of older candidates for the priesthood will not alter that reality because they too are entering the secret world that prefers an adolescent emotionality.

Those who claim that celibacy is adequately taught through the whole system of regulated hours, spiritual direction, and confession, are misguided. Priests have not been well served by that system. It is rare for any young priest to hear the direct witness of an older celibate such as, "I know what celibacy is; this is the process I have experienced, and this is how I have achieved it." Without living role models with whom to identify explicitly in the area of handling one's sexual drive, the priest is left to the secret arena and isolation of his own fantasy, where fear and guilt proliferate and sap his psychic energy.

I. F. Stone pointed out: "You cannot have secrecy and accountability at the same time." There is no other single element as destructive to sexual responsibility among clergy as the system of secrecy that shields behavior and reinforces denial.

Increasingly during the 1980s and '90s, celibacy was touched upon in the context of moral theology class—2 weeks in a semester. One- or 3-day seminars are used, sometimes including outside consultants to address issues. These seminars are well intentioned but insufficient to deal with the understanding and mastery required by the celibate goal.

It is not at all obvious that canon law is really observed in regard to training for celibacy. Canon 247 states, "The students are to be prepared through suitable education to observe the state of celibacy, and they are also to learn to honor it as a special gift of God. . . . They are to be duly informed of the duties and burdens of sacred ministers of the Church; no difficulty of the priestly life is to be kept back from them." A big order for a few days, or even a few years.

One study of Catholic clergy reported that 68 percent agreed "that the traditional way of presenting the vow of chastity during their religious training often allowed for the development of impersonalism and false spirituality" (Greeley, 1972, p. 363).

A guide prepared by the Bishops' Committee on Priestly Life and Ministry of the National Conference of Catholic Bishops acknowledged the intrinsic nature of sexuality—a step forward.

To be a human person is to grow, develop, and mature throughout the life span from cradle to grave. To be a human person is to be a sexual person—the marvelous mystery of human sexuality permeates every moment of human existence. . . . The human person is so profoundly affected by sexuality that it must be considered as one of the factors which give to each individual's life the principal traits that distinguish it (National Conference of Catholic Bishops, 1983, p. 7).

Two years earlier, the conference decreed but *did not implement* the following guidelines for the training of seminarians for celibacy:

This education should deal specifically with such topics as the nature of sexuality, growth toward sexual maturity, marital and celibate chastity, the single state, premarital and extramarital sexual relationships, and homosexuality. . . . It is clear that confidence in being able to live out the response of celibacy is based on God alone. Seminarians, with a sensitive appreciation of women and their natural attraction to them, will base their determination to lead a celibate life on their special love for Christ. (National Conference of Catholic Bishops, 1982, pp. 24–5)

These are exactly the questions that should, but cannot be discussed under the current doctrinal stance to the church.

ABSTINENCE

Most training for celibacy remains deficient. Celibacy is not simply sexual abstinence, any more than honesty is simply not stealing. A few years ago a rock star, on a late-night talk show, expounded on the "new celibacy." He said that for the first time since he was a teenager he had been abstinent for a whole month. He waxed eloquent on the sense of freedom and relaxation he was experiencing. Some authors extol periodic sexual abstinence for health and adjustment reasons (cf. Williams, 1999; Wolter, 1992). And the history of celibacy is not exclusively the narrative of Catholic clerics (Abbott, 1999/2000).

Priests know instinctively—even if they lack a complete comprehension of its nature—that sexual abstinence alone is not celibacy. One middle-aged priest voiced the concern of many when he said, "I don't want to be celibate by default—just too tired and bored to have sex."

There are many people who are sexually abstinent for shorter or longer periods of time—some for healthy, loving reasons, others through neurotic fear or even psychotic disarray, others from necessity—but they would never view celibacy as desirable, much less as an ideal.

Important vexing questions remain hidden within the secret world. How are priests able to be celibate? How many priests keep the law, and how many attain the ideal?

LAW AND IDEAL

Two similarities exist between the *law* and the *ideal* of celibacy: The first is that each remains operative regardless of whether celibacy is practiced or not. The second is that a person must work to effect either in his life.

The few brief canons that deal with clerical celibacy and those concerning clerical spirituality are probably sufficient to sustain a celibate lifestyle for those who observe them with full understanding and commitment.

Canon law decrees that priests must be celibate. It is not always observed. Regardless, every priest in our study was bound by that law—specifically, canon 277:

> Clerics are obliged to observe perfect and perpetual continence for the sake of the kingdom of heaven and therefore are obliged to observe celibacy, which is a special gift of God, by which sacred ministers can adhere more easily to Christ with an undivided heart and can more freely dedicate themselves to the service of God and humankind. . . . Clerics are to conduct themselves with due prudence in associating with persons whose company could endanger their obligation to observe continence or could cause scandal for the faithful.

The question that is debated more and more in clerical circles is whether one can legislate a charism. The response from an authority is that the charism *must* be presumed to be present prior to ordination (Canon Law No. 1037). *The law* is clear: it requires perfect and perpetual abstinence in order to serve like Christ.

CHRIST THE IDEAL

The moral ideal for every Christian is Christ. The priest is meant to serve others as Christ did. A personal relationship and identification in the end give meaning and possibility to this striving. Priests are the first to admit the impossibility of celibacy without a personal relationship with Christ. (Those not acquainted with this mode of spiritual expression can focus on the essential psychological element—the capacity for and achievement of a personal relationship.)

We all know that distance and time do not destroy mature relationships in spite of the great difficulty maintenance of them demands. St. Paul, even though he never met Christ, knew him well. St. John the evangelist, who was a friend of Christ, remained vibrantly alive in that relationship, years beyond the physical separation of the two men. (I John 1:3–4).

The history of religion—apostles and popes included—shows that celibacy is not necessary for the maintenance of a meaningful relationship and identification with Christ. However, celibacy is not possible without the capacity for involvement with some reality beyond the self. And celibacy must be productive in the service of one's fellow humans. These elements were essential to Gandhi's celibacy in a different religious tradition.

The ideal of the priesthood articulated in the 4th century went like this: "The soul of a priest ought to be purer than the very rays of the sun, so that the Holy Spirit will not abandon him, and so that he may be able to say 'It is no longer I that live, but Christ that liveth in me'" (Jurgens, 1955, p. 92). This lofty ideal is at the heart of the decision of many men who wish to be priests—their sense that they wish to be *like* Christ. Naturally, this intention does not occur in pure culture. Their motivation is mixed with whole spectra of emotions and ambitions—both holy and selfish—that need to be refined by the process of seeking that ideal.

LOVE

Writers extol the nature of celibate love: "So love is to say yes to another, to say yes not merely with the lips or even with the heart, but with one's whole being. The yes is uttered before the total giving, and yet it is the yes which guarantees the certainty of love" (Raguin 1974, p. 11). The images ring true, but the day-to-day directives are completely vague. What the ideal means as applied by a particular person and how it is achieved in the face of conflicting demands are nowhere spelled out.

The goal of Christian celibacy is the enhancement of love. The nature of love makes easy philosophy, but complex reality. "What in primitive religions had served to idealize the natural functions of man now became a means of transcending nature. Love turned into a *super*natural device, and in Christianity it became the very essence of God. "In the ancient and the medieval world philosophical idealizations were primarily transcendental" (Singer, 1984, p. 42).

The celibate, removed from sexual activity and involvement, is forced to grapple with that transcendental nature of love. That struggle has proven pregnant for Western civilization and culture precisely because the transcendent reality of love had to be translated and activated into projects that transform him, but making him a "man for others," a man of service to humanity.

DEFINITION OF CELIBACY

These are roots of any viable definition of celibacy. My definition of celibacy includes seven essential interrelated elements:

> Celibacy is a freely chosen dynamic state, usually vowed, that involves an honest and sustained attempt to live without direct sexual gratification in order to serve others productively for a spiritual motive.

1. Freely Chosen

To be free in sexual matters is not easy. There were many priests in our study who said after years in the priesthood that they had had no real idea of what celibacy was all about when they were ordained. They had been happy as seminarians and somehow assumed that a supportive environment would follow them into their pastoral settings. The fact that one is not initially free or not fully aware does not vitiate one's pursuit of celibacy.

To be celibate a person should be free from sexual dependency—that is, his sexual orientation and internal adjustment should not interfere with his physical or mental health, his interpersonal relationships, or his effective and efficient functioning. This does not mean that he must be virginal; but one who has been subject to any compulsive sexual behavior such as pedophilia, committed homosexuality, or heterosexual activity without regard for the reality of relationships will have a hard time choosing the state of celibacy convincingly. Celibacy is not a running away from sex. It knowingly embraces reality with the subjective conviction that one existentially is not able to do otherwise. And one freely accepts that.

In short, it is the sense of personal vocation. Freedom is itself a process. Gandhi (1960) records the struggle in a way to which other celibates can relate when he says:

> The spirit in me pulls one way, the flesh in me pulls in the opposite direction. There is freedom from the action of these two forces, but that freedom is attainable only by slow and painful stages. I cannot attain freedom by a mechanical refusal to act, but only by intelligent action in a detached manner. This struggle resolves itself into an incessant crucifixion of the flesh so that the spirit may become entirely free. (p. 71)

Freedom requires knowledge of one's embodiment, an acknowledgment that humans are sexed beings. It demands sexual realism and self-determination—all areas that have been neglected in seminary training.

Marriage and celibacy are meant to lead Christians to the "freedom of the children of God." There is an acute need for cooperation between married and celibates in the sexual training of those thinking about freedom and celibate dedication.

2. Dynamic State

Life and sexuality are dynamic. Demands and opportunities always change. Struggle is necessary to enter and live in a "state," that is, a lifelong situation that is free of sexual involvement. The process of engaging celibacy differs after 5 years from after 1; or 25 versus 10. The process is to become a celibate, not just be celibate.

The neglect of the sense of dynamism in celibate pursuit has harmed those who want to be celibate, and those with whom they associate. The constantly changing circumstances and demands of living—growth and development—require adaptation and new coping mechanisms.

Traditionally great emphasis has been placed on the "state" of celibacy. All of the idealistic treatments emphasize the stability and constancy of the practice. The sense of unchanging demand for compliance leads churchmen to shy away from dealing with the complexities and challenges that engaging the reality of sexual nature requires. Fear and avoidance are not helpful in making rational decisions. They don't support or encourage growth. Neglecting the *dynamic* undermines the *state*.

3. Usually Vowed

Although there may be exceptional instances where celibacy is pursued without a conscious or public declaration, I do not know of many. For Catholic priests, the vow precedes ordination as a requirement, and the church places such emphasis on the vow that it remains even if one loses the clerical state. According to canon 291, "Loss of the clerical state does not entail a dispensation from the obligation of celibacy, which is granted by the Roman Pontiff alone" (*Code of Canon Law*, 1984, p. 103).

There is something about the public nature of the commitment and the declaration of one's intent that is necessary for the efficaciousness of the endeavor. Celibacy is not meant to be a harbor for the fearful or a refuge for the sexually incompetent, but a witness by those dedicated and concerned for humanity. A powerful impact is made, even on nonbelievers, when a believer is so convinced of his cause and so dedicated to his beliefs that he is willing to give up all sexual pleasures in their behalf. It is the kind of admiration one has for those who give up their lives for the country they believe in or for the person they love. The connection between martyrdom and celibacy is not accidental. There has to be an element of the heroic striving in both, and there has to be a relatedness to the community. It declares the most private—sex—as a most public promise. One example of this:

A few years ago a young religious sister shared the following experience. She was enrolled at a state university in a course entitled "Human Sexuality." She attended the class anonymously and was unrecognized as a sister. For reasons unknown (and probably unknowable), the students were required to share with the class the wildest sexual encounter they had experienced. Sister resolved to stand her ground and admit the awful truth—she had never had a sexual encounter.

As this exhibitionists' round-robin made its way to her, she disclosed her dreadful secret. The students thought they had been prepared for everything, but not for this! Chastity was just too far out. Between their gasps of incomprehension and guffaws of unbelief, she managed to explain that she was a religious sister. The response of the group completely reversed. Her classmates were delighted, awestruck, and deeply moved. They all agreed that she should stay right where she was and not have an encounter. Even the most jaded were impressed to know that someone, somewhere, had managed to preserve her humanity and yet be chaste for the Kingdom of God (Groeschel 1985, p. 11).

In his autobiography, Gandhi eloquently describes the difference between his practice of celibacy during his 5 years of trial and after his subsequent vow. The vow made a profound difference internally.

4. An Honest and Sustained Attempt

The fulfillment of the vow of celibacy is not accomplished by the public declaration. The constant daily living and implementation of leading a sexless life demand a quality of control and inner freedom which is devoid of self-deception and rationalization. In short, it takes a kind of integrity that has balance, self-knowledge, consistency, and commitment.

A key factor is the equilibrium of needs and demands. Many priests throw themselves into their work without regard for their other personal needs. All of their sexual energy is thus translated into their work effort. Breakdown and oftentimes rebound are inevitable. This unbalanced approach is matched at the other extreme by priests who feel that because they are deprived of sexual gratification they have a right to every other comfort.

Celibacy requires that a person find a parity among internal versus external demands, individual versus communal forces, and immediate versus ultimate needs—not an easy task for anyone. However, if one is to renounce sexual gratification as a means of tension reduction, then the building of relationships and the transmission of spiritual life challenge that person to a level of creative living not commonly experienced.

Self-knowledge is absolutely indispensable for the celibate pursuit. Denial is the great betrayer of celibacy.

Accepting and living with the reality that God made us bodily creatures does not mean that we must voluntarily indulge in sexual pleasure. It does mean recognizing that our sexuality will often be felt and experienced in many ways. Because sexual expression in its highest form is linked with tender emotions and the need for intimacy, the person seeking to be a chaste celibate need not suppress tenderness and emotion while seeking to avoid pregenital or genital behavior. As in most areas of human accomplishment, advance is along a knife-edge, avoiding on the one hand an unrealistic Puritanism and on the other an indulgence of inappropriate behavior which is disguised as virtue. I have come to suspect both the angelic battle of the 1940s and the "third way" of the 1970s as being denials of sexual reality (Groeschel, 1985, pp. 35–36).

The celibate must face honestly his physical and spiritual assets and liabilities. A deep search of one's personal history and a social awareness will keep the daily struggle in perspective.

There is an intensely private and personal side to the sustained attempt to be celibate. Some transgressions can be incorporated into the *attempt* to be celibate, but a sexual incident that can very quickly turn into a pattern obliterates celibacy as a reality. The priest, for instance, who regularly, even though infrequently, seeks out a sexual liaison, is not a practicing celibate. There are scores of examples of priests who have had to abandon celibacy for a time in order to find out what it is and later practice it, but that abandonment must be honestly acknowledged lest the public image become a cover for hypocrisy.

The masturbations pose a specific and special problem for the celibate. Although masturbatory activity is technically and legally forbidden in celibate practice, our study shows that it is a common activity even among those who in every other regard observe celibacy and strive honestly to attain it.

Each person pursuing celibacy develops adaptive patterns that are consistent with his characterological formation. Some personality structures are more readily compatible with the discipline required of a celibate. Others have to work harder for constancy. The impulsive or narcissistic character will have great difficulty to incorporate the necessary constancy self-control demands. These qualities are very frequently observed in priests who sexually abuse minors.

Commitment to others and to one's self is measured by the allegiances and loyalties one has; but above all by the quality of one's existing relationships and the capacity one has to develop new ones. Sustained celibate living is really not possible in a schizoid vacuum. Without the commitment to others, celibacy breaks down, if not in technique, at least in its goal.

5. To Live without Direct Sexual Gratification

The core of celibacy involves necessary sublimation. The sexual instinct of the celibate is defused and directed to the service of other pursuits. Not a few priests have said that celibacy means that they will not *marry*. They hold that *chastity*—that is, the virtue of purity—is reserved for those who, like nuns, take a specific vow of chastity. As celibates (unmarried), therefore, they feel they can engage in sexual activity without breaking their vow or violating their *state* in spite of the fact that they may sin. This is simple rationalization and has no merit.

At first glance celibacy seems an impossible and even outlandish course of life. For most people direct sexual pleasure is a necessary component of their personal growth and development and a means of loving and serving. Upon reflection, however, one realizes how many of the joys of life and truly meaningful interactions do not involve direct sexual gratification: the love between parents and children, brothers and sisters, and friends; and work and career accomplishments. In addition, there are those few persons who are so in touch with the transcendent that they achieve profound relatedness and universal love of other humans almost constitutionally.

6. In Order to Serve Others Productively

Sexual denial that is without a social or community goal is meaning-less and probably not possible. Again, celibacy is not merely absti-nence. By its essence it has to be *on account of something*, and that something has to be perceived as valuable and worth the sacrifice. Canon law speaks about "chastity assumed for the sake of the king-dom of heaven." It establishes the person as a sign of the future. It produces an undivided heart. Perfect continence in celibacy is in-tended to facilitate meaning and usefulness (*Code of Canon Law*, 1984, #227).

Celibacy reaches beyond self. It aims first at the familial model of early Christianity, where all men and women are brothers and sisters, genuinely loving, and serving because Christ is present in each. Geni-tal behavior is excluded not because it is evil—that was a later devel-opment consolidated by St. Augustine (cf. Pagels, 1988)—but because of the relative superiority of building up the kingdom of God—that what Christ taught could become a reality so "that all may be one" (John 17:23). Celibacy is meant to be witness to these values.

It is also meant to be a witness to the ability of grace to overcome nature and to the fact that courage can surmount biological impera-tives, that hope is stronger than death, and that one can give even one's life (and energies) for others. Although not all priests today agree that celibacy frees them for unencumbered service to others (cf. Hoge, 1987), there is an essential link between being free *"from"* sex-ual demands and being free *"for"* service.

By embracing celibacy, one can eschew relationship bonds that impose an exclusive mutuality. A commitment to universality of ac-cessibility is inherent in celibacy. It values all humanity indepen-dently of external merit or presentation. Rich and poor, healthy and sick, saints and sinners all have equal claim to the celibate. Love translated into universal relatedness: this is the core of celibacy's free-dom for service.

Celibacy demands a single-heartedness. Intended is the singleness of purpose of one who has discovered the pearl of great price and is willing to sell everything to possess it. That kind of dedication has its parallel in the service of others—the athlete, the actor, the scholar.

Persons of excellence in every field sacrifice deeply and focus all their available energy and efforts toward the achievement of their goal. That dedication, bringing fame and fortune sometimes, is extolled and understood even if it cannot always be emulated.

The depth of the aloneness that must be embraced to support celibacy cannot be minimized. "Celibate people have a special relationship to loneliness because they make a commitment to enter life's moments of loneliness more completely and more vulnerably than is possible for the married" (Clark, 1982, p. 55). There is no way to practice and achieve celibacy other than by penetrating the aloneness, not merely sustaining it. Aloneness taps the wellsprings of spirituality and leads to the sixth essential element of my definition.

7. For a Spiritual Motive

There should be no question about this: Celibacy is not proposed as a natural phenomenon. Several priests recalled that they were told in school that every boy is called to the priesthood but only a few respond. The priesthood may be an option for every Christian; celibacy is not. Celibacy is a highly specialized gift that presumes an awareness of existence and reality beyond the ordinary as well as a charism—that is, a special gift of grace and of spiritual witness. The priest will want to know, eventually, if his sexual struggle is with the development of his genuine charism, or if it is a conflict arising from a discipline he accepted as part of his ministerial role without the benefit of the special gift.

Priests believe in grace. A charism is a grace and not a product of nature, although it is usually supported by a special combination of genetic endowment, environmental luck, and deep subjective awareness that one "cannot do other."

Surprisingly, there is not a great deal of direct literary witness to the experience. We have the scriptural witness of Christ's life of love. St. Paul, who was most likely over 40 years old and widowed at the time of his conversion, is most explicit in his decision to remain celibate rather than to remarry. I have always liked this explicit description of Gandhi's discovery of his celibate vocation:

> It was in South Africa that Gandhi learned to translate . . . tremendous
> ideals into effective action. . . . Night and day, carrying . . . stretchers
> across the vast deserted hill country of Natal, he plunged himself deep
> into prayer and self-examination in a fervent search for greater strength
> with which to serve.
>
> (Easwaran, 1972, pp. 37–38)

The intensity of his desire led him to the source of power itself. Deep in meditation Gandhi began to see how much of his vital energy was locked up in the sexual drive. In a flood of insight he realized that sex is not just a physical instinct, but an expression of the tremendous spiritual force behind all love and creativity which the Hindu scriptures call kundalini, the life force of evolution. All his life it had been his master, buffeting him this way and that beyond his control. But in the silence of the Natal hills, with all his burning desire to serve focused by weeks of tending to the wounded and dying, Gandhi found the strength to tap this power at its source. Then and there he resolved to be its master, and never let it dictate to him again. It was a decision which resolved his deepest tensions, and released all the love within him into his conscious control. He had begun to transform the last of his passions into spiritual power.

There is currently a sharp debate in theological circles about the legal requirement of celibacy for the priesthood. There are many priests who firmly believe they are called to the ministry of the priesthood and at the same time called to the married state.

I remember psychoanalyst Dr. Gregory Zilboorg commenting on a consultation he had conducted with a Jesuit scholastic. He judged him "obviously schizophrenic." His conclusive proof was that the man wanted to be both a priest and married. Zilboorg's diagnosis might have been correct, but his criterion would be very unreliable in any consultation office today. I have always wondered, incidentally, whether that patient was truly psychotic or merely ahead of his time!

This distinction between celibacy as a discipline and as a charism has always existed. The shift in support systems that used to surround clerical life brings the question into painful focus for many priests. Privilege, prestige, educational advantage, social, political, and spiritual power, exclusivity, and secrecy all conspired to form a protective barrier for the priest dealing with his sexual drives. Within such a system it was not so essential to deal with the distinction between charism and discipline. The celibate charism will always remain, as it has in the Buddhist tradition; however, the discipline primarily—and even secondarily the charism—is greatly strained without significant external supports.

Seminary education has been gravely remiss—certainly from the psychological perspective—by not examining actively enough the distinction between charism and discipline. The church also does itself a grave disservice as well as personal injustice by requiring the practice of celibacy without actually supporting it (cf. Sipe, 1988, pp. 45–47).

Only a spiritual (i.e., transcendent) motivation can sustain celibate striving. Gandhi makes this clear in his pursuit. Only a love that can match or exceed what is possible with sexual love can sustain celibacy.

Legal and ideal frameworks situate celibacy. The ideal defies easy understanding or easy practice. As with all ideals, some merely profess, some strive, and a few achieve. Our definition of celibacy is operational. It does not impose on either the ideal or legal constraints, but makes both more attainable. This chapter gives the reader sufficient background to proceed to the second question of our study. How is celibacy really practiced and not practiced by those who profess it?

The sexual turbulence of the past half-century, with its discoveries and consciousness of equality will have its lasting impact on celibate practice and achievement. The generation of priests who were part of this time have been in a unique position to expose and examine their celibate practice. A closer examination of celibate practice is inevitable in the wake of the exposure of the abuse of minors. More revelations about the dynamics of celibacy will come. They are a necessary contribution to the understanding of this mysterious "sign of contradiction" that coexists with and participates in *culture and history* (Cf. Williams, 1999; Abbott, 1999/2000).

How Do Those Who Profess Celibacy Practice It?

We usually think of Freud as saying the restrictions of conventional morality are bad for man since they prevent him from carrying out his sexual desires. In point of fact . . . Freud is saying . . . man does not learn to love in a full and mature manner insofar as his passions remain in a crude, infantile state which keeps him from being fully human, fully able to give himself in love.

—Thomas Merton

I have no reason to doubt the validity of those figures.

—Jose Cardinal Sanchez (1993)

Freud and psychoanalysis had a tremendous influence on thought and behavior in the 20th century. By mid-century his contributions had gained broad acceptance, even among religionists. The development of psychological awareness and the acceptance of discussions about sex made this study possible.

Psychotherapy brought sex out of the confessional where it was secret, and subject to the moral judgment, into an arena where thought, behavior, and motivation was subject to unfettered exploration and self-evaluation. It was *the new confession*. It breached the secret system—secrets were leaking out. Priests could now speak of their goals, growth, and distress to an objective "ear." They had to tell not just *what* they did, but *why*.

Priests shared their personal sexual concerns *and* the sexual secrets of the system in a confidential setting, not under the control of the church. And they talked about sex to others. The sexual concerns of folks who came to them for advice took on new meaning as they grew in appreciation of psychological dimensions to pastoral problems.

Bishops and religious superiors consulted a number of Catholic psychiatrists (and others) about some of their men who presented difficult management problems. Some had personal stresses from which they sought relief. As comfort with the new helping science grew some superiors wanted their own men to be trained in the new skills in order to apply them to spiritual direction. Psychiatry intruded into the secret system. Psychiatry—still extremely conscious of the centrality of sex—was penetrating the system.

Legal procedures and press coverage about priests who have abused minors has opened the secret world of celibacy to broad public scrutiny. There are responsible and informed voices that have made profound historical and psychological observations about how the celibate system works (Wills, 2000; Kennedy, 2001). Authoritative observations have been recorded from within the Vatican without any effort to make quantifiable estimates of behaviors (The Millenari, 2000). But the world is observing in new ways and with unique intensity the celibate/sexual world of priests.

LEVELS OF OBSERVATION

In my research of celibacy, I organized my data into five levels of observation. I base my estimates of the celibate/sexual practice of priests and my analysis of the structure of Roman Catholic clerical life on this data.

> *First Level*: Firsthand experiences of priests.
> *Second Level*: Firsthand experiences of sexual partners of priests.
> *Third Level*: Reports from qualified observers.
> *Fourth Level*: Autobiographical and biographical accounts in private and group settings.
> *Fifth Level:* Validation. Public record.

First Level Observation: FIRSTHAND EXPERIENCE OF PRIESTS. The group of reporters who formed the core contribution to knowledge about the celibate practice within the Roman Catholic Church are those who were involved in the process of living it. Those who wanted their stories told are priests who shared their ongoing experience of life. Part of this group was involved in psychotherapy or counseling. They discussed and shared the complexities of their celibate/sexual development in that context. Others shared their life experience outside any form of therapy.

Second Level Observation: FIRSTHAND EXPERIENCE OF SEXUAL PARTNERS OF PRIESTS. From the very beginning, I noted firsthand experience reported by men and women who had been involved sexually with priests. These included priests, nuns, and seminarians, married and single women, and married and single men. I retained this information almost instinctively. At first I was ignorant of the real significance of the data. But it provided information from the celibate/sexual structure of the priesthood about that group of men who would not self-report their adjustment or activity. Throughout the period from 1960 to 1985 few of these people thought of themselves as "victims"; certainly not in the well-defined sense of 2000. Likewise, the appellation "survivor" was not available to support this group during those years. Litigation was not a serious consideration for the vast majority of these people. Although this group was working out relational conflicts, many talked about their involvement as a matter of course in recording their psychosocial histories.

Some reported the priest or brother to a bishop or religious superior. They seldom received any satisfaction or compensation for their abuse. In some cases child support was provided for a birth that involved one of its clergy. I began to realize the value of these accounts as reliable and authentic observations of priests' behavior because there was no secondary gain from sharing them. This group of informants alerted me to the scope of sexual involvement of priests with minors.

Third Level Observation: QUALIFIED OBSERVERS. One group of reporters were people who were not direct participants in the sexual behavior of priests but were in positions to observe the celibate/sexual conduct of priests. That is fellow clergy, housekeepers, concerned superiors or clinicians who spoke in case study fashion about priests where the anonymity of the patient and confidentiality of the therapeutic bond could remain in tact. These reports were extremely important because often reports from housekeepers, assistant pastors, or fellow clergy were made to religious superiors, chancery officials or bishops, and ignored.

The tendency on the part of the hierarchical system to disregard these kinds of reports reinforces a secret system, inhibits public disclosure, and defends and perpetuates abusers. It was clear to me that many superiors did not want to "know" the actual facts, (culpable ignorance). Some regarded sexual transgressions as a normal, if unfortunate, part of clerical life. Sexual activity was common enough so that it did not merit special attention, unless there was threat of public scandal. Intimidation of the victim or person reporting was commonly the first line of defense. There are significant numbers of instances where the person reporting abuse was chastised for speaking up. I experienced this kind of reception three times. Victims were often blamed for the abuse they suffered and humiliated for coming forward.

During the 1960s, '70s, and '80s priests increasingly sought counseling, psychotherapy, or psychoanalysis as a means to growth and development. Many wished to enhance their celibate commitment, and facilitate their emotional maturity. Others requested treatment for troublesome symptoms, while others were sent to treatment (or hospitalization) because they were troublesome, in trouble that might cause scandal, or had manifested behavioral or psychiatric symptoms that progressed to an unacceptable level.

Some clinicians shared case histories in a teaching mode. Preeminent among this group who taught me was Leo H. Bartemeier, M.D. He possessed breadth of knowledge and depth of experience with the treatment of Catholic clergy. He did numerous consultations with bishops and religious superiors. He mentored me during my 5 years at Seton Institute; I employed his services for 2 hours a week from 1972 through 1978. During this time he shared his full experience from working with clergy and supplied my study with background and case material from as early as 1917 and most especially from 1930 onward. He also assisted me in sorting and analyzing the data that I had amassed.

Some priests' histories were presented by clinicians who were inexperienced with the treatment of Catholic priests; they were in the process of consulting another clinician who knew about treatment issues of clergymen. In all, case studies from 25 psychologists, psychiatrists, and psychoanalysts were available to me during the course of my study; many of these cases were presented in the setting of Seton Psychiatric Institute or at St. John's University Institute for Mental Health between 1965 and 1970.

Fourth Level of Revelation: AUTOBIOGRAPHY AND BIOGRAPHICAL REPORTS. Priests and superiors who were not in therapy shared their stories. Sexual aspects of life are mostly spoken of in private. But reports of celibate/sexual disclosure also developed within open but restricted group settings. Some experiences are more easily shared with a stranger. There are times when sharing is most easily encouraged within a group of peers. In this regard, the examiner of a culture must be accepted as a participant-observer. The era between the 1960s and the 1990s was remarkable in its fashionableness of sharing personal feelings. The group sensitivity movement, the development of group therapy, and the proliferation of self-help groups as well as management styles favored mutual self-exposure and process thinking.

In every culture there are avenues of communication between members of an "in" group. Besides direct verbal expression of celibate/sexual facts, there are as canon law indicates "suspicions, rumors, complaints, and reports of sexual activity" that a bishop or religious superior is obliged to investigate. Group settings are often the arena for sorting out fact from fiction.

Opportunities for self-revelation proliferated in religious houses and Catholic dioceses during this time in the form of informal support groups, workshops, and meetings that encouraged open and frank disclosure of personal concerns and viewpoints. These situations, while they did not offer the depth afforded by long-term involvement with reporting subjects in individual settings or psychotherapy, did often reveal intense perspectives from real life struggles with celibacy and sexuality. Participants shared concerns that were frequently eased by a kind of consensual validation. Masturbation, sexual attractions or affairs, questions about sexual orientation could be tested out and subjected to peer evaluation. Some groups formed or evolved into specialized support systems; that is, groups of priests who had struggled with alcoholism or a gay orientation.

The mental health disciplines and the psychological sciences (especially psychoanalysis) were undoubtedly overvalued during the decades of the '50s, '60s, and '70s. The helping professions were subjected to over-expectations. These circumstances allowed clinicians unprecedented entrée into the inner workings of celibate/sexual life during this era. My studies reflect these sets of circumstances.

Fifth Level Process: VALIDATION. My estimates of the celibate/ sexual behavior of priests are based on observations and revelations within the four levels mentioned above. They produced approximately fifteen hundred narratives about the sexual/celibate adjustment of priests: approximately one-third (497) involved priests who were in some type of therapy; another third (512) were priests not in therapy; and one-third (504) were from sexual partners or victims of clergy. I refined my definition of celibacy and established my estimates of celibate/sexual behaviors and outlined the process of achievement of celibacy by 1985.

My estimates were not made from a random sample population nor were the observations made in the form of a survey or a poll. Nonetheless, these estimates can be validated. First of all, those who have lived a celibate/sexual life and existed within the celibate culture can verify practice in their lives and experience. They can estimate the celibate/sexual adjustments within their group.

Exposure of clergy sexual activity and sexual scandals has proliferated in the media since 1985, remarkably so since 2002. By exploring certain examples the media validates that sexual activity by clergy does indeed exist. The media is selective in its reporting and cannot establish numerical estimates for the group. But public incidence can contribute to validation of broader observations.

Court reports in criminal or civil proceedings provide another source of validation of sexual abuse and confirm the existence of sexual activity by some priests. Analysis of the numbers revealed in these arenas and the record of allegations by victims has contributed to numerical estimates. Records of reports of priests who abused minors exceed 1,800. These figures will, of necessity, always be incomplete. Public exposure of failure cannot vitiate the obvious achievements of clergy and celibate practice that does exist within a goodly proportion of those who profess it.

Numerical valuations are important factors in organizing and validating data. Scientific studies must be verifiable, measurable, and replicable. Ethnography meets these criteria. There will be future studies using other methods, randomly selected subjects, and formal standardized questions that address the questions that I have explored ethnographically. They can be productive in ways that complete the work I have done in the delicate area of sex among a group who profess celibacy. Until that time, I submit my estimates of the celibate/sexual practice of Catholic clergy as a baseline for careful consideration.

NUMERICAL SUMMARY

I considered reports of or from a total 2,776 priests from five levels of observation for my estimates of celibate/sexual behavior. My goal always was to provide a baseline for understanding the practice, process, and achievement of celibacy. Of these 2,776 priests:

The 512 priests not in therapy were between the ages of 26 and 78. This group contributed information on levels of observation 1, 2, 3, and 4. Their narratives were invaluable for the understanding of the celibate process and for the achievement of celibacy among Roman Catholic priests in the United States.

Three hundred five priests had some form of therapeutic contact with the principal investigator and, from this context, contributed data to levels of observation 1, 2, and 3.

Material from case study reports of 192 priests in psychotherapy with analysts, psychiatrists, and psychologists added primary and corroborating data for level 3 observations.

The 504 people who had been sexual partners or victims of priests or were in a position to observe it directly provided an essential and valuable fund of data for level 2 and 3 observations.

One thousand two hundred sixty-three priests belonged to 10 religious groups (diocesan or religious) in which I had sufficient, knowledgeable contacts (bishop, major superior, novice master, personnel director, vocations director, or other) who supplied observations and estimates of the sexual functioning of men in their groups. Reports from these groups, along with reports from private and public sources, contributed to level 5 validation of our estimates from other data.

ESTIMATES OF SEXUAL BEHAVIOR

I estimate that *at any one time 50 percent of priests are practicing celibacy* (in accord with the definition I proposed in chapter 4.)

Two percent (2%) of vowed clergy can be said to have *achieved* celibacy—that is, they have successfully negotiated each step of celibate development at a more or less appropriate stage of development and are characterologically so firmly established that their state is, for all intents and purposes, irreversible.

Another group of priests—eight percent (8%)—has consolidated celibate practice beyond the point of expectable reversal in spite of some past failures.

An additional forty percent (40%) of priests do practice celibacy, but their practice is not established enough to mark it as either consolidated or achieved. And indeed, these priests are open to sexual reversals and experimentation as well as progress.

My first premise leads to the conclusion that at any one time half of the priest population involve themselves with sexual activity of some sort.

Thirty percent (30%) of priests are involved in heterosexual relationships, associations, experimentation or patterns of behavior.

Fifteen percent (15%) of priests are involved with homosexual relationships, experimentation, or patterns of behavior.

Five percent (5%) of priests are involved with problematic sexual behaviors—transvestitism, exhibitionism, pornography, or compulsive masturbation.

Heterosexual Behaviors. Of the priests who are heterosexually active, two-thirds (or 20% of the priest population) are involved either in a more or less stable sexual relationship with a woman or, alternatively, with sequential women in an identifiable pattern of behavior (estimate from all sources). The additional third (8 to 10% of priests) are at a stage of heterosexual exploration that often involves incidental sexual contacts. The latter resembles dating and predating behavior, where no relationship exists. Nor have these priests established a pattern of sexual involvement. This behavior can be the extent of the priest's experimentation, or it can evolve into a pattern of sexual activity or even a relationship. Included in this number are priests who get involved with minors.

Homosexual Behaviors. From the data I have I estimate that thirty percent (30%) of all clergy have a homosexual orientation. Other knowledgeable observers tend to register higher numbers (Cozzens, 1998). I think that some observers do not take into account the number of sexually undifferentiated men in the priesthood. Approximately half of the priests who would describe themselves as homosexual either practice celibacy or have consolidated or achieved celibacy, and have done so in the same proportion as priests who have a heterosexual orientation.

Approximately 15 percent of clergy involve themselves in homosexual activity (projected from all sources). Eight percent (8%) of clergy have a stable homosexual relationship. Some of these relationships involve genuine friendship and loyalty, without interfering with the practice of their ministry. Priests experience the involvement as an aid to their lives and vocations. Priests involved with women express the same sentiments. In both categories priests experience little or no guilt about their behavior. (Or at least do not express sufficient motivation to change it.) Some priests in this category do experience guilt about the sexual acts and periodically use sacramental confession or some means of spiritual direction. However, the pattern and the behavior described remain relatively stable over long periods of time.

Three percent (3%) of priests experiment with sexual relationships of relatively short duration. The behaviors represented can be experimental and involve short-term relationships with relatively appropriate partners. If these relationships involve anonymous partners they are not indiscriminate or dangerous. Alcohol and drugs drastically change this dynamic.

Four percent (4%) of behavior by homosexual clergy is conflicted to the extreme, impulsive, anonymous, dangerous, or all of the above. Frequently a cycle of guilt and repeated promises of reform plague this behavior. In its extreme, self-loathing and fear drive this behavior. Alcohol and drugs are a common in this dynamic.

A large proportion of *situational* and *transitional* actions occur in the unique homosocial atmosphere and structure of the clerical subculture. These account for discrepancies between homosexual behavior and orientation. Some men who experiment in the clerical culture later accurately identify themselves and function consistently as heterosexual. Also, there is a small percent of men who involve themselves in heterosexual activity who later identify themselves as homosexually oriented.

Some homosexually oriented men do not involve themselves with other people. They nonetheless act out sexual fantasy, often via pornography and compulsive masturbation.

Priests and Minors. Six percent (6%) of priests involve themselves sexually with minors. The minor may be either male or female, so the behavior can be either homosexual or heterosexual depending on sex of the victim. Twice as many victims are adolescents as are prepubescent children.

Of the six percent (6%) of priests involved with children or minors, two percent (2%) have a basic heterosexual orientation; four percent (4%) have a homosexual orientation. But the paraphilia is so clearly dominant that sexual orientation is a secondary question. There certainly is no connection between orientation and object of sexual excitation. Homosexually oriented men are no more likely to be abusers than heterosexuals.

Celibacy/Sexuality—a Poll. A poll of 5,000 priests conducted by the *Los Angeles Times* in October 2002 received responses from 1,851 participants (a 37% response rate). The final question was: "Is celibacy a problem?"

Answers:
32%—Not a problem, do not waver.
47%—Takes time to achieve, an ongoing journey.
14%—Try to follow it, don't always succeed
2%—Celibacy is not relevant to the priesthood; don't follow it.

In the same poll 23 percent of younger priests categorized themselves as "gay or on the homosexual side." Fifteen percent of the current clergy chose that self-identity.

NARRATIVES

The narratives that follow are from the histories as told by informants. They have given permission for inclusion. In some instances, the histories are of people now deceased. Other examples are so common that the example cited is an accurate representation of a whole subgroup.

In all cases, the identity of informants is carefully guarded. The reader should be aware that there is no likelihood that he or she will guess the informants' identities. There is, however, a very good chance that the informed student will recognize someone "like" that. In fact, if this study has really tapped the essences of the practice, process, and achievement of celibacy, *every* priest will find himself included, and *no* person will find himself exposed.

PART II

PRACTICE VERSUS PROFESSION

4

THE MASTURBATIONS

Nec tangere nec tangi (Neither touch nor be touched)

—Giulio di Medici

Masturbation is the most common and frequently used sexual behavior of celibates. At times, masturbation is employed with other sexual elements—voyeurism, exhibitionism, transvestism, and pornography—but sometimes it is the celibate's exclusive or occasional sexual expression.

The first survey of masturbatory activity among celibates, that I am aware of, was conducted in the 1950s by a seminarian from the archdiocese of St. Paul.

In 1969, Dr. William Masters told me about a survey of 200 celibates, the results of which revealed that 198 of them reported having masturbated at least once during the previous year. Of the other two, Dr. Masters said, "I don't think they understood the question!"

In the late 1970s, Father Michael Peterson, M.D., a priest of the archdiocese of Washington, DC, conducted several informal surveys of his own (unpublished work) and spoke of masturbation as an often practiced and usual activity among seminarians and young clergy.

I estimate that 80 percent of clergy masturbate occasionally (numbers based on information from clergy sources only). Knowledgeable people, including priests, react to this estimate with a "So what?" Unfortunately, the question is not that simple for the serious student of celibacy. Regardless of whether masturbation is frequent or infrequent among celibates, three pressing issues must be faced. First, the traditional assertion that masturbation is essentially pathological. Secondly, the teaching that—even if it is not pathological among the very young—it is an immature activity. Third, the moral stance that masturbation is intrinsically selfish and sinful because it violates nature.

Even those who consider masturbation a basically normal activity, necessary for healthy development, are aware that it *can* also be a sign of distress. Freud originally considered it "dangerous," and saw it as the cause of neurasthenia—a neurosis marked by anxiety and lassitude.

In clarifying Freud's stance, Fenichel (1954) called masturbation a *normal* symptom, "if it appears at certain intervals and only if sexual acts with objects [persons] are not possible. It is a *pathological* symptom under other circumstances, and has to be understood as a sign that the capacity for satisfaction is disturbed. . . . And really, there is no mental disorder in which the symptom of pathological masturbation does not occur. The psychic value [significance] of pathological masturbation can be manifold" (p. 86). Fenichel's comments are why I refer to the masturbations in the plural—the plural challenges us to distinguish this sexual behavior beyond categories of normal versus pathological, mature versus immature, and virtue versus sin.

NATURE

Masturbation is normal and universal among healthy infants. In fact, it is necessary for development. It would be ridiculous to hold that an infant should discover every other appendage and orifice of his body and selectively neglect his genitals. As early as 1949, Spitz and Wolf wrote about autoerotic activity in one's first year of life. The results of their observations are especially significant since they established the link between good object relationships and the manifestations of spontaneous genital play at that age. They determined that "a certain level of development is a prerequisite for the appearance of genital play" (p. 91), and "the closer the mother-child relation . . . the more infants we find manifesting genital play" (p. 97). By contrast, a parallel link exists between the deprivation of good mothering and the lack of an infant's development. In Spitz and Wolf's words:

> [Autoerotic activities] are absent when object relations are absent; when object relations are so constantly contradictory that object formation is made impossible, rocking results. When object relations change in an intermittent manner fecal play results. When object relations are "normal," genital play results. (p. 119)

Although this infantile autoerotic activity is not masturbation as such, it is both a precursor of and necessary to the establishment of a sense of self. Kleeman (1965) says of self-stimulation in the 1st year of life, "a slightly different way to conceptualize this is that good maternal-infant relations facilitate the discharge of maturational drive representatives in the form of self-stimulation" (p. 241).

From their observations of infants and children, Margaret Mahler and her colleagues (1975) noted that it is probably of developmental significance that a boy becomes acutely aware of his ability to have erections at the same time that he develops mastery over his own body by walking. A little boy's exploration of his own penis during the first part of his second year seems at first "an experience of unmitigated pleasure. At the beginning of the third year, the masturbation takes on the quality of 'checking their penises for reassurance'" (p. 105).

In normal boys, this self-stimulation leads naturally toward clear masturbatory activity that is appropriate in their 3rd to 5th years. Their self-discovery is progressive and complicated, and is intricately intertwined with their entire developmental process (Kleeman, 1966). It is sufficient for our purpose here to remember that a boy's discovery of his penis has profound implications for the formation of his male identity—that is, the establishment of his core gender identity—and of healthy object relationships throughout his life. It is not a process that ends in infancy. Freud (1953a) refers to the "second phase of infantile masturbation" around the 4th year that may continue until suppressed or "without interruption" until puberty (p. 189).

It is generally conceded that adolescence is the ordinary stage of development for the consolidation of one's sexual identity and solidification of career goals. Aristotle believed that adolescent masturbation fostered maturity and manhood (DeMause, 1974, p. 46). It is also common knowledge that masturbation is a well-nigh universal activity of normal adolescence. Few authorities would hold otherwise. It is normal at this age, Fenichel (1954) says, because

[i]t is the best discharge children can have. If tendencies to masturbate do not appear at all, one can be sure that a serious repression has already taken place. And if the educators prohibit masturbation altogether, they

push the child into a state of tension, which is difficult to sustain. And more than that: They create in the child's mind the idea that sexual matters are bad and dangerous. They motivate the child to repress his instincts in the future, and in this way cause neuroses and deformations of the child's personality. (p. 85)

PATHOLOGY

Most health professionals and clergy now believe that masturbation itself is natural; however, it does involve some psychic compromise, and can become pathological. Fenichel (1954) described the problems:

> But it is true that there are certain other dangers attendant on masturbation—dangers which are mostly less important than the dangers that are caused by prohibition of masturbation—and they become actual only in pathological forms of masturbation.
>
> 1. The tolerance to sustain tensions is diminished if one is accustomed to flee from every tension immediately into masturbation.
> 2. If reality is customarily replaced by fantasy, this circumstance causes or increases introversion; that means a general withdrawal from reality. Masturbation may furthermore fixate the disturbance of the subject's relations to his objects, of which it (the masturbation) was a consequence.
> 3. If masturbation is performed with a bad conscience and anxiety which prevent its running its natural course, this circumstance has, as I have described, pathological consequences.
>
> But we also said before that a normal person must be able to masturbate if circumstances prevent sexual object relations. . . . (p. 86)

In most priests, masturbation is not a symptom of severe pathology, although clearly some reports can only be understood as involving some disturbance. There are priests for whom masturbation forms the only available means of sexual tension reduction. They only know how to work. Play has not been part of their developmental skill. Their social interactions are restricted.

Some priests deny themselves nothing in the way of creature comforts. They lack a capacity to delay gratification in any area of their lives. Sometimes these men went through a period of severe self-denial while they were in training and now compensate themselves for their sacrifice.

A number of priests reported experiencing sexual excitement while they heard confessions. Most could tolerate the discomfort. Some reported having a spontaneous emission and others reported masturbating at the site.

Stringent religious restrictions on masturbation—because it is deemed "unnatural" and a mortal sin—can lead to unhealthy compromises in order to control the impulse. Paul Hendrickson (1983) tells of the devout confessor who tried to help his students fight their tendency to masturbate by having them hold a crucifix in one hand while stroking their own genitals with the other—to the point of short of ejaculation. By avoiding discharge, the student could evidence his choice between pleasure and religious goals. The confessor also offered to let the students practice in his presence during confession. This custom was not unusual. Many confessors rationalized that they were helping anxious young men to be comfortable with their bodies by exposing themselves to the priest or allowing him to measure their penis, and so forth.

Severe anxiety regarding masturbation can be overwhelming to some priests. They masturbate only under great internal pressure, with no fantasy and with little pleasure. Afterward they feel compelled to go to confession immediately, sometimes at great disruption to their lives and reality. One priest reported endangering his life by a late night search for another priest to forgive his sin. This kind of tension is pathological. But, as one priest pointed out, he had been taught that a single act of masturbation was sufficient for him to lose his soul and destroy all the good he had ever done. When understood in that context, his anxiety becomes a logical response to the doctrine he learned and obsessively obeyed.

Striving to avoid "transgressing nature" leads some priests to elaborate ways of circumventing the law. Rationalizations abound: if he does not touch his genitals with his hands the masturbation doesn't count; or if he goes only so far in his touching, and then the ejaculation happens "by accident," he is not responsible. Therefore, behaviors such as anal manipulation or scratching, genital pressure on a pillow, encouraging a partial erection, or simply allowing the water pressure of a shower or whirlpool to do the arousing make the experience acceptable. In these instances, the pathology derives not from the masturbation, but from the anxiety that leads to such convoluted reasoning.

In some cases, the anxiety can become so severe that all means of masturbation are impossible for the individual. Such inhibition at the expense of all psychic functioning is neither healthy nor reasonable. One disturbed priest who was hospitalized had been asked prior to his ordination when he confessed masturbating, "When are you going to grow up?" At that moment he vowed never to masturbate again. Over the next 10 years, an increasing amount of his psychic energy was consumed while he kept his vow and in the process lost his effectiveness in every other area of his professional life. During his hospitalization, he had to break his vow to regain his sanity and initiate a satisfying ministry.

Anxiety can cause such a preoccupation with control that extreme means can either be fantasized or actually carried out. Besides fasting, severe asceticism and self-flagellation were a part of some priests' training prior to the mid1960s. Few priests continue these practices, but some record wishing that they could be castrated to relieve their sexual tension. One celibate did in fact castrate himself, precipitating his admission to a psychiatric hospital.

Although the dynamic is not identical, there is an ancient precedent for castration in the service of celibacy, epitomized by the 3rd-century theologian Origen. And of course Abélard (1079–1142) was involuntarily castrated when Héloise's guardian uncle thought Abélard had abandoned her after her secret marriage. The castration was in reprisal for sexually educating the canon's niece, Héloise, and for violating with her the celibacy his position of university professor demanded. The mutilation succeeded in curtailing his sexual activity and ardor, but did little to cool Héloise's devotion for him. She spent the rest of her life in a convent.

Masturbation that usually occurs in conjunction with pathological patterns of sexual behavior, is secondary to the pathology, and should be distinguished from the behaviors described above.

MATURITY AND IMMATURITY

There are those who say that masturbation is, at best, an immature sexual activity, even if it is not a sign of illness. After talking with hundreds of priests, I have come to the conclusion that sometimes masturbation can be an expression of maturity at any age (and at times may be virtuous).

How does masturbation contribute to maturity? Play and transitional objects hold a very important place in helping a child deal with reality. Fenichel (1954) describes the situation as follows:

> Playing is a very important matter for children. The child learns to master reality by playing. What the child has experienced passively in the past or what he expects to happen in the future—that he plays actively. The tensions which have been set by passive experiences or which will be set by future events, could overwhelm him. But he himself sets this kind of tension in a smaller degree by playing, so that he can learn to master it gradually. Playing is the way to learn to master the world. By playing, a child learns to bear increasing self-imposed tension, becoming thereby slowly able to withstand reality.
>
> But in my opinion it is to a certain degree correct to say that masturbation *is* sexual play. By masturbating the child learns to master sexual tension. One often hears the idea that the masturbating child loses self-control and becomes a victim of his bad instincts. I consider that the opposite is true: if masturbation has no pathological character (as described above) it is a means by which the child learns to control his sexual instincts. (p. 87)

One must be careful to distinguish between masturbation and other forms of play since, as Winnicott (1971) points out, the latter has a quality of sublimation that masturbation lacks (p. 45).

There are priests who can accept that masturbation among infants is an appropriate activity to help the infants traverse the distance between their subjective world and external reality. Without belaboring psychoanalytic theory, these priests are instinctively aware of psychic equivalents to the beloved mother and her breast. There is, in addition, the need for transitional phenomena to help children cope with reality and the need to endure the pain of giving up things to gain autonomy and build bridges between the subjective and objective so as ultimately to operate as total human beings (Winnicott, 1965, pp. 143–5). These priests understand the relationship of play and mastery.

Likewise, many priests acknowledge that masturbatory activity in adolescence is age-appropriate behavior. Winnicott says, the adolescent "is essentially an isolate. It is from a position of isolation that a beginning is made which may result in relationships between individuals, and eventually in socialization." This isolation colors all the sexual experience of the young adolescent boy who, in his psychic cocoon, does not know what kind of butterfly he will become—homosexual, heterosexual, or frankly narcissistic. Masturbation is part of practicing for an adult sexual life and relationship—future reality tested in fantasy. He continues, "urgent masturbatory activity may be at this stage a repeated getting rid of sex, rather than a form of sex experience" (1965, p. 81). Masturbation can simply reduce sexual tension enough for the adolescent to avoid, at least temporarily, having to make an internal sexual commitment.

Many priests empathize deeply with this phase of the maturational process and exist for years in this state of suspended sexuality. Their training period sanctifies their isolation without establishing a truly spiritual relationship or solidifying their sexual identities. Here the adolescent process may be played out, but in *super slow motion,* one action frame at a time. Other priests delay the whole identity process until after they complete seminary studies, when at some future time the floodwaters of adolescence break through their dam of repression.

A priest had been a successful and affable student during his seminary years, during which time he had not masturbated, and had no memory of *ever* having done so. For the first 3 years after his ordination, he was relatively happy in his ministry, part of which involved hearing the confessions of adolescents. He became curious about masturbation, because so many of the young people he admired confessed frequent masturbation. The priest began to read books on sex—something he had avoided doing. He had, in fact, never allowed himself to think about the whole area of sexuality. When 28 years old, this man discovered masturbation. Along with it he was inundated by all the thoughts and questions he had been side-stepping. He became profoundly confused, feeling deceived by the teachers and the system he had taken literally. By confronting his previous denial, avoidance, and over-dependence, he began to re-evaluate his life in light of his new-found sexuality.

This phenomenon is common. Repression and denial sustain a man in unchallenged celibacy for long periods of time. It is especially so among men of superior intellect who do well in their studies and are successful in the clerical system. They are popular with their peers and superiors. A number of this group of informants registered anger—also adolescent-like—at the system they believed betrayed them. Having kept all the rules of that system, the men were surprised and felt sabotaged by the force of their internal fire. These were men who thought they had come to terms with their celibacy because of their intellectual success. As one man said, "I have never before had a problem I could not reason my way through." Body, emotion, and sex were foreign territories where all the acquired skills now apparently had no meaning or effectiveness. The coin of the realm had changed.

Some priests react strongly against their own sexual impulses and, at least temporarily, reinforce their resolve by reaction formation. They rebuke with disdain adolescents who confide their masturbations. Harking back to the pathological model, others threaten the penitents with impending insanity if they continue their self-stimulation. Both of these kinds of responses have decreased over the decades. Now more priests seem to be in tune with the cartoon that showed two boys sitting on a curb, their feet planted firmly in the gutter, with one boy saying to the other, "The way I understand it, you go crazy if you don't do it."

The line between pathology and immaturity seems to blur when it comes to masturbation. I remember hearing a retreat master who had long experience both as a hospital chaplain and as a minister to the inner city indigent. He drew a picture of the futility and deprivation of masturbating by telling how these poor souls masturbated even on their death bed while he was administering the last sacraments. The equation in his mind was clear: Masturbation equals deprivation equals death, much in the same way the medical manuals of the

1800s equated all manner of ailments with "the habit," as it was called. Today, what most health care workers who attend the dying know is that masturbation near the time of death is a common phenomenon without moral implication. The process of dying is regressive. Union with the Ultimate Other also entails a trip backward to the womb; thus, the life circle is complete (Schnaper, 1984, p. 282).

Clergy were not alone in relegating masturbation to the category of the pathological and immature. Entrance to the Naval Academy as recently as 1947 was barred to anyone who, on medical examination, was found to masturbate habitually. (How this is discovered on physical examination remains unclear to me.) *The Boy Scout Manual* dropped its negative reference to masturbation only in 1973.

Quite simply, under ordinary circumstances, masturbation can be a natural, healthy, unselfish act, expected at *any* stage of life as a part of the process of growth, self-definition, and normal sexual function. The basic question really is how well a person relates to reality and to other people.

The place of masturbation in the life of a person vowed to celibacy becomes a serious conundrum. Does it violate celibacy? Two bishops from the same diocese, required to give legal disposition in 1988, were asked that very question. One answered, "Yes," and the other "No." The correct response is probably "Yes *and* no."

Like the informant described earlier, there are priests who claim never to have masturbated. (A few of these men are victims of Kallmann's syndrome.) Others are psychically so defended that they deny or rationalize away their sexual reality; they are not consciously lying. Still others simply *do* lie. Winnicott (1971) warns that anyone who investigates these areas must be prepared for lies. I have records of several priests who indeed had not masturbated either in their adolescence or adult lives. Their profoundly restricted personalities rather than their lack of masturbation led them into a period of severe mental illness. During their treatment, their ability to masturbate was seen as a sign of health, maturation, and growth.

My estimate is that at any one time, 20 percent of priests are involved in masturbatory patterns that are manifestations of sexual immaturity. These patterns may include the pathological elements Fenichel (1954) mentioned: overuse as an exclusive tension-reducing maneuver; isolation and preference of sexual fantasy over sexual reality; and extreme forms of anxiety. This group of 20 percent does not include healthy masturbation or other forms of sexual behavior that concomitantly involve masturbation.

NOCTURNAL EMISSIONS

In order for the church's teaching on sex and masturbation to be credible, involuntary or nocturnal emissions would have to provide, in Kinsey's words (Kinsey, Pomeroy, Wardell, & Martin, 1948), "sufficient release to keep an individual physically and mentally balanced." I have no evidence that this is the case. I hope our study will provide the impetus for further refinement of data from observant celibates to determine the place of nocturnal emissions in the life course of a male. American priests are the logical group to provide this service to science and to clarify a moral position the Church adamantly defends without sufficient cause.

> "It would . . . be of exceeding scientific importance to have histories from a sufficient sample of highly restrained individuals, particularly of those who are celibate. Without such data it is, of course, impossible to depend upon general statements which have been made on this point, especially when they come from persons who are interested in defending moral or social philosophies." (Kinsey et al., 1948, p. 528)

As with all sexual issues, the moral questions surrounding nocturnal emissions are not new. I remember long discussions from my own seminary days. A question such as: "If one awakes during an ejaculation and enjoys the experience, does it become mortally sinful?" This question has a tradition dating to the 4th century. Athanasius treated nocturnal emissions as natural, and did not consider them sinful (Quasten, 1960, p. 328). Timothy of Alexandria, an early writer whose opinions on this matter were confirmed by the Sixth and Seventh Ecumenical Councils, wrote:

> A layman who has suffered a nocturnal emission should not have Communion if this is because he has himself by deliberate choice entertained

desire for a woman in his heart. But if the reason is temptation from the demon, then he may have Communion. (Russell, 1981, p. 135)

A 3rd-century cleric, Dionysius of Alexandria, held the same modulated view. Two important elements of moral development were manifest in the controversy: (1) the growing responsibility of the self-awareness that good and evil did not reside outside the self; and (2) the question of what is natural regarding sexual functioning.

Very early in Christian tradition, the celibate ideal was outlined by the Thebaid—monks living in the Egyptian desert. A discourse dating from the 4th century elaborates on the subject, and sets the standard:

1. Take care that no one who has pondered on the image of a woman during the night dare to approach the sacred Mysteries, in case any of you has had a dream while entertaining such an image.

2. For seminal emissions do take place unconsciously without the stimulus of imagined forms, occurring not from deliberate choice but involuntarily. They arise naturally and flow forth from an excess of matter. They are therefore not to be classed as sinful. But imaginings are the result of deliberate choice and are a sign of an evil disposition.

3. Now a monk . . . must even transcend the law of nature and must certainly not fall into the slightest pollution of the flesh. On the contrary, he must mortify the flesh and not allow an excess of seminal fluid to accumulate. We should therefore try to keep the fluid depleted by the prolongation of fasting. Otherwise, it arouses our sensual appetites.

4. A monk must have nothing whatever to do with the sensual appetites. Otherwise how would he differ from men living in the world? We often see laymen abstaining from pleasures for the sake of their health or for some other rational motive. How much more should the monk take care of the health of his soul and his mind and his spirit. (Russell, 1981, p. xx)

There has been no clear path to the refinement of these issues in moral thought. A 9th-century cleric, John the Faster, still embraced the most severe position by forbidding communion to any man who had experienced a nocturnal emission, regardless of his subjective involvement.

Modern moralists tend to dismiss the controversy as inconsequential and thereby miss a core problem in the theory of sexuality: What is natural? And by missing this question, they avoid the related issue of the place of sexual pleasure in human development.

FASTING

Most ascetic authors draw a connection between fasting and controlling the sexual appetite. There is evidence that the link existed early in Christian tradition. It is probable that some of the early monks were anorectic and experienced the elation and euphoria of negative nitrogen balance, ketosis, or chemical reactions that alter mood in severe diet restriction. Rudolph Bell (1985) explored the effects of anorexia in certain of the female saints.

In talking about his own celibate struggle, Gandhi said that if a man can control his appetite for food, he can control all of his instincts:

> But if it [celibacy] was a matter of ever-increasing joy, let no one believe that it was an easy thing for me. Even when I am past fifty-six years, I realize how hard a thing it is. Every day I realize more and more that it is like walking on the sword's edge, and I see every moment the necessity for eternal vigilance.
>
> Control of the palate is the first essential in the observation of the vow. I found that complete control of the palate made the observance very easy, and so I now pursued my dietetic experiments not merely from the vegetarian's but also from the *brahmachari's* [celibate's] point of view. (Gandhi, 1960)

Mental attitude as well as dietary restriction is essential to celibate practice. Gandhi sounds much like the early desert Fathers in his admonitions:

> Fasting can help to curb animal passion, only if it is undertaken with a view to self-restraint. Some of my friends have actually found their animal passion and palate stimulated as an after-effect of fasts. That is to

say, fasting is futile unless it is accompanied by an incessant longing for self-restraint.

Fasting and similar discipline is, therefore, one of the means to the end of self-restraint, but it is not all, and if physical fasting is not accompanied by mental fasting, it is bound to end in hypocrisy and disaster. (1980, p. 40)

Priest informants who had been POWs during World War II reported that they experienced either a significant diminution or complete cessation of their sex drive during their capture; their nocturnal emissions also stopped. They associated the change with their severely restricted diet. As one priest said, "During that time, I never once dreamt about sex; I always dreamt about food."

From the 1940s through the 1960s, priests in training were cautioned against the use of certain spices or condiments that might increase their sexual desire or cause nocturnal emissions. There were many jokes and rumors (with some justification in certain places) to the effect that saltpeter was added to the seminarians' food to reduce their sexual response. Fasting was regulated by church law, during Advent, Lent, and the vigils of certain feasts, for example.

Some religious orders still maintain stricter dietary regimens among their members than those followed by other celibates. There is no evidence that the stricter diet causes an appreciable difference in the rate of nocturnal emissions or masturbation in the two groups.

SPONTANEOUS EMISSIONS

There are individuals whose powers of imagination are sufficient to cause an emission. One celibate, 35 years old at the time of his interview with us, could sit in a library, his room, or even church, and without any physical movement at all could bring on an ejaculation. He struggled greatly with the morality of this ability and worried about his "normality." He would not allow himself to "masturbate" and never consciously used his hand to stimulate himself. He had joined the seminary as a teenager and his first conscious memory of sexual excitement was awakening from a nocturnal emission. Over the years he developed an ingenious compromise by re-creating dreams in his imagination. Visual stimulation—especially movies—were invariably sexually arousing to him. He had no other sexual contact or activity.

Another priest frequently experienced an erection while he was saying Mass and, on occasion, had a spontaneous ejaculation at the time of consecration or communion. He was greatly troubled by the experience, since his conscious thoughts were on his prayer and on the ritual he was performing. He was a spiritual man, not neurotic in any observable areas of his functioning. He used confession and incorporated into his spiritual goals occasional masturbation to reduce his excess sexual tension, forestalling the surprise of a spontaneous emission at Mass. At 45 years of age, he felt he knew himself and the rhythm of his life sufficiently to modulate his masturbation in the service of his vocation.

A third priest, in his late 20s, would fall asleep at his desk while preparing a sermon and would awaken at times during an emission. He wondered if he had some unconscious participation in the occurrence and felt he really did not have his sexuality "sorted out yet."

Some conscientious priests who have not allowed themselves to masturbate while awake have reported that they do so "in their sleep." They are half-aware of their involuntary movements on awakening, or they wake up shortly after the experience. All of the men reporting this behavior masturbated prior to their vow of celibacy and have reproduced in sleep the body movements that were part of their previous conscious pattern. The degree of responsibility each feels varies from extreme guilt, as though the act had happened in full consciousness, to guiltlessness—the latter men feeling that the experience is as involuntary as any other nocturnal emission.

There is an ancient story from the Fathers of the desert in which a convert awakens "with his hand full of white fluid." The elder explains to the troubled neophyte that it is merely an unconscious remnant of his former way of life, and does not invalidate his spiritual resolve to follow a life of celibacy. Obviously, there is continuity in the elements of the struggle to live without directly sought sexual pleasure, just as there is a persistence to the functioning of nature. Culture has only limited influence on the interaction between ideal and nature.

VICE AND VIRTUE

The claim that masturbation can be virtuous may seem revolutionary at first blush, but only the unreflective or inexperienced clinician or moralist can hold that it is intrinsically evil and inherently unhealthy. Sin was the unquestionable epithet attached to "self-abuse," "pollution," or simply "playing with oneself"—mortal sins all. The direst of punishments of Hell would befall one who succumbed to this temptation. A classic pamphlet commonly distributed at the spiritual retreats of teenage boys in the 1950s was entitled *The Greatest Sin*.

One might think that such a title would be reserved for a booklet on genocide, or perhaps rape. Racial injustice or any number of sins against humanity might also come to mind. But no. This was a treatise on masturbation. Generations of young boys became alternately terrified and disappointed that at 13 years of age they had already committed their greatest sin. One can almost admire those brave souls who defied such hyperbole, as well as those who used the book as a how-to manual. A few teenagers had the good sense to recognize the distortion—those who had already developed a firm direction in their sense of self-mastery.

This tradition of crowning masturbation as the king of sins is not recent. It is connected with the attempt to establish power via guilt. In writing about the 14th century, Barbara Tuchman (1978) says of Jean Gerson, the most eminent French theologian of the time:

> He advised confessors to arouse a sense of guilt in children with regard to their sexual habits so that they might recognize the need for penitence. Masturbation, even without ejaculation, was a sin that "takes away a child's virginity even more than if at the same age he had gone with a woman." The absence of a sense of guilt about it in children was a situation that must be changed. They must not hear coarse conversation or be allowed to kiss and fondle each other nor sleep in the same bed with the opposite sex, nor with adults even of the same sex. Gerson had six sisters, all of whom chose to remain unmarried in holy virginity. Some powerful family influence was surely at work here from which this strong personality emerged. (pp. 479–80)

The idea that masturbation is "worse" than fornication is based on the incomplete theology of sexuality that views procreation as the only end of all sexual acts. One can see the lengths to which this lacuna in moral teaching spread in a Vatican document entitled *Instruction on Respect for Human Life in Its Origin and on the Dignity of Procreation: Replies to Certain Questions of the Day* (Rhinelander, 1987). The collection of sperm through masturbation, even for medically valid reasons, is forbidden. The document states:

> Artificial insemination as a substitute for the conjugal act is prohibited by reason of the voluntarily achieved dissociation of the two meanings of the conjugal act. Masturbation, through which the sperm is normally obtained, is another sign of this dissociation; even when it is done for the purpose of procreation, the act remains deprived of its unitive meaning: It lacks the sexual relationship called for by the moral order, namely the relationship which realizes the full sense of mutual self-giving and human procreation in the context of true love.

When translated into practical interaction between two Christian people, those solemn words form a procrustean bed of very undignified make-up indeed. The only Vatican-approved method of collecting sperm for any medical reason is one devised by Dr. Ricardo Asch, as described in *The New York Times* on March 21, 1987:

> The method . . . requires the use of a special condom with a small perforation, which captures some sperm for processing in a laboratory by fertility specialists, while also allowing some of the sperm to escape, a necessary requirement of any treatment program facing the moral judgment of the Church. (Rhinelander, 1987, p. B10)

Anyone who sees this method as more dignified than masturbation, as a means of collecting sperm has no realization of what the conjugal act means to most married couples. To have sexual relations in order to pump sperm into a perforated condom for a laboratory sample is both a gross disregard and insensitivity for a woman and her dignity. She is simply used to obey the letter of a misguided law.

However, seeing masturbation as anything but grave sin poses a major threat to the entire structure of the church's teaching on sexuality. If all sex outside conjugal intercourse for the purpose of procreation is deemed sinful, a simple, clear-cut, *act-oriented* morality remains stable and unequivocal. Moral control is secure. Any variation—especially one grounded in male physiology, where ejaculation is physically determinable, if only by nocturnal emission—poses a serious threat to traditional order and control.

Confronting the problem of the masturbations is crucial for the understanding of celibacy. If it is intrinsically evil, as the church teaches, and yet is so commonly practiced across the broad spectrum of age, celibacy becomes a sham.

GUILT

Priests demonstrate a spectrum of guilt reactions to their masturbatory activity—a spectrum that has no demonstrable relationship to the act or its circumstance. One priest may be completely devoid of any guilt feeling after some very pathological masturbatory activity (i.e., in the confessional or in connection with child pornography), while another may have deep pangs of conscience over an isolated incident occurring in complete privacy and in the face of great stress.

For priests, masturbation has always been a subject of jokes among themselves, as well as a fascinating subject of moral exploration, as in "how to deal with it as a confessional matter" when directing penitents. Personal sharing with other priests has become common. The following is an example from the early 1980s.

Ten priests were gathered at a parish house for cocktails before dinner. One of the youngest priests announced, "I always like to masturbate when I shower; it makes me feel clean inside and out." The statement caused a conspicuous silence and a series of awkward coughs. For some priests, masturbation is still a subject that holds guilt and embarrassment, if not confusion and anxiety.

Masturbation can be a concomitant of any orientation or involvement—heterosexual or homosexual. For many priests, it is the main sexual activity for extended periods of time.

One group of priests reports no guilt at all about masturbation. These are decent, hardworking men, but would probably not be described as "holy" by anyone. They have very little in the way of a spiritual life, and not much religious motivation. They are natural men, who can be quite dedicated to the work of the church, although their strength lies in administration rather than in morality. Masturbation seems to keep them from other forms of sexual involvement, at least for long periods. Celibacy as a spiritual ideal has little meaning and does not become a great obstacle to their daily functioning.

The capacity for sexual denial found among priests seems unmatched in any other group of single men. On initial inquiry some priests will claim either that they have never masturbated or at least are not doing so currently. Only on subsequent interviews will they reveal that there is indeed a history of some form of self-stimulation. Yet these men are not lying. They exhibit a profound denial about their sexual activity because of the anxiety and passivity surrounding it. As they proceed through their interviews and the pattern of their tension reduction emerges, they describe behavior that somehow "doesn't count" as masturbation—activity before they go to sleep, when they awaken, while they are bathing or going to the bathroom. The masturbation is subsumed under another natural function, sometimes not involving the use of their hands. Since it is not incorporated into their consciousness and usually "just happens" without conscious sexual fantasy, it cannot be incorporated into their spiritual striving. Their resultant guilt feelings are transferred to another activity, that is, to the way they handle money, or to a general feeling of unworthiness.

Another group of priests, who would be judged as hypocrites if their activity were known, masturbate regularly, using sexual fantasy, while expounding adamantly to others about the sinful nature of both masturbation and other indulged sexual thoughts. Some of these priests quite simply are hypocritical, placing on others' shoulders a moral burden they themselves refuse to carry. However, the contradiction among other priests is not that easy to categorize. Some have completely split the masturbation off from the rest of their lives, ideals, and values. Although they retain consciousness of both sides of their behavior, there is no link in their awareness between the two. Literally, their own sexual activity is never internally subjected to the critical faculties that are very available for their direction of and preaching to others. Somerset Maugham's preacher in "Rain" is a dramatic portrayal of this dynamic in the extreme. These latter priests are almost overwhelmed by guilt if and when the split is exposed.

Some priests rationalize their masturbation. They retain a conviction that the activity is sinful, but excuse themselves from sin. An example is a priest who said if he resisted a temptation to masturbate for 4 days, there was no sin after that time. It is not logical to justify an act that one teaches is "intrinsically evil" and "unnatural" by merely delaying it.

Some priests do not feel or teach that masturbation is intrinsically evil, nor do they intellectually consider it unnatural. They treat others' concerns about it reasonably and gently. Among this group are those who feel "it is just not a big deal," or that it is "of minor moral consequence." Many priests arrive at this conclusion after years of dealing with the spiritual and moral concerns of lay persons. They are able to treat themselves with the same gentleness and reason they apply to their parishioners.

Other priests use quite a different standard with themselves. They feel tremendously guilty and make every effort to go to confession before they say Mass, or as soon as possible after masturbation. Many times these men have no awareness of sexual fantasy when they masturbate; it is the unconscious sexual fantasy behind their act that causes their feeling of guilt. Therefore, simple reassurance does little to relieve these men of their anxiety, but sometimes, spiritual maturity, either with or without psychotherapeutic intervention, can bring the unconscious fantasy into awareness where it can be subjected to ego integration.

There are those priests who incorporate masturbation into their life of service, who are more or less conscious of their sexual fantasies, and have freely chosen to masturbate as a necessary activity in their lives. These men are divided into two distinct subgroups:

The first group is made up of those priests who see masturbation as the lesser of two evils. Although they desire to be celibate, they have found their fantasy life (or in their words, their desires and temptations) *too* strong. Previously they have wandered into sexual behaviors they found ego-alien and incompatible with their lives. For them, masturbation has become an acceptable substitute for homosexual or heterosexual activity.

Either on their own or sometimes with the understanding guidance of a confessor or psychotherapist, they have learned that masturbation is more ego-syntonic than an involvement with a student or a stranger. By isolating their sexual problems in a way that frees some psychic energy, these priests are able to expand the nonconflicted areas of their egos and allow the possibility of more sublimation in their professional lives.

The other subgroup is that of priests who are accepting of both nature and spirit. They have profound spiritual lives, are conscientious about daily prayer, and submit their every instinct and motivation to introspection and self-analysis. They tend to be mature, solid in self-identity, and with a record of healthy and appropriate relationships with both men and women. They are capable of a high degree of sublimation. Not satisfied with a choice between the lesser of two evils, and with no essential paraphilia or perversion for which to compensate, these men strive for integration. For them masturbation takes on the quality of virtue. It is consciously willed and directed by love.

One priest reported that his first insight into the real nature of masturbation and its possibility as a virtue, not just the vice he had been taught it was, occurred while he was serving as an Air Force chaplain at a base during the U-2 flights. The temporary duty demanded that the men be separated from their wives, and have no contact with them or their families by telephone or letter for weeks at a time. However, the men were permitted some night or weekend passes to a town near the base. A few of the men confided to the chaplain that they masturbated while thinking of their wives as a protection against the temptation to seek out prostitutes or local girls in the town.

Another priest, in his late 30s, entered treatment for depression. He was creative in his ministry, mature in his interpersonal relationships, and dedicated to his vocation and to his parishioners. A priest friend had recently "burned out," and had had to take a leave of absence from his work. Our priest had many of the same pressures and challenges as his friend, and was afraid he was going to burn out too. However, after a course of brief therapy, his depressed feelings lifted and his enthusiasm and confidence returned.

He thought he was ready to leave treatment, but confided that there was something he "did not want to talk about." Naturally, the therapist encouraged him to pursue that area, and the priest revealed that he masturbated occasionally and was unsure as to what to do about it. This observant priest prayed quite naturally before most of his daily activities—eating, sleeping, studying, and preaching. He had not thought about praying before masturbating. He began to do so at the therapist's suggestion, and once he had incorporated his masturbation into his life goals, he experienced a degree of relief and integration he had not known before. He said it was only after praying about his masturbation that he really understood the ritual words he uttered daily at the moment of consecration in the Mass, "This is my Body." It was for him a profound religious experience to identify himself with Christ as a *real human* being.

Later he reported that his ministry had never been so energized or meaningful. Subsequently, he shared his insights with some of his priest friends, none of whom had thought of their own masturbation in these terms. They also were encouraged by his thoughts.

A like-minded priest who was not in psychotherapy shared the following entry from his journal:

I've been thinking a lot about spirit and flesh and the relationship that results. I know that theology splits the two in order to understand them.

Now there is the "whole-person." We are spirit-life, or spirit and flesh. What are we going to attach ourselves to? We must be in the flesh but dedicated to the spirit. This has implications for my personal life, Christian living, religious life, and social justice.

As for me, I've had to let go of friendships, material things, . . . But the more of those things I let go of, the more I'm left to deal with myself. My supports and crutches are gone, and it's just me and the Lord.

Let me share some reflections on celibacy.

Masturbation is to celibacy what intercourse is to marriage. Intercourse in marriage celebrates love, forgiveness, dependency, fun, togetherness, unity, and commitment of my body to another. Masturbation in celibacy is not so much a celebration but a reminder of my humanness, dependency on God, humility, loneliness, and commitment of my body to God—it's not as real and concrete as another person, but then I believe it can support my growth in dependency on God. It's kind of like saying, "God, it's only me in here, but it's all I have and it's for you and your people."

Intercourse is personal, private, and shared with another person I deeply love and respect. It takes a while for a relationship to move to that point. Masturbation is personal, private, and shared only with myself as a celibate as many things are because that's the life-style. It brings me face to face with myself. Do I still want it? Is it still worth it?

If intercourse in marriage is the ideal sexual response, then masturbation in celibacy is less than ideal—but it is the sexual response celibates are committed to by virtue of their celibate vow. Masturbation as a sexual response may not last all of a celibate's life, just like intercourse may not last all of a married person's life. If celibacy is to have masturbation as a sexual response, then we cannot talk of celibacy by default—there is no such thing.

Letting go is the ideal for the celibate so that the total giving of self to God may be accomplished through my humanity. That God is the desired goal is unquestionable and whatever stands in the way of that can be accepted or seen as understandably necessary for a while but only until I don't need it as a crutch or until I can depend totally on God who gives me life—brings me to life—calls me to life.

I have to live the life of the spirit if I am to understand the struggle of letting go and what it means . . . I must understand the struggle first and enter into it myself before I can tell people that it's life-giving and good for them.

New life comes when letting go happens. In the end I even pray to let go of masturbation—see it as a necessary part of human growth and development, but not as a desired goal of the celibate life-style—the movement toward.

The majority of American priests in their pastoral practices do not treat masturbation as a gravely serious sin. Although many of them feel guilt about their own masturbation or are confused about it, most priests do masturbate, at least occasionally. This activity can be a symptom of pathology and immaturity, but can also be a sign of maturation and even virtue. It is clear that some priests must masturbate if they are to achieve celibacy. That is a paradox that was most difficult for me to define, but the evidence presented by the lives of many priests makes that conclusion inevitable.

5

PRIESTS AND WOMEN

Si non caste, tamen caute (If not chastely, at least carefully)
—Albert, Archbishop of Hamburg, 1040

THE HETEROSEXUAL PRESUMPTION

There are two presumptions about Roman Catholic priests: that a majority of men who pursue a life of celibacy are heterosexual in orientation; and that heterosexual impulses, distractions, or "temptations," if you will, pose the greatest threat to the practice of celibacy. Both assumptions are justified in my study. All groups sampled demonstrated a 2 to 1 ratio of heterosexual to homosexual orientation and behavior.

But the heterosexual presumption is under serious attack at the beginning of the 3rd millennium when it has been threatened by the opposite presumption, namely, that the majority of priests are homosexual. The politicization of sexual issues generally, and homosexuality specifically since 1950 has given rise to open speculation. Discussion of homosexuality among clerics has been spearheaded not from forces or interests outside the clergy, but from strong, credible voices within the ranks of priests.

I hold to my judgment that the heterosexual presumption is still basically valid for the priesthood as a profession.

Two landmark studies on the Catholic priests in the United States pointed out that "the priests in the United States are ordinary men" faced with extraordinary ideals and demands. (*Sociological Investigations* 1972, and *Psychological Investigations* 1972) Studies on the priesthood attempt to be fair. No one is eager to label people as sick, deviant, or different. Studies seek to find the solid humanness that sustains us all.

However, subsequent research on the clergy has not matured on the solid foundation laid down by these early studies. Father Andrew Greeley's early work ferreted out *opinions* about celibacy and *attitudes* toward sexual morality (although not behavior). But in the popular press (1983b), he minimizes the differences between the married state and celibacy when he says:

> It is no more impossible, if we are happy in our work, than fidelity is for a normally heterosexual married man (or woman, for that matter) who is reasonably satisfied in his (or her) marriage. Which is to say that there are times when it is only mildly difficult and other times when it is extremely difficult indeed. (p. 6)

Greeley also feels that there is every reason to believe that priests in the United States keep their celibacy; "While celibacy is not necessarily honored all the time, perhaps, it is nonetheless the normal behavior of most American priests," he says (1983b). It is that *not necessarily all the time* that needs to be respected, understood, and researched.

Celibate fidelity and married fidelity are *not* parallel sexually. Both infidelities may involve a betrayal of trust or promise; but the experience of celibacy and of marriage are psychic horses of very different colors.

To be precise, they are not even both horses. Celibacy and active sexual involvement operate on two separate circuits of tension reduction. To blur this fact minimizes the significance of reality and perniciously undermines the achievement of both. Celibates do not help themselves or each other when they deny the reality of this difference.

The average healthy and stable vowed celibate has to use inordinate amounts of unconscious mental defenses to move from the celibate mode to an active sexual mode: denial, rationalization, reaction formation, and splitting are the most common.

A married person, even to be unfaithful, does not have to go through a shift in psychic mode. Direct sexual activity—already chosen—is free from the need to defend it. The married man may have conflicts over his choice of partner; he may have guilt; but he does not move from one psychic mode to another.

Celibacy cannot be kept in place without honesty. If the celibate chooses sexual activity, some distinct mental mechanism must be employed to keep him "balanced" while he compromises the incompatibility between some sexual activity and *no* sexual activity. Celibacy that does not involve the attempt to channel sexual energy into nonsexual outlets is a sham and pretence. Periodic sexual abstinence is not celibacy.

Second, it is not usual or ordinary to be celibate. One is *different*, if one chooses to live one's life—even for the highest of motives—without direct sexual gratification. Spiritual tradition is constant: a celibate is a man set apart. Special grace (charism) is given him. To argue that celibates are ordinary men is simply to avoid the questions of *what is different* about the person who chooses to live without sex, and what *nature* the grace of celibacy transforms.

Research published by the National Conference of Catholic Bishops points to traits that are stronger among seminarians studying for the priesthood than among the general population:

1. Dependency—a tendency to depend on others rather than on oneself.
2. Low sexual interest in the complementary sex.
3. Heightened aesthetic interest as opposed to athletic or mechanical pursuits.
4. Mother dominance, or a prevalence of a dominant unconscious mother image (an idealized view of women) (Hoge, Potvin, & Ferry, 1984, p. 23).

These tendencies seem to be connected with the *role* of minister, regardless of which religion he represents. Noncelibate seminarians show similar characteristics on testing.

The question that seems to frighten everyone is whether or not these characteristics invalidate the heterosexual presumption of the ministry. In other words, is this finding a reflection of a larger homosexual component among the clergy than in the general population? The answer is yes.

Traditional polarized definitions of heterosexual and homosexual are inadequate when we enter into a deeper exploration of what celibacy is and how it is protected.

Estimates vary widely. But these psychological dispositions, interests, and attitudes have to be reconciled with celibacy. It is one thing to be open to marriage; quite another—regardless of one's testing profile—to put oneself in a structure and organization that allow no place for women or for direct sexual gratification.

One commentator makes this sound simple when he says:

> Is celibacy difficult? For some priests. I don't think so. Like some married men, some celibate priests don't find women all that attractive sexually. They can do without them rather easily. Others are so caught up in the game of ecclesiastical power that they transfer the urge for pleasure to that all-consuming game. There have always been a few priests whose sexual orientation is in the other direction, and most of those also keep their vows. (Greeley, 1983b)

Attitudes toward women, power, and the homosexualities are not, I have found, that easily dismissed by priests who are talking directly about their celibate-sexual lives and struggles.

Third, the priest commits himself and is absorbed into a clerical organization/hierarchical structure that is not heterosexually balanced. Both sexes are not regarded equally. This is so at the highest echelons of the Vatican and in the smallest parish.

Idealization of a mother image—that reaches its psychological perfection in devotion to the Blessed Virgin Mary—is often purchased at the price of devaluing all other women.

Lack of interest in the complementary sex can translate institutionally into disregard for, and even hostility toward, women. Seminaries were bastions against women. If a woman *defiled* a male cloister—it had to be reconsecrated. Woman becomes the evil one—the source of sin and temptation.

Women are eliminated as social equals, in spite of a number of women employed as public relation officers, chancellors, or canon law consultants. A homosocial support system prevails. Most women remain to be served pastorally, or to play subservient roles as cook, housekeeper, or secretary. A priest's chance for advancing politically is dependent upon his committing himself to an exclusive structure socially insulated from women. Hierarchically, there is no place for women.

Those who say the military ranks and the halls of government share in this pattern are correct. However, the possibilities for sexual alliance and influence—wife and children—make the military and political arenas vastly different from the church.

Clergy are dependent on the organization and structure of Mother Church. For many this bond is an affiliation of glorious loyalty as well as an umbilical cord of monumental force. Forged from a close alliance with *mother*, often reinforced by deep devotion to the Blessed Virgin Mary, Mother Church becomes an idealized source of spiritual and economic strength and nourishment. Unadorned, that ideal, of course, strips every other woman of adult sexual identification. They become "mothers"—sexually unavailable in fantasy. Women celibates can be the brides of Christ and they can find and serve Christ in their ministries. Therefore, a heterosexual ideational structure is available to them within the context of their celibacy. Male celibates are in a more difficult stance heterosexually.

Power brokers are all male: God/father; Jesus/son; Spirit/male love; pope and bishop. An enduring model for priests is the Roman paterfamilias, (or feudal lord) who held power over the life and death of his household, free and slave alike (Veyne, 1987). The desire to participate in this male strength and dominance has preserved the presumption of the heterosexuality of the celibate priesthood.

Kennedy and Heckler's research (1972) did not specifically focus on the celibate/sexual behaviors of priests, but the respondents provide clues to their level of psychosexual development. Celibacy was approached as "hardly separable from the context of the priest's overall understanding of himself, his faith commitment, and his attitude toward his vocation" (p. 32). Inherent in that statement are precisely the elements pointed out above—homosocial organization, and power structure, and the identification with Christ. A priest's sexual abstinence or behavior proceeds out of this context. The maintenance of the system socially and hierarchically is often at the expense of women or the sacrifice of self-maturity.

SPLITTING AND SECRECY

Two patterns mark priests' sexual relationships: *splitting* and *secrecy*. The priest psychically separates his sexual behavior from his professional life. This splitting allows him to carry on his daily work with a degree of efficiency and comfort. The sexual relationship is often kept secret from others especially the public. Even when he shares it with friend or confessor, part becomes public, but something in his mind remains secret. The secret element protects the splitting, reinforcing the denial of the conflict in a double mode of operation—celibate on duty, noncelibate off.

Rationalization flourishes under the cover of secrecy: "Sex is good"; "I am now a better priest"; "No one is being harmed"; "It helps me understand and love others better." Long-term relationships are accepted as an "arrangement" by other priests who know about the situation.

The official structure reinforces the splitting by minimizing guilt, and encouraging the denial and rationalization. "The avoidance of scandal" is the primary goal when the sexual activity of a priest comes to the attention of authority, and standard solutions usually involve sending the priest away—on retreat, to another district, or even to a mental hospital.

HETEROSEXUAL RELATIONSHIPS

There is no question that some priests—cardinals and bishops, too—have sexual relationships with women. These liaisons can endure for years with willing partners, be less long lasting, or be furtive and exploitative.

It would be incorrect to think that priests or bishops who have long-term relationships with women are unsuccessful in their vocation. The following is a description of a priest who had a 40-year mutually satisfying love relationship with one woman.

> Father was a lover of life, a vital and enthusiastic man, an excellent and fascinating speaker, an intellectual, a teacher and writer, an athlete, a motivator, a generous friend.
>
> He was a very committed priest. He was opinionated and strong-willed; he never said "no" when people needed him. People always wanted to be around Father. He also served as a chaplain in World War II and as a Judge on the Matrimonial Court, and was active in many other religious and educational functions.

He loved golf and magic tricks and electronic toys, and had a very special place in his heart for children.

No one can capture the essence of this wonderful human being in such a short space, but perhaps this might give you some flavor of his dynamic personality.

He was very proud of his 50 years as a priest—50 years of service to God and his Church.

He had many wonderful women friends and a very clear picture of the value of women as mothers and religious persons. But I question whether his training and/or the vision of the Church gave him a full and mature view of all that women can be and have to offer the Church. I feel that his lack of full appreciation of the appropriate role of women was a part of what made him sexually vulnerable.

Housekeepers

This group of hardworking and dedicated women has been maligned and often unjustly accused of being the sexual partners of the priests they serve. Most are not—which, of course, does not mean that the practice is unknown. The problem of the living arrangements for priests and bishops is an old one. Legislation by the early church councils regulated the clerical household and in some instances limited the women living there to close relatives. Obviously, there were abuses, especially with the growing custom of dedicated virgin women serving in the houses. (Fox, 1987, p. 369)

Many early tracts were addressed to the clerics and condemned the custom followed by some priests of having consecrated virgins in their homes to keep house for them, pretending to live with them as sisters in devotion. (Quasten, 1960, p. 464)

Church authorities' efforts to protect women were absent from reports in our study. On the contrary, we have dozens of informants who were told by a bishop or pastor that if they had a problem with celibacy, they should take a housekeeper, or a mistress. Arrangements that were private and did not give scandal were seen as preferable alternatives to resignation from the priesthood. Time after time, superiors ignored the personal relationship of the sexual involvement, and the emotional implications of the priest's behavior. "Make a retreat!" is common advice; "Look at all you stand to lose"; or even "What would your mother think?" are misguided attempts to help where real understanding of the struggle fails.

A 37-year-old priest informant had spent the first 10 years of his priesthood on the staff of a diocesan high school. He was popular and successful, and had received several indications from his bishop that there were greater things in store for him in the future. The bishop, subsequently infuriated when this man signed a statement of disagreement with the papal encyclical *Humanae Vitae*, transferred the priest from his high school post to a small parish of 30 families. The priest said he thought he "would go crazy" there. Accustomed to the high-pitched demands of adolescents, classes, sports activities, and the congenial community of other teachers, he could not adjust to the new unstructured and, for him, unchallenging environment. Although he was developing his celibate commitment adequately with regular prayer and confession, he knew he did not have the spiritual reserves to withstand the change.

In his first parish assignment, there had been a girl in one of his classes who had joined the convent. He and she had maintained an appropriate, warm, but casual contact over the years. After eight years in the convent, and prior to her solemn vows, the girl, who was now a young woman of 27, decided to leave religious life. In the meantime, in the loneliness of his new position, the priest became aware of this relationship in a new way. There was specialness to it that he had not previously noticed. With his growing insight and infatuation as they explored their friendship, the priest consulted his confessor before he and the woman initiated any sexual activity. The advice: "Take her as your housekeeper. If anything happens, God will understand. It's better than leaving the priesthood." He was saddened and shocked at the total disregard for the woman.

Most housekeeping arrangements that end up as sexual relationships do not start out that way by design. Loneliness, unexpected compatibility, and simply growth in appreciation from proximity seem to draw some men into a satisfying sexual liaison that is compatible with their work. Many of these relationships last into old age. Morris L. West portrayed this phenomenon with sensitivity and accuracy in his novel *Devil's Advocate* (1959). Informants in our study told stories strikingly similar in affect and development.

Married Women

For priests without sexual experience prior to their ordination, married women are the most frequent sources of their first sexual relationship. Next in frequency are alliances with younger women (even minors) who themselves have had limited sexual experience.

The naturalness of a priest as a family friend is often the context in which a sexual relationship grows. This seemingly safe arrangement is extolled even by serious priests, who say:

> If a young married woman has a confidant relationship with a priest, her own marital satisfaction is, on the average, higher than is the satisfaction of a woman who does not have such a relationship. Moreover, the husband of the woman who has a priest-confidant is more likely to report a high level of sexual fulfillment than is a husband whose wife is not in such a relationship.
>
> Both the husband and the wife profit from the wife's relationship with a celibate priest. (Greeley, 1983b)

Our informants confirm both the frequency and the viability of these relationships, but they also report that the friendship does not always remain nonsexual. Marriage is frequently the setting for a long-term love relationship with a priest, although at other times it is only a brief excursion into sexuality and part of a priest's experimentation and education.

One relationship that ended with the death of the priest and divorce for the woman may seem extreme, but the dynamic is not. The priest was in his early 40s, and was befriended by a couple and their five children. The priest was a welcome companion to the husband on the golf course on Wednesday afternoons and Saturday mornings. He related well to the children—the younger ones were fascinated by the stories he would tell, and the teenagers could argue freely with him. He was a family delight. It was one of those situations that Greeley glorifies, in which the wife becomes the priest's confidant, even as he becomes hers. Everyone in this particular family felt better and functioned more efficiently because Father was a part of them. It was accidental that he and the wife became lovers, or at least neither had consciously planned it.

A series of business trips had left the already busy husband distressed and pressured. The wife, in turn, was left feeling neglected, and the priest's own work stress was weighing heavily on him. In the home setting the wife and the priest shared drinks at this time, as they had always done. They began to express their feelings for each other—something that had not occurred before, $1\frac{1}{2}$ years into their acquaintance.

The sexual liaison between them continued for 4 years. It was disrupted when the priest suffered a fatal heart attack. He had been serving as the financial officer of his religious community, and shared the internal matters of his community—financial and otherwise with his partner. Having purchased a home in his own name, but with the community's funds, he promised to give it to her. When the priest died, she insisted that the religious community honor that promise or she would publicize what she knew. The religious superiors acquiesced to her threats, and her husband divorced her.

Another situation involving a 12-year relationship between a priest and a married woman had a different outcome. This woman had moved into the priest's parish. She had several young children—the reason she gave for not leaving her abusive husband. She felt she was a woman of parts—"part daughter, part beaten wife, part broken mommy, and part a woman and compassionate person." She felt held together and proudest of "the part that was a lover of a special man." She suffered great pain when the priest was transferred to a new parish, quite some distance from her home. She lamented:

> The 12 years prior to this one were beyond a doubt the best years of my life. I grew and had a reason to live. Church and priest. Or the other way around. I was wanted and needed and loved by both. I guess priest and Church all ran together; I couldn't imagine a life without either one.
>
> I would give almost anything to have them again. But that is impossible. I'll never have them again. Now I don't know what to look for to fill the space that they left. There is a big part of my life that doesn't exist any more. I guess

a woman who suddenly becomes a widow goes through pretty much the same thing. I guess I'm a very insecure person not to be able to pick up and get on with living. I should be finished with my grief by now; it's been almost a year. I can't seem to be able to take the first step, and I'm terribly afraid. I said I just wanted to be left alone. It's lonely by yourself. You can't live just for yourself. There's nobody to do anything for. Nobody to make something for. Father has visited and stayed all night with me, but it's not at all the same. I resent that he lives in a place I'm not a part of. That he does things I'm not involved in.

She also added that she knew Father would find a new friend in his new parish.

I was not the first, and I know I won't be the last. I always knew that. But I also know his needs. He can't get along without a woman. I wouldn't expect him to.

That sentiment is relatively common among married women involved with priests. Some are quite nonpossessive. One woman told of the joy she experienced in her long relationship with a priest and ended her account with these words:

Well, why not find another church? Easier said than done. It all comes back to Father. See what happens when you fall in love with a priest? He made me happy. He was my best friend. He gave me things to do to keep me busy. He cooked me dinners. Told me stories. Introduced me to interesting people. Listened to me ramble on about things. Asked my opinion. Gave me a wink when he thought no one was looking. I miss him very much.

Few husbands appear to be conscious of the sexual dimension of their wives' friendships with the priests. When the couple is "caught," often the husband becomes angry, and the wife's relationship with the priest ends.

The priest's involvement with the whole family is part of this dynamic. If the whole family is included socially while the relationship continues, everyone—including the husband—feels safe. This balance is also possible with a divorced woman or one who is widowed, with her extended family taking the place of the husband.

However, when the family bond is ruptured by strain, competition, by the wife or husband requesting a divorce, or if the priest's equilibrium is shaken by vocational dissatisfaction, the pattern fails.

An example of this disruption occurred when a suspicious husband became increasingly distressed because he sensed a growing competition between himself and his parish priest. His wife seemed to be too defensive. The couple were in their late 20s and the priest was approaching 50. One day the husband came home from work at noon—not at all his habit—to find the priest and his wife in bed. The priest, making his exit as hastily as possible, said, "My son, come to my office and we can talk about this calmly." The young man was not pacified.

Religious and Co-Workers

Those who work together, share the same values, and have similar training and goals can come to admire and understand each other more profoundly than those outside their shared vocations. From these satisfying working relationships between priests and religious women there can develop a special closeness overreaching the bounds of celibacy.

Contrary to some popular opinion, most nuns do not have sexual relationships with priests. Now, however, many more church jobs—besides teaching in grade school or high school—have opened up for nuns. Rectory assistance, team ministries, and diocesan offices, as well as secular positions, put many nuns outside community life for extended periods of the workday or even for months at a time—and outside the protective atmosphere and more easily maintained community system of spiritual and physical restraints.

But, history is not devoid of examples of sexual relationships between priests and co-workers. Early Christian literature is rife with concern for virgins. They were the bishops' responsibility. By the year 250, abuses against virginity were common. St. Cyprian wrote: "Frequently the Church mourns over her virgins as a result, she groans at their scandalous and hateful stories" (Fox 1987, p. 373).

The burden of the loss of virginity seems eternally to rest with the woman. Certainly, after St. Augustine, the idea of women and sex as the sources of evil was solidified in the Western theological mind (cf. Pagels, 1988, Chapter 5). And early literature

> ... insists that canonical women ... must not have men residing permanently with them under the same roof. Chrysostom admits that there has been no great amount of actual wrongdoing, but points out that scandal must inevitably arise. Though the treatises breathe an apostolic zeal for a reform of the clergy, their language is often harsh and biting, comparing such houses even with brothels. Palladius mentions that "this caused great indignation to those among the clergy who were without the love of God, and blazing with passion." (Quasten, 1960, p. 464)

One pastor had a sexual relationship of several years' duration with the principal of his grade school. Each kept a very rigorous daily schedule, but set aside time every week for each other. Their sexual interaction was regulated like clockwork, just as the rest of their lives.

When ordinary work brings two people into a satisfying shared opportunity for limited social contact appropriate to each person's state, the sexual component can be incorporated and maintained with a minimum of effort as long as the shared work goal remains reasonably predominant. If that focus shifts, then marriage is an alternative—which, of course, ordinarily, but not necessarily, disrupts their ecclesiastical vocations (cf. covert marriage, below).

Nuns are not the only female co-workers of priests who share their religious ideals and values. Other women—married or single—can participate in a sexual relationship whose dynamic has a focus of family rather than the shared work goals.

Priests traditionally have had more social latitude than nuns. Association with lay women, especially those who are professionals or church-related, is usually accepted without question if the work relatedness is in order and no other "danger" signals are emitted. Travel with priests, even for extended periods, is not uncommon among this group.

Many women in this co-worker group are energetic, loving, and conscientious in their occupations. However, also included among them are those who have burned out in their work and have found a sexual relationship as one way of going on.

To the Served

Pastoral work is a source of great satisfaction. Teaching, preaching, counseling, crisis intervention, comforting, and facilitating the growth of people is what many a priest states "I was ordained for." The sociological study of priests said that 80 percent felt that their ministry was aided by celibacy—that because of celibacy they had an enhanced measure of availability of both time and energy. The denial of sexual gratification should in theory promote their development toward the goal of universal love for all mankind.

> ... the overwhelming majority of the priests agree that celibacy provides a priest with more time to be available to the people, but slightly less than half think that celibacy is essential to fulfill the potential of the priesthood, and only one-third think that the nature of the priest's relationship with God excludes companionship with another in marriage. On the other hand, approximately half think that celibacy may be harmful to some priests and half also think that many men are kept from the priesthood by the requirement of celibacy. (Greeley, 1972)

Denied physical and emotional satisfaction in other areas of life, a priest can be driven to over-invest emotionally in those he serves. This, coupled with a basic ambivalence can lead to a special kind of relationship—an unexpected treasure, not sought out, but found while conscientiously tilling the field.

A 46-year-old priest, who had a remarkable life history of active and energetic work as a pastor and chaplain, had a host of devoted and appropriately loving and grateful followers whom he had rescued from various precarious life crises. With insight and humor, he said of himself, "I walk down the street and all the stray dogs and cats follow me. There must be something in my personality—that's been my priesthood too, only with people. And I love it." He became sexually involved with a woman half his age while counseling her. An abusive and abandoning boyfriend had impregnated her. The priest was captivated by her predicament. He had a similar affair earlier in his priesthood, but this time he described himself as "head over heels" in love for the first time in his life.

When he was 15 he promised his dying mother he would become a priest and "save" people. He grew to feel a genuine aptitude for the work and the life as a priest. He could not duplicate the opportunity for work satisfaction in any other setting.

He and his young friend continued their relationship for several years. It was mutually gratifying and retained the quality of the helper and the helped, while incorporating sexual satisfaction for them both.

Another priest had contact with the study for 10 years prior to his death at age 65. He had a 30-year relationship that began when the woman was 16 years old. Then the girl—a member of his parish—made a serious suicide attempt. Her whole family credited the priest with saving her life, and she became a devoted and active parishioner. The priest presided at her marriage, baptized her children, attended to all of their first communions, and was the honored guest at their weddings.

This picture is what everyone saw. In truth, this woman was his first and only source of sexual satisfaction. She ministered to him and his needs as she grew in sexual experience and maturity in her marriage. There was a genuine friendship between the two, and they enjoyed and shared the ballet, theatre, and gourmet restaurants—things that did not interest her husband, and that at times the family could not afford.

Fundamentally, the relationship began and remained on a level of a good priest serving his parishioner. He felt that this unique personal relationship helped him to carry on his ministry. He denied ever thinking of leaving the ministry to marry. He could not have had an affectionate and sexual relationship with anyone who did not understand the importance to him of the priesthood and its work. His companion did not want to marry him. She wanted to be the perfect parishioner and, in addition, wanted to "minister" to him in some way.

This situation is not isolated. The dynamic is represented with frequency in our study population. Two points are salient. First, the relationship usually begins with an initially profound pastoral experience of genuine spiritual significance for both parties. Convert instruction, spiritual direction, counseling; a confessional exchange that leads to a life change, comforting at the time of death, loss, or illness of a loved one—all can become unique for the priest who has served the same function with hundreds of others. However, there is something "special" about the serving of "*this*" woman. And, of course, there is mutuality in the specialness.

Second, two people who are basically content, with his or her living circumstances share the specialness of their spiritual and sexual experience. He does not want to be anything but a priest or bishop. She does not want to be other than a special parishioner. The genuineness of the bond and the compatibility of mutual needs make this kind of relationship remarkably durable.

The Outsider

Priests who assiduously avoid sexual contact with women in their social circle—co-workers, parishioners—at times find a relationship in a surprising quarter. They find safety and excitement in the uniqueness of a sexual relationship with a woman from a religious background, value system, or social circumstance entirely different from their own. They are attracted by not being treated in the manner to which they are accustomed. Some of these men find a freedom of self-expression for the first time in their lives—sometimes after years of ministry and celibate practice. These women are either unacquainted with or not overwhelmed by the social reverence and reserve that surround a priest. To them, he is "just another man," and it is this lack of constraint that seems to be refreshing and attractive.

A 50-year-old priest entered into a sexual relationship with a woman—an avowed atheist—whom he met at a convention. She was "not like any other woman" he had ever encountered. She related to him as an intelligent and interesting man, not as a priest. She was singularly unimpressed by the trappings and ready answers others seemed to relish. For the priest, she was a first—enabling him to make challenging and stimulating exchanges. He was delighted with her intelligence and by her view of life, so unlike his own. "I'm in love for the first time," he confided, "and it's the most wonderful experience!" Although he had some trouble adjusting the relationship to the demands of his ministry, it endured for 3 years.

Women who share religious values but different religious traditions also bring the quality of taboo-breaking to the relationship. Women of the priest's usual acquaintance, although attractive to him, may not be as free to defy or at least question openly his life assumptions, including his celibate practice.

A priest ordained for 12 years met a woman—a hostess at a restaurant—while he was on vacation in a large city several hundred miles from his own diocese. He was not wearing his clerical garb at the time, nor did he present himself as a priest. He was simply a man on vacation. Several pleasant days of socializing provided the foundation for a growing friendship between the two. Raised in a large fundamentalist family in the mountain country, she was a young widow with four children. He was the product of an urban Catholic ghetto. They met on territory that was far removed from either's roots and embarked on an 18-year relationship that involved regular telephone contact and a monthly visit of 3 or 4 days. The priest became a surrogate father to all her children, who called him "Uncle" as they grew to adulthood.

The outsider status and geography allowed the relationship to coexist with his continuing priestly commitment and a minimum of guilt.

The Asexual Marriage

We are extrapolating from reported sexual relationships those features that allow relationships to continue for extended periods of time in spite of vowed celibacy without resorting to either unnecessary psychiatric or moral judgment.

Power and prestige rather than lust or adult sexual strivings seem to be at the core of some relationships priests have with women. Our report records only the *known* behavior of priests.

Tentatively included in this category is the friendship of Pope Pius XII with a Holy Cross sister named Pascalina. It is an example of a durable man-woman relationship that may or may not have included direct sexual exchange. As far as the psychic structure of the relationship is concerned it makes little difference. Their acquaintance lasted from 1917 when she was 23 years old until the pope's death in 1958. They lived together both in Munich and in the Vatican (Murphy, 1985). These long-term affective relationships are not infrequent among the ranks of ordinary priests or men in authority.

I have often heard it said, "Power is the lust of the clergy." The core of the dynamic of the asexual marriage is that, to one degree or another, power replaces adult sexual strivings. Fenichel commented:

> The exaggerated striving for power and prestige has, in such persons, a history that leads back again into infantile sexuality. Power and prestige are needed as defenses against an anxiety that has become connected with infantile sexual strivings. (1945, p. 244)

A perceptive and articulate exponent of the dynamic between power and sex in the priesthood wrote:

> Asexuality connotes a lack of personal development, an immaturity characterized by a failure to achieve adequate differentiation of sexual identity. It is observed in many persons who use power to dominate others. The gratification experienced from this asexual model of functioning is in some sense a substitute for mature sexual gratification. (Kennedy, 1986)

The same author weaves a sensitive portrayal of this viewpoint in the novel *Father's Day* (1981). There the choice the priest must make is not between a sexual relationship and a celibate existence, but between power and a woman. The essence of the relationship described is bound up with authority—some personal, but essentially institutional and bureaucratic—through which the priest realizes his existence as a man.

To maintain such a relationship, both parties need to acknowledge that the authority or power system is supreme. Both must derive their primary meaning and satisfaction from their alliance with the power structure. In an article, "The Problem with No Name," Kennedy comments (1988):

> As ecclesiastical leaders move uneasily around the issue of women's equality in the Church, they reveal not only something about themselves, but something about the deepest historical authoritarian instincts of the bureaucratic Church. (pp. 423–24)

In our study, both priests and women who revealed this kind of power-based relationship reported that for them sexual intercourse was always secondary and could be absent entirely for long periods of time. In general, deep, affective and often romantic bonds are reinforced by regular contact and sharing, and since physical affection is limited, the relationships can flourish at a great distance and sustain prolonged separations.

The telephone is the great gift to such people. Every emotion and secret is shared, and the parties have no doubts that each is the other's best friend. In most emotional ways, the relationship is like a marriage—long term, but based on a shared alliance with and devotion to the authority structure of the church. Also in practice there is what amounts to a tacit agreement that neither party will elevate adult sexuality above a minimal level.

Covert Marriage

There are some priests who enter into civil marriages and continue their ministries within the ordinary church structure. Awareness of these secret marriages is surprisingly easy to come by. They have increased appreciably over the period of our study—especially among chaplains in the military, where celibacy has little cultural meaning, and where personal freedom and security are enhanced or at least protected in their isolation from routine ecclesiastical supervisors.

Frequent among our informants reporting legal marriage was their desire to be "honest," or to provide for the security of the women they loved and the legitimacy of their children. They strove—several successfully and for many years—to continue their assigned ministries. Some hoped they could live their double-lives until their retirement. In every instance, the priests were aware of the ecclesiastical penalty for "a cleric who attempted marriage even if only civilly" (Canon Law No. 194, 1:3). They knew they could be removed from office—but, as one said, "only if I get caught."

Marriage in spite of legal prohibition is not new. Among the many historical accounts, one from around the year 1206 reads as follows:

> Although Lambert was a priest, he made no secret of being married, and he had at least two sons, both of whom became priests like himself. This was a century after the Gregorian offensive against concubinage among the clergy, and demonstrates the distance between ecclesiastical theory and practice in the matter of morals. (Duby, 1983, p. 253)

One has to face the question, How much has changed over a millennium?

HETEROSEXUAL BEHAVIORS

Not all heterosexual activity of priests takes place within the context of a durable relationship. Some sexual activity forms behavior patterns limited in their essence by the constraints of the priests' emotional immaturity, compulsion, impulsivity, or psychopathology. In each instance, the primary focus is on the *act*—the relationship is in the service of sex rather than the other way around.

Some priests say that they went through a sexual "practice phase" prior to the formation of a continuing involvement with a woman. Others used their practice to find meaning in celibacy. Other priests continue sexual activity that is immature, transient, exploitative, or narcissistic, and from which they learn little.

Transitional Behavior (The Prove-Myself Experience)

There is a kind of sexual involvement that can last for a few months or even a few years with the same person, yet remains a transitional sexual encounter for its entire duration. The goal is not mutuality. The sex is either in the service of the priest's *growing up* or his *re-dedication* to his vocation—a sadder if wiser priest. The woman is essentially a tool of his growth or salvation. She is used. Many younger women are exploited in this process.

In the early 1980s, seminarians coined the phrase "The Greeley Syndrome." When I asked them what they meant by this, they said, "I have to have sex with a woman, be conflicted, and then reject her so I can get back to celibacy and be a bishop." They devised that from reading his novels. That "syndrome" sums up the quality of much of the initial sexual activity of priests.

A priest ensconces himself in a protective position where marriage or a permanent sexual union is theoretically impossible. One priest who had his first sexual experience said, "Thank God I have the security of my priesthood while I go through all this turmoil!"

A priest, who had been ordained 3 years, was aiding a young couple grieving the loss of their child. He became sexually involved with the woman. On her side, she needed special reassurance and support in her crisis—which her equally grief-stricken husband could not provide. The priest needed to grow up sexually. Although the involvement lasted for a year and was meaningful for both the woman and the priest, the priest was aware that there was no permanency asked or promised, nor equality of emotion exchanged.

The core of transitional sex is the *act*—substituting for a genuine pastoral involvement by the priest, and providing a stand-in for the woman's husband. Later, the priest was able to identify the nature of his experience. He believed he had "proved" something about himself and felt more secure in that he was now "like other men" and would be more sympathetic to his parishioners' marital distresses and sexual tensions.

This kind of transitional sexual involvement is almost taken for granted in a certain phase of clerical development. One young woman, working at a parish, became distressed by the sexual advances of the curate. There were many things about him that attracted her, but she did not want to become involved, nor did she want to lose her job. When I asked why she did not talk to the pastor about her situation, she replied, "I can't do that; he's involved with my mother."

Another young woman related that she had sexual involvement with three priests. Each encounter lasted about a year. She expressed pride in the educational service she had provided to each. But she become distressed when she became more deeply attached to one of the priests than she had intended. He was unwilling to commit himself emotionally to a deeper relationship. Previously she had been able to accept rejection because of her devotion to the church and the priesthood. In this instance, however, she experienced deprivation, and found it not to her liking.

An example of the casualness with which encounters are sometimes viewed was that of a deacon who had been referred for psychiatric evaluation by the rector of his seminary. The deacon had become involved with a married woman who worked around the facility. He had been seen necking with her in a car not far from the campus. When he was interviewed, the deacon insisted that he wanted to continue in the program to ordination in spite of the sexual liaison. He was embarrassed by the exposure and frightened by the woman's husband, who had heard rumors of the young man's activity.

When postponement of ordination was recommended on several grounds, including the student's ambivalence demonstrated by his sexual encounter, the rector disagreed and replied, "He has been a good student and wants to proceed. A thing like this is not sufficient to keep a man from ordination. It can be a *good growth experience*. I think he's learned his lesson." The student was ordained and remained in contact with our study for 3 years thereafter. During that time, he became aware that the rector himself had periodic sexual friendships, which in the older man's words, "kept him human."

Salient in all of these examples is the unevenness of involvement, expectation, gratification, and dedication to the priesthood. Sometimes it is the woman who recognizes the importance of the priesthood to her partner and is, therefore, unwilling to make the relationship permanent or equal. She "saves the priest" for his vocation by treating the sexual encounter as a phase of his learning.

There are several accounts in the *World of the Desert Fathers* (1986) that demonstrate this phenomenon. One account follows.

> The abbot sent a brother on an errand. Arriving at a place that had water, he found a woman washing clothes. Overcome, he asked her if he might sleep with her. She said to him, "Listening to you is easy, but I could be the cause of great suffering for you." He said to her, "How?" She answered, "After committing the deed, your conscience will strike you, and either you will give up on yourself, or it will require great effort for you to reach the state which is yours now: therefore, before you experience that hurt, go on your way in peace." When he heard this he was struck with contrition and thanked both God and her wisdom. He went to his abbot, informed him of the event, and he too marveled. And the brother urged the rest not to go out of the monastery, and so he himself remained in the monastery, not going out, until death. (p. 14)

This story dates from around the year 300 and leads us to a consideration of another type of sexual behavior.

Curiosity and Immaturity

Some behavior is even further removed from a relationship than the transitional dynamic. It is immature conduct and is driven essentially by curiosity. Curious and immature priests can have a band of priest friends to whom they can confide their distress. These are the priests who are encouraged by their buddies, for example, "Go and get it out of your system. You'll find it's not so great."

There is some precedent in ancient wisdom for this advice. An old Talmudic saying counsels the following:

> Many suggestions, courses of action, and admonitions are offered by the talmudists to combat this powerful and controlling basic urge. Nonetheless, in their wisdom, they were cognizant of the force of compulsion and the "irresistible impulse." For the person who struggled sincerely but unsuccessfully with his impulse, they offered advice. . . . He was to dress in black (as a sign of mourning) and go to a strange place where no one would know him and discharge his desire. Although it was acknowledged that God was aware, even when one sinned in secret, a man was admonished to sin in a place where he was not known, lest he set an example and encourage others to sin . . . (Schnaper, 1970, p. 192).

It is clear that *act* rather than a *person* is central to tension reduction.

A woman lost her father when she was 16 years old, after which she became unruly and promiscuous for about 3 years. Upon entering college, she determined to change her life, and became devout, attending daily Mass and participating enthusiastically in religious activities. She chose a young priest as her confessor, and during her annual retreat, made a general confession to him of all her past sins. Subsequently, the priest became more attentive to her and by the end of the year had unburdened himself to her, confiding to her his sexual inexperience. He asked her to teach him to French kiss, since he had never done it.

Dependent personalities are prominent here. Priests in this category need to be agreeable and approved of, and have great fear of rejection. They don't like to be alone and are more willing to take advice from others than to make decisions for themselves. They can conform well to the clerical system during seminary training. Their need for approval and fear of criticism make them conformists and good organization men. They do not want any relationship that disrupts the system, but their sexual curiosity can be piqued beyond endurance once they become exposed to the lives and problems of people they serve in a parish or school. In addition, if they feel at all disappointed in or disapproved of by the clerical system or by those they count on within it, they look for other avenues for acceptance.

The loner is prone to sexual behavior that involves no relationship but satisfies his curiosity or immaturity. Prostitutes are sometimes employed to gratify this urge. Loners are men who find a refuge in the clerical system rather than companionship or shared goals and values. They can be considered a bit odd, and different from the average priest. They do not have close friends and tend to be suspicious— both factors that can be misread by others as signs of spirituality. Because they generally conform to the system and do their job, their discomfort with people and their eccentricities are tolerated and in some cases even extolled as "holy." Their sexual life will be episodic, secret, and completely devoid of personal feeling. Pornography is a source of their education.

A priest displaying these characteristics went periodically to massage parlors where he was fellated at the culmination of each encounter. The satisfaction of his sexual curiosity was limited to this experience. Even when the women would offer him intercourse, he would decline. His psychic immaturity was locked into a level of impersonal exchange.

Hardworking, devoted priests who are willing to sacrifice everything for the perfect accomplishment of their work can also be vulnerable to immature, curiosity-satisfying sexual encounters. These men are over-conscientious and even scrupulous. They exhibit a rigidity in their lives and their relationships and prefer hard work to recreation and friendship. They are men of the letter and are, accordingly, valuable lieutenants in the clerical army because of their devotion to detail, rules, and order. Their inflexibility can be interpreted as conviction, and their restricted ability to express affection as discipline and objectivity. These men agonize over their sexual transgressions, which they painfully see as sinful. They do not have the time for the development of a sexual relationship and are not prone to deny or split off sexual activity from their consciousness. A sexual encounter sends them to conscientious repentance and a renewed dedication to their work and to their usually well-ordered lives. But the cycle becomes a pattern.

One priest informant of this type was not only active in ordinary priestly activities, but in addition dedicated himself to a spiritual group of laymen and priests (Opus Dei), which demanded further sacrifices of his time, energy, and resources. Each month he would fit into his already crowded schedule a day of spiritual renewal with this group. Then, on the way home, he would stop at several bars where women would be available for sexual activity. He was fascinated by the atmosphere and clientele of these bars, so different from the ambience of his own life. Most of the time he would simply have a drink, talk with the women, and then refuse sex—almost as if he were testing his power to resist temptation. Once in a while, however, he would have sex, return guiltily to his residence, wake a fellow priest, and make a confession.

Anxiety, Depression, Mania, and Stress

There are certain emotional symptoms that at times are so intimately bound up with the sexual activity of priests that it is difficult to know which is the cause and which the effect. For the vowed celibate, sexual activity is a forbidden outlet for tension reduction. If his ordinary channels of tension reduction fail, or if stress becomes periodically overwhelming, the priest becomes more vulnerable to his sexual desires.

The priesthood is a vocation of concern—if not worry—over the condition of the human race and its salvation. Worry and anxiety can seem natural to the conscientious priest, and at what point he crosses the emotional line between justifiable concern and pathological anxiety is not always easy to detect. Those who have had a long involvement in the medical care of priests say that these men can suffer multiple physical symptoms—digestive upset, shortness of breath, heart palpitations, dizziness, difficulty concentrating or sleeping, irritability, and exhaustion. These symptoms can indicate anxiety, but will often be treated first as manifestations of physical disease.

When the priest is threatened with loss of internal control, his anxiety symptoms can increase and lead him to justify or rationalize some sexual activity intended to reduce them. Such outlets ironically can lead to even more sexual frustration and anxiety. As a result, the priest's fear of sexual contact or release can be so inhibiting that it can develop into a true panic.

A priest in his early 30s became so concerned about his sexual thoughts and so fearful of sexual contamination that he grew unable to distribute Holy Communion lest he touch a woman's lips or hand in the process. Eventually he had to be reassigned to a position that obviated duties that would rouse his distress.

There are a certain number of priests who are truly agoraphobic, but still can function adequately within the confines of some clerical assignment—usually in a community setting. They experience genuine panic attacks any place outside their "home." It is the combination of their sexual aversion, dependence on their priestly state, and fear of separation from it that holds them in place. Their sexual activity is infrequent and almost always impersonal.

Although depression often diminishes the sexual drive, for some priests a depressed mood is the trigger for *increased* sexual activity. Because of its self-destructive nature, I speculate that this behavior is directly connected with their sexual control and uncompensated or unsublimated instinct.

One monsignor who was well known in his locale became depressed and began frequenting a part of town harboring bars and brothels, where he and his car were easily recognized. His activity came to the attention of church authorities, who recommended that he seek professional help. In treatment, his depression was diagnosed and a subsequent course of medication and psychotherapy restored him to his former level of celibate functioning.

A priest in his 40s who had considerable ecclesiastical responsibility became depressed, exhibiting the classic signs of weight loss, early morning awakening, fatigue, and persistent thoughts of death. In spite of encouragement by his subordinates, he resisted any medical treatment. Instead, he became sexually involved with a divorced woman, whom he experienced as compassionate and understanding. Several times a day his telephone conversations with her seemed to buoy him up, temporarily relieving his mood and aiding his ability to work.

In retrospect, after his eventual treatment, he acknowledged that this relationship had been sexual, detrimental to his career, and punishing to him personally—confirming his sense of unworthiness and increasing his already overwhelming sense of guilt.

Another priest was encouraged by his brother—who was also a priest—to experience sex with a woman. He was reluctant to follow his brother's suggestions. Eventually, however, he acquiesced, and became involved with a woman who was eager to initiate him into the rites of sex. Afterward, the priest became severely depressed and required hospitalization. During the course of his stay, he came to terms with his celibate decision, and realized that, unlike his brother, he was unable to combine his priesthood with sexual activity. Subsequent to his release, his celibate resolve remained, and his depression lifted.

Two priests not able to assuage their guilt after sexual experimentation committed suicide. Hypomania and frankly manic episodes involving increased sexual activity are also recorded in some priests.

One busy and productive priest entered into a period of unusually fierce professional activity. Since he was successful and extraordinarily resourceful in his ministry, it was not initially noticed that his expansiveness had become out of line. He initiated several ambitious projects that he had been thinking and talking about previously. He decreased his sleep time and stepped up his work schedule to meet the new demands. Other priests grew concerned about him when he began telephoning them at midnight and later, sometimes talking about the same matters again and again. During this frenetic time, he also became sexually involved with a woman. Eventual treatment with lithium carbonate and psychotherapy allowed him to reduce his activity and simplify his schedule to their former levels. He continued his successful career.

Sometimes a change in a priest's sexual activity can have a hormonal root. One priest who became sexually active was subsequently diagnosed with Graves's disease (hyperthyroidism). Treatment with surgery and regulation with synthetic thyroid enabled him to resume his ordinary functioning.

Both within and outside of the celibate discipline, the relationship, balance, and interaction between mind and body are delicate and quite mysterious. We have a great deal to learn about how biochemistry and mood affect sexual functioning, and also how they in turn are influenced by sexual deprivation.

Idealization, Impulsiveness, and Narcissistic Behavior

There are priests who go largely undiagnosed, but who could most appropriately be put in the category of borderline personality—and indeed are so classified if they come to psychiatric attention. They are often at the center of conflict or controversy within a group; or, to be more precise, they are effective in splitting a group into factions. This kind of priest overidealizes those to whom he wishes to become close, only to denigrate and devalue them later on. He has a profound capacity for the psychic mechanism of denial, and in this way keeps his sexual activity—which is mostly impulsive in character—out of his conscious integration. He is a man who literally does not know who he is. His identity is not solidified, and he is as likely to be involved in homosexual as in heterosexual behavior. This kind of priest finds it difficult to be by himself, yet his friendships and associations are marked by intensity and instability.

I do not know that more of this personality type is represented in the priesthood than in the general population—but it is not less represented. Tolerance for lack of self-definition and sexual differentiation make the priesthood compatible with it. The sense of emptiness these men experience seeks amelioration in the ideals of selfless service. The church offers ample opportunity for idealization and devaluation. One's rage and anger can be directed with impunity against sin and sinners. Invariably, however, it is the impulsiveness of these men rather than any of their other disagreeable traits that is least tolerable in the clerical system. Impulsive sexual exploits most frequently trip them in the end.

A young priest informant had a history of assignments, each of which usually began with great promise, but ended in acrimony and strife. Throughout his career, he maintained a coterie of staunch supporters who were delighted with his quick wit and agile mind. Always more promising than productive, and most impressive on a first or brief contact, the priest managed to come through a series of community skirmishes barely scathed. He invariably set up conflict between two power figures. He was the focus of a split between these men. In the end, one was relieved of his duties.

His pattern in ministry was one that raised questions in successive parishes. He would surprise the congregation and colleagues with his fits of rage—sometimes in private, but most from the pulpit—that caused controversy among the other priests or both consternation and alienation in a segment of the congregation. His sexual contacts were impulsive. They would always demand attention, and he would eventually be reassigned to another house, where he would repeat the same behavior. He had little insight and presented a formidable administrative and therapeutic challenge.

A number of these men never come to treatment. They remain minor malcontents, accumulating florid histories and much administrative attention over the period of their lives.

Other priests in this category are self-aggrandizing and have a remarkable overestimation of themselves, their work, and their value. They feel they are special and unique. Their vocations as "another Christ" and recipients of the highest calling serve to validate their conviction of self-importance. They take advantage of others because they feel they are *entitled* to do so. Thus, the clerical role of these priests lends itself to their personal ends. Many people are willing and eager to serve the church by "doing for the priests."

One priest who, among other accoutrements, enjoyed lavish furnishings in his private apartment, expensive Oriental rugs, and a complete Waterford crystal bar set, said, "They're not for me personally. They're because of Christ." Sex and a Mercedes Benz can also be justified by the same reasoning.

The attention these people need is accessible to them by virtue of their role and not because of merit. They have rich fantasy lives involving idealized power, love, and success—themes that their sermons tend to reveal. When they "fall in love," it is with deep appreciation for their own needs and experience and markedly little for those of their partners.

Such priests tend to be critical and demanding of others, yet are sensitive themselves to any slight, criticism, or correction from someone else. As priests they can do adequate work for the church. In instances where they identify closely with their projects, they can accomplish remarkable things. Dr. Richard Gilmartin, a psychiatrist who has treated many priests, refers to this phenomenon as "altruism in the service of narcissism."

These men are not noted for their celibate achievement. They really do not believe that the rules that apply to others—or even about which they preach—apply to them. At the same time, their demandingness does not lend itself to a mutuality that fosters relationships. That is why I have categorized this group with "behaviors" instead of with "relationships." This pattern and its variants are so familiar to the average thoughtful reader that no examples need to be supplied here.

The Gantry Syndrome

In his 1927 novel *Elmer Gantry*, Sinclair Lewis portrayed a charming, dynamic, shallow yet convincing cleric who is opportunistic and promiscuous. A small number of priests fit this description well. They often have charisma and tremendous dramatic ability. They really do put on a good show, and can demand respect and popularity in both clerical and lay circles. But what they say and preach is so irrevocably split from what they do that "hypocrite" becomes simply an adjective rather than a judgmental term when applied to them.

One charming priest who was interviewed for a period of several months had had sexual relations with 22 women. A follow-up record several years later revealed that although his sexual activity had diminished, his basic behavior pattern was essentially unchanged.

These priests are sequentially involved with a number of women over the period of their lives. They do not consider themselves promiscuous. Priests who are promiscuous like Gantry experience no regrets and exhibit little perturbation. Even after being caught their pattern persists.

The characterological deficits behind these behaviors are not very amenable to known forms of treatment, although "conversions" have been reported. An environment with clear and stable limits is needed to maintain this type of person in any celibate resolve.

PATTERNS OF ASSOCIATION

There are priests who have respectful, healthy, and satisfying friendships with women, all within the structures of celibate dedication. The history of religion records major examples. The New Testament places Mary and Martha and Mary Magdalene in close association with Christ. St. Paul refers with affection and regard to Phoebe (Romans 16), whom he calls his sister. Virgins and widows were important elements in the early Christian communities from the middle of the 2nd century. By the 3rd century, celibate priests and Christian virgins lived under the same roof and in mixed communities. Remarkable spiritual friendships between celibate men and women are noted in the biographies of the founders of religious orders—St. Francis of Assisi and St. Clare, or St. Francis de Sales and St. Jane de Chantal, for example.

These relationships are so thoroughly directed to spiritual goals, and the sublimation of sexual instinct clearly manifest in the productivity and integrity of dedicated service, that they literally are above question. I will deal with this phenomenon in the section on the achievement of celibacy.

My concern here is with a type of association that is more ambiguous. Some associations have elements of shared spiritual strivings or elements of sexual sublimation, but the social and sexual elements are still viable. They can overshadow the celibate elements. These associations are clearly dating patterns or thinly veiled excursions into social experimentation that skirt the edges of sexual involvement.

To some extent, the patterns of association between priests and women will be influenced by the fashion of the day—what is considered appropriate in one era will not be countenanced in another. For example, King Henry II failed in his attempt to discredit Thomas à Becket—the Archbishop of Canterbury in the late 12th century—by trying to compromise Becket's chastity with one of the king's mistresses. Although Becket's youthful behavior had been indistinguishable in its lusty zeal from the behavior of the other youths of his time, as an adult he proved capable and versatile. Several of his biographers note "his lavish generosity and his extreme desire for popularity. They are unanimous, citing their witnesses, that he never lost his chastity, but three of them remark that he followed the fashions of his companions *in the use of emotional language and affectionate caresses*" [italics mine] (Knowles, 1970, p. 9). What talk and caresses precisely were in fashion in 1170? The implication is that, whatever they were, they would not be fashionable or appropriate during every age.

Fashions do change. What can be humorous on one occasion becomes gross or even repugnant at another time or in a different context. Certainly the association of priests with women shifted considerably between 1960 and 2002.

One group of five priests was typical of the early 1960s. The priests were all in their mid to late 30s, and each held a responsible position in his diocese. They worked hard and took their social cues from the schedule of parish and diocesan activities—confirmations, weddings, parish missions, bazaars, fund-raising dinners, communion breakfasts, priests' retreats, and so on. Their general demeanor with women was friendly, if formal. They were not familiar, and allowed only a warm handshake rather than an embrace except from family members, and often not kisses even from them.

Twice a year they would vacation in a group of three to five. Sometimes their focus was golf, skiing, or some other sport. During this time they would shed their clerical collars, don mufti (lay clothes), and socialize in bars and spas as though they were not priests. Protected by the group, they could venture into conversations and brief encounters with women they met. The unspoken rules of the game allowed for some intimate sexual exchange—necking and petting, but not intercourse—as though somehow intercourse but not the rest would be a violation of the celibate trust.

The limits of celibacy could be tested, but the group rules had to prevail. If one of the group became too troubled by sexual desire, he was advised by the rest to go find a woman somewhere and get it out of his system, but the group setting was simply for "play" within the safety of priestly association.

The late 1960s and early 1970s saw a metamorphosis from the dating-like behavior within groups of priests to the frank pairing of priests and women in a clear pattern called "the third way" (described by Pierre Teilhard de Chardin, S.J.). Neither marriage nor traditional celibate practice, this third way allowed for, and even extolled, close personal relationships between priests and women that included all the behavior open to any other dating couple—shared intellectual goals, leisure time, and socializing. The relationship was not intended to lead to sexual intercourse, and marriage was never its goal.

In the pseudo-psychological 1970s, a "deep, meaningful relationship" with a woman became *de rigueur* for the bright, young, restless cleric. It was a kind of adolescent rebellion within the bounds of the law. Affectionate language and caresses were legitimate; intercourse was not. One priest told the press, "Through these relationships you might say that the Roman Catholic Church is allowing its latent heterosexuality to come out" (*Newsweek*, December 3, 1973). The third-way pairing—without group protection and with little life experience preceding it, and with no integration possible between a celibate spirituality and sexual immaturity—was a treacherous ideal to maintain. Frequently it evolved into one of the sexual relationships or behaviors mentioned earlier, or would lead to the priest's giving up his vocation.

The third way and its dangers were not unique to this period. Cyprian—Bishop of Carthage in the early 200s—was alarmed by a parallel practice.

In bishoprics near Carthage, young virgins were cohabiting with Christian men, with clerics, even, and deacons, with whom they were said to be sleeping chastely in the same bed. The risks were obvious, and Cyprian was quick to deplore them (Fox, 1987, p. 169).

In some instances an episode of third way experimentation led to a priest's re-evaluation of his vocation and subsequent rededication to celibate living. One priest in his early 50s commented on his experience during that era: "I kissed everyone, and hugged everyone. I just thought it was the mature thing to do. I'm more conservative now; it's hard to keep all hugs and kisses nonsexual."

Many men who left the priesthood credit their experience in the third way as the catalyst for their departure. They entered into an honest relationship, thinking it could be reconciled with their celibate ideal. They welcomed the openness and the psychological and social support given the practice by psychologists and moralists, but then found themselves incapable of keeping a comfortable balance.

Nuns enjoyed increasing freedom. They attended summer school on university campuses far from the familiar schedule and ambience of the convent. They discarded traditional religious habits. This created an atmosphere and setting where like-minded, similarly valued, and mutually concerned priests and nuns could meet and associate. The zeitgeist was one that did away with the externals and nonessentials of spiritual life and celibacy, in favor of greater maturity and self-reliance.

However, some people discovered how intricately intertwined their internal observance of celibacy was with the external structure they had unconsciously come to depend on. When structure was removed, inherent immaturity was revealed for re-evaluation and redefinition—which did not always lead back to a more mature celibate commitment. At times the restructuring became a springboard into a more or less secret sexual relationship as described previously. In other cases, it became a failed attempt at a relationship that in turn initiated a pattern of sexual experimentation.

In significant numbers, the formation of a real relationship led observant priests to choose marriage over the priesthood. Many of these priests entered the third way in good—if naïve—conscience, but they were men who could not easily tolerate a secret or dual existence. They had been happy and effective in the priesthood and refused to compromise either themselves or, more significantly, the women they genuinely loved. Of course, some priests also chose marriage or a relationship as a way out of an unhappy existence and a misguided vocation.

Regardless of unconscious factors that motivate two people who share a conscious ideal of celibacy to initiate a close "meaningful" relationship that has neither sex nor marriage as its goal, inevitable psychic conflicts result when they find themselves in a mutually inclusive affectionate bond. Choices must be made.

Political, economic, and social structures surrounding celibacy and providing some of its external support fluctuate from era to era and place to place in the church. In spite of heterosexual strivings, some priests have found that the economic and socio-political advantages of their vocation simply outweigh the risks of existence outside the clerical structure. Priests of the 1970s and 80s were dubbed "the last of the vested gentry."

Frank Bonnike, who founded CORPUS (Corps of Reserve Priests United for Service) left the priesthood himself in 1973 and was identified in the national media as "the former president of the National Federation of Priests' Councils . . . among those third-way priests who are unwilling to live a public lie. 'I was happy as a celibate,' Bonnike wrote recently to friends in a letter announcing his plans to marry Janet Proteau, a former nun. 'I do not wish to be an unhappy or a compromising one. Once I discovered myself closer to God because of Janet, I knew I could not just be open with Him about our relationship, but that I had to be open about it before people, too' " (*Newsweek*, December 3, 1973, p. 110B).

A good number of priests who are now married desire to continue in the active priesthood as married men. Some of them were among the most observant of celibacy for most of their ministries.

But not all former celibates achieve good marriages. Marriage for some results in regret and pain for both parties. Divorce sometimes results. A member of the Roman Curia told me that one of the reasons Rome became resistant, and obstructed priests' requests for dispensations from their vows was the large number of requests for reinstatement to the priesthood from priests who had been dispensed previously.

Nevertheless, priests continue to leave the priesthood in substantial numbers—most of them to marry. Fifty percent of American priests leave by the 25th anniversary of their ordination.

The isolation, silence, and reflection demanded by men in contemplative orders (Trappists, Carthusians, Camaldolese) increase their fantasies to an exquisite pitch. Even among the cloistered, the association with women can transcend fantasy.

Thomas Merton developed an intense affective relationship with a young nurse he met in 1966 while he was a surgical patient. The relationship is important for an understanding of the dynamic of celibacy, because it flowered after Merton had pursued a celibate life for more than 25 years. The sexual struggles of one who has left a rich legacy of literary and spiritual significance add a dimension of understanding not duplicable in other life accounts. Merton knew this, and explicitly stated in his trust that his relationship with this woman should not be permanently suppressed, only delayed in its disclosure.

Merton's biographer quoted him regarding this love:

It needs to be known too, for it is part of me. My need for love, my loneliness, my inner division, the struggle in which solitude is at once a
problem and a "solution." And perhaps not a perfect solution either.
(Mott, 1984, p. 458)

Merton described in detail the process of his love affair with M
and his internal struggle to understand it in relationship to his ongoing vocation as a priest (Merton vol. 6, 1997, pp. 303-48). In the
midst of it he recorded, "I stood there among all the others, soberly
aware of myself as a priest who has a woman" (p. 79).

Currently the patterns of dating association are less blatant, more
subdued, and yet not quite secret. Many nuns report the frank invita-
tions by priests to enter into a "buddy" relationship. In a sexually conscious and explicit age, these relationships, plus the group dating
patterns described earlier, persist as a protection against sexual naïveté
and the homosocial structure.

The *use* of the woman for one's growth, experience, or recreation is
not acceptable to many young priests.

Likewise, the *third-way theme* is still humming along. A 60-year-
old pastor approached a young nun who worked on his parish staff
and carefully explained to her that he would like to have a nonsexual
friendship with her—that he wanted a companion for dinner, for visiting museums, and for attending athletic events. Although the nun
had no doubt as to the sincerity of the pastor's conscious intentions,
she was too attuned to the unconscious human agendas to be comfortable with the invitation. Therein lies the crux of the heterosexual
patterns of association between priests and women. It is not in the
conscious intent to embrace both the celibate ideal and a mature
friendship with a woman, but in the unconscious sexual striving and
immature attitudes toward women and the unsublimated elements of
the priest's life and spirituality.

Church authority views women as the greatest danger to the priesthood and celibacy. Of course, the real danger is not women, but
church structure whose authority is sexually underdeveloped.

6

WHEN PRIESTS BECOME FATHERS

My hope is that when He comes again, He will still be human enough to shed a clown's gentle tears over the broken toys—that once were women and children.

—Morris L. West

BIRTHS

An archbishop who was being deposed—in a case of one of his priests who abused minors—admitted that he had had sex with several young women. He quickly added that he always used "protection." In some cases, however, sexual intercourse with a priest leads to conception and birth, even in spite of caution, contraception, and the conscious intent *not* to have a baby. Priests and bishops do impregnate women. This is not merely a recent phenomenon, nor is it as uncommon as church officials would have the public think. The church and its social services have at times vigorously opposed open adoption records in part to protect the identity of priest parenthood.

The first report I reviewed was in 1966. A staff member of a large archdiocesan foundling home—a nun—said that six of the residents were nuns, all waiting to deliver their babies. The father in each case was a priest. Since that time I have had the opportunity to review scores of cases where priests became fathers.

One priest, at age 32, was the epitome of naïveté in sexual matters. He reported that at the time of his ordination at age 26, he believed that every act of intercourse created a pregnancy. He comforted himself that since he would not have wanted more than five or six children if he had married, celibacy would not be such a great sacrifice. He experienced seminary life positively, threw himself into his parish assignment with enthusiasm, and was well received, especially by the young people in his parish community. A 17-year-old girl in one of his high school release-time classes developed a strong attraction for him. He reacted in a fashion more befitting an adolescent than a man in his 30s. Since he was active and observant in all areas of his clerical life, the "crush" seemed to other observers to have been absorbed, when in fact it flourished as a growing underground relationship.

During its 2nd year, the relationship gained the attention of some parishioners and other priests in the parish house. The couple was seen walking together hand-in-hand, sitting very close at the local community softball games, and being overattentive to each other at parish functions. By the time the priest was formally called on the carpet for his demeanor, he had learned that not every act of intercourse ends in pregnancy. Soon the girl became pregnant. The small Catholic community responded with both shock and understanding. The priest was reassigned to a parish some distance away. The girl, now 19, went to a large city to a home for unwed mothers. She remained in that city and later married someone she met there at her work.

The naïveté of this man was dramatic, but only in degree. Report after report of priests' sexual involvements with women is marked with a quality of remarkable ingenuousness, in part due to the priests' massive denial of sexual feelings. This quality becomes a two-edged sword: the childlike innocence of the young priest's sexual inexperience is perceived correctly, making him both attractive and vulnerable. Again, the unpredictable onset of the priest's delayed adolescent development makes his psychosexual maturing difficult—or at the very least complicated—for himself and for others.

Another informant was the mother of a priest. One day a woman appeared at her door carrying a baby. "I would like you to meet your grandson," she said. Having only one son—a priest—the mother was flabbergasted and unbelieving. When she confronted her son, he finally admitted his ongoing relationship with this woman, who, in fact, was married. A remarkable facet of this case history is that this child was one of three born to the woman and the priest. The woman's husband was tolerant of her relationship with the priest. He was willing to bring up the children and act as if convinced that they were indeed his own. The priest and the wife were open and clear about their relationship to the priest's mother, who eventually accepted both the relationship and her grandchildren. His sexual friendship or the pregnancies did not interrupt the priest's career, nor was his companion's marriage perceptibly affected.

Another case involved a young seminarian who, at 18 years, sought the identity of his biological parents. He knew he had spent the first 3 years of his life in an orphanage before living with his adoptive family. His adoptive parents were supportive, but his efforts encountered one resistance after another from the Catholic Charities' officials through whom he had been placed for adoption. He pursued their clue that his father was dead. But he discovered that the man had been a priest. Finally, he was able to locate his biological mother—still living, but very protective of the fact that she had conceived a child out of wedlock. She was not willing to include him in her current life, but she was helpful in confirming the identity of his father. The priest's history made the seminarian proud of his father and his clerical accomplishments.

Another case came to light in the context of a family mystery. The son of a divorced couple was sent to live with his grandparents in a large city. The household included an unmarried aunt and her son. The newcomer to the household began to suspect that his cousin's father was the parish priest. The grandparents, knowing the truth, were eager to keep the secret and had participated in the cover story that their daughter had been secretly married to a soldier who left her pregnant and then died. When it was clear that the young grandson saw through the ruse and observed the ongoing relationship with the priest, he became a threat to the stability of the family. The grandparents panicked and made him promise to perpetuate the cover story.

The most common pattern reported is that the pregnancy destroys the relationship, each party usually going his or her way. The child is frequently given up for adoption. Offending priests do not necessarily grow in respect for women by their experience. But I have seen that the experience for certain priests can be incorporated into renewed dedication to celibacy in the tradition of St. Augustine. It can, however, also serve as no more than a rite of passage that produces a more cautious and sexually aware man.

ABORTION

Official Vatican teaching on abortion is clear and unequivocal. Abortion is forbidden. The only exception is when the life of the mother is clearly endangered.

> The earliest American Catholic stand on abortion was that of Francis P. Kenrick, the Bishop of Philadelphia, who, in 1841 declared that there were no "therapeutic" indications for abortion. Two deaths, in his view, were better than one murder. (Luker, 1984, pp. 58–9)

Most bishops today would not hold to that rigorous a standard. An early testimony to the Church's position is from Athenagoras of Athens:

> "When we say that those women who use drugs to bring on abortion commit murder and will have to give an account to God for the abortion, on what principle should we commit murder? For it does not belong to the same person to regard the very fetus in the womb as a created being, and therefore an object of God's care, and when it has passed into life, to kill it; and not expose an infant because those who expose them are chargeable with child-murder, and on the other hand, when it has been reared, to destroy it. But we are in all things always alike and the same, submitting ourselves to reason and not ruling over it. . . ." [Quasten says] It is very important that Athenagoras refers here to the fetus as a created being. According to Roman law of that time it was not considered a being at all, and had no right to existence. (Quasten, 1950, pp. 234–5)

This was in 177. But the circumstance was not simply that of doctrinal exposition. The Christian minority was under severe persecutory attack and one of the arguments against them was that they were baby killers. In later centuries, the Christian majority would use this same accusation to assail the Jewish minority.

Hippolytus of Rome (circa 215–35) attacked Pope Callistus for his laxity in ordaining priests who had been married two or three times. He also criticized the pope for looking with mercy on sinful bishops and pardoning adultery and fornication after penance. But he vents his real wrath on women who call themselves Catholic after an abortion:

He [Pope Callistus] permitted females, if they were unwedded and burned with passion at an age at all events unbecoming, or if they were not disposed to overturn their own dignity through a legal marriage, that they might have whomsoever they would choose as a bedfellow, whether slave or free, and that a woman, though not legally married, might consider such a companion as a husband. Whence women, reputed believers, began to resort to drugs for producing sterility, and to gird themselves round, so as to expel what was being conceived on account of their not wishing to have a child either by a slave or by a paltry fellow, for the sake of their family and excessive wealth. Behold, into how great impiety that lawless one has proceeded, by inculcating adultery and murder at the same time! And withal, after such audacious acts, they, lost to all shame, attempt to call themselves a Catholic Church." (Quasten, 1953, p. 206)

Abortions were not unknown even in the Middle Ages, when Christianity held its greatest social and political sway. *Artes muliebres* (women's arts) were the closely guarded secrets passed on from woman to woman and included mixtures that allowed women to remain barren (Duby, 1983, p. 268).

Throughout this report, I have aimed to have priests speak for themselves about their own celibate/sexual practice. I have taken equal care to allow women to speak for themselves, both theoretically and by practical exposition in regard to abortion and childbirth.

Although there is a significant, substantial, and vocal group that supports the Vatican view on abortion, the majority of Catholics do not endorse it without reservation. Dr. Ralph Lane analyzed survey data gathered between 1972 and 1982 by the Chicago-based National Opinion Research Center. About 90 percent of Catholics approve of legal abortion, at least under certain circumstances. Chittister and Marty (1983), found in their local but landmark study of Christian belief as applied to practice that

... almost three-quarters (70%) of the population accept abortion, only 15% believe that it should be entirely a matter of personal choice. Almost half (45%) would permit abortion only in extreme cases. Whatever their definitions of "extreme," this 45% does not look upon abortion casually. Nor is it a matter of clear consensus even among the majority who accept abortion as sometimes moral. But it is, at least in Minnesota, admissible in the church community, even to more than one-third (35%) of the Roman Catholic population, to more than three-fourths of the Lutherans (77%), Baptists (78%), and Covenant Church members (78%).

A closely reasoned position articulated by Dr. Elizabeth R. Hatcher (personal communication, 1989), a Catholic woman staff physician from the Menninger Foundation, represents a view not uncommon among lay Catholics:

> Most moralists would agree that the subjective morality of abortion is affected by a host of variables: the degree to which the woman understands what she is doing, the medical problems involved, the motive, the stage of pregnancy, the question of whether the woman consented freely to the intercourse that produced the pregnancy, whether she tried to use a responsible form of contraception, what socioeconomic pressures she may be under, and so on. Given a real case and asked to decide the degree of evildoing (if any) with respect to this abortion, we would have to assess all those circumstances.

Attackers of legal abortion would simplify this issue by reducing it to the proposition that human life with all the rights of an adult begins at conception. But this proposition cannot be proven. Moreover, for Catholics it "is not, strictly speaking, a matter of dogma," as moral theologian Bernard Haering concedes, however reluctantly. Learned geneticists have supported this proposition in testimony before Senate committees—and equally learned scientists have disagreed. The proposition cannot be proven because the evidence is ambiguous. The morality of abortion is almost inescapably a subjective issue.

I do not perceive the issue in terms of "pro" or "anti," of "life" or "not life," or "abortion on demand" or "no abortion." I think in terms of a continuum of life from viral to bacterial to vegetative to animal to human, and a continuum of human life from one generation to the next. Since our brain functions make possible most processes of organ and system physiology (except heartbeat) and constitute everything that is "human" about us (our consciousness of pain, our emotions, our thinking, our self-reflection), I think it is safe to define human life as beginning with the start of brain function (EEG waves) near the start of the second trimester. "Almost 90% of abortions in the United States are performed during the first trimester"—before the start of fetal brain function (Katchadourian & Lunde, 1980).

Pregnancy is a complex interdependence of the already established adult life of the woman (and the lives of her family and her community) with the developing life of the fetus. The real needs of both the woman and the fetus must be regarded. In the unfortunate case where needs conflict, a judgment call must be made.

Some examples: An irresponsibly pregnant unwed teenage girl might worsen her problems by an irresponsible abortion 6 weeks into her pregnancy. Her sexual activity may be a symptom of an emotional problem. Counseling may show her that carrying her child to term would be a fulfilling, responsible act. But in this early phase of pregnancy the final choice, made after reasonable deliberation, should be the woman's.

A different case: A responsibly pregnant married woman with children may suffer hyperemesis gravidarum—morning sickness so severe that she must be hospitalized (one case in 200 pregnancies). This condition can become so acute that she will die without an abortion (Katchadourian & Lunde, 1980). In this case, an abortion seems morally necessary. Since morning sickness occurs mainly in the first 6 to 8 weeks of pregnancy, many consider such an abortion is not taking a human life.

After the first trimester, the reasons for abortion must be grave, since now the needs of the developing *human* life are outweighed by the needs of already established human lives. A threat to the physical survival of the mother seems a justifiable reason for late abortion. The ethical principle that the end does not justify the means has been used against such abortions. This principle is indefensible here, since we are forced to choose between the lesser of evils, and to do nothing is as much a human act as to intervene. Moreover, the indifference to the meaning and value of the mother's life in these circumstances reflects church sexism.

Catastrophic fetal disease also presents a much debated motive for late abortion. "About 5 percent of all infants born live will have some sort of serious birth defect or will develop mental retardation" (Katchadourian & Lunde, 1980). It is fortunate that chronic villus biopsy, which permits diagnosis of many fetal diseases early in pregnancy, is now quite safe and accurate.

A catastrophic fetal disease is a permanent condition that will take the child's life before adulthood or destroy its capacity for self-care. An example is Tay-Sachs disease, a degenerative disease of the nervous system. "By about eight months [after birth], symptoms of severe listlessness set in. Blindness usually occurs within the first year. Afflicted children rarely survive past their fifth year" (Curtis, 1979). Such a birth is a tragedy. The emotional and financial cost to the family is staggering.

Many unjustifiable abortions doubtless take place. We need good demographic research on this issue. Good sex and prenatal education is associated with a lower abortion rate. Does abortion cause emotional scars or suicidal tendencies in women? Are abortion and emotional problems the result of deeper, underlying causes? Women, having a medically unnecessary abortion, should be impartially counseled when contemplating abortion.

A practical reason for a permissive abortion law is that, legal or not, women will have abortions. Before the 1973 Supreme Court *Roe v. Wade* decision, "Kinsey found that about 23 percent of the white women he sampled had an illegal abortion by the time they finished their reproductive years" (Katchadourian & Lunde, 1980). Illegal abortions endanger the lives of women while profiting organized crime.

> The issue is not whether to allow abortions. They will take place whatever the law. The issue is how to manage a situation that can be either a serious medical dilemma or a symptom of important socio-psychological problems—or both. And in the last analysis, the issue is decided in the consciences of individuals.

Abortion as a doctrinal issue has not received open debate in Catholic academic circles, where there is clearly a variance of opinion and reasoning. The celibate clergyman is poised between a clear doctrinal and disciplinary stand on the part of church authority and, on the part of his church members, either defiant or reverent disagreement and deliberate, thoughtless, or reluctant behavior. Many priests do not think much about abortion. Some are leaders of movements to champion and amplify the church's current stance; and a few are persistent in seeking to clarify the issues both doctrinally and pastorally. Some priests involved in pregnancies choose abortion; their reasoning may be more akin to Hatcher's than the Vatican's, or it may be thoughtless panic.

Dozens of priests have chosen to have the fetus they fathered aborted. Several physicians who are acquainted with Catholic clergy have reported this phenomenon.

One priest who had an ongoing and stable sexual relationship with his housekeeper, impregnated her twice and each time they decided to abort the fetus. Neither was willing or able at the time to alter their living circumstances to make the care and raising of a child possible. Although both had their regrets, they felt family obligations, the priestly vocation, and avoidance of scandal outweighed other moral considerations.

Another priest had a 2-year love relationship that grew out of a work assignment. The woman was an active member of a Protestant parish. When she became accidentally pregnant, she was eager to marry and raise their child. When the priest refused, the woman agreed with some reluctance to terminate the pregnancy rather than lose the relationship entirely.

A young woman in graduate school became sexually involved with a visiting professor—a priest. She became pregnant just as she was about to complete her studies and he was to return to his tenured position at his university. They both agonized extensively over the decision, but in the end chose abortion. She was not eager to cut short her career at that particular point in her life, while he was very conscious of the negative effects a pregnancy and his departure from the priesthood would have on his ailing mother, who was financially and emotionally dependent on him. These rationalizations did not relieve any of the genuine pain of their decision, nor account for the unconscious striving of both of them to be free to marry.

One woman was irate and regretful after the abortion she chose. She was involved in a long-term sexual relationship with a priest who was being promoted consistently up the ecclesiastical ladder. She was both secure and proud of his professional accomplishments and supported his work with sacrifice and enthusiasm. She was shocked and disappointed when she found out she was pregnant. He was furious.

She quickly sought an abortion out of fear, rather than thinking it through clearly or discussing her decision with him. Her later anger resulted from his failure to support her when she needed it most, as well as at all the unresolved unconscious factors surrounding the relationship and pregnancy in the first place. She continued the relationship with the priest, feeling that the abortion was her punishment for it.

One woman wanted to tell her story in her own words.

I met Father Mark about two years after my divorce from my husband, Jim, who had been a Protestant pastor. I had always been drawn to the Catholic Church, even when I was a child—which is another whole story—but when I was dating my husband, he told me I'd have to stay Protestant if I wanted to marry him. Protestant pastors couldn't have Catholic wives. So after my divorce there weren't any obstacles any more to my taking instructions in Catholicism and I signed up.

I made my decision to join the Church too late to be part of the already-in-progress instruction class, and I had a real crazy travel schedule with my job, so I was relegated to once-a-week-whenever-I-was-in-town sessions with Father Mark, who was the assistant pastor.

My initial reaction was disappointment because I always pictured myself sitting at the feet of a patriarch type and here I was with a man who was just my age—thirty-five at the time. I'm mentioning this so you'll understand that I didn't choose to take instructions from Father Mark because I was interested in him—that really hadn't entered the picture at all.

My instructions went pretty quickly. Because of the eleven years I had spent married to Jim, I already had a good grasp of the sacraments, and both Mark and I relaxed pretty quickly into talking about how the particulars of the Church were applied to reality in the world. We found that we saw life the same way, and even knew a lot of the same people—he had traveled in some of the same circles either a year ahead of or a year behind Jim and me, and it surprised both of us that we had never bumped into each other before. We began to laugh a lot—thought the same people were terrific and the same people were idiots—he was so different from my husband, from whom I had obviously grown distant enough to divorce.

I couldn't tell you exactly when I realized that I was in love with Mark or he with me. Jim and I had known quite a few priests during our marriage, and I guess I had demythologized them unlike people who grow up in the

Catholic Church. Mark also told me how much he valued our time together, since I was "different"—a real person to him, probably also because of my own clergy background.

Right after I was brought into the Church on Easter, Mark asked if I would go to a ball game with him. I said I didn't realize priests could date. He said he had never had a date in his life, but couldn't see any reason for us not to do things together—we had become friends after all. I was delighted that our relationship was going to continue.

I know now that we were both kidding ourselves. After two years on the singles scene, I had grown to hate all the bullshit out there, and saw Mark as such a refreshing change—I really thought I could compartmentalize our friendship and treat him like I treated my girl-friends. God only knows what lies he was telling himself.

He seemed to be everything that Jim was not—or rather everything that I had thought Jim was and then found out he wasn't. I was probably trying to replace Jim, who had been such a dismal failure as a husband, and whose existence reminded me of my dismal failure as a wife. Mark I guess was going to be the new Jim—my second chance—my opportunity to "get it right" this time. Mark was kind and honest and warm and funny and nurturing—all the things I thought Jim was when I first knew him.

After a few months Mark and I became lovers. Mark had never been to bed with anyone before, and always cried and said it could never happen again after we made love. We tried all kinds of schemes and bargains to keep him celibate—we'd spend more time outside my apartment, or not have drinks, or only "go so far," like a couple of teenagers. Except that the more sexual we became, the guiltier he got, and then he became so paranoid about being seen with me and having people suspect the truth about us, that if we wanted to see each other at all, it had to be in my apartment. And then we'd both pretend to be surprised when we'd end up in bed. I remember dumb things like during one of our periods of being abstinent, Mark suggested that we go stretch out on my bed, because it would be more comfortable up there, or that we take a shower together because it was a sticky night. Some celibacy! And then the old guilt trip and script would kick in, and he'd blame me for going along with him—like I was supposed to stop him when I loved him and wanted to sleep with him.

The longer I stayed with Mark, the more I doubted my own sexuality and sexual reality testing. Here I was—having been married all those years, and having had a normal heterosexual adolescence, being made to feel guilty by someone who had the emotional and sexual mindset of a fourteen-year old. Mark was like the worst of all my teenage years—a kid inside a man's body. And yet I loved him—I guess I couldn't accept that he had about twenty years of catching up to do. He was so wise in so many other areas—and I refused to accept that he was really two people—(1) the priest with all the priestly qualities I had grown to admire; and (2) an adolescent who was cheating on his girlfriend—or in this case, his wife, the Church.

The real killer, however, was in the third year of our relationship when I became pregnant—a diaphragm failure. It took Mark a while to accept that I really was pregnant—he kept hoping all the tests were wrong. I told him we had four choices: (1) I could have the baby and raise it with my other two children; (2) I could have the baby and give it up for adoption; (3) We could marry and raise the child together; (4) I could have an abortion. Without batting an eye, he told me to have the abortion. He couldn't marry me, couldn't help raise the baby, couldn't face what people would think of him if they knew.

I was so sad and mixed up, I did have the abortion. Mark wouldn't come with me to the hospital. One of my girlfriends did. That night he came by my apartment—he wanted ME to comfort HIM. I couldn't believe it. He dissolved into a pool of tears about how could this have happened to HIM when he had tried to be so good his whole damn life. I remember that I needed some milk for the kids—they stayed with their dad for a few days during all this—and I asked Mark to drive me to the nearby market to get some. I wasn't supposed to drive for a few days. Do you know he refused? He was afraid of what people would think if they saw me in his car! Here I had just aborted his baby about twelve hours before that and he's worried about my face in his car window.

As a footnote, I should mention that Jim knew about the abortion and was a lot more understanding and probing about it than Mark. Jim has never thrown it in my face, never told the kids; he talked to me for hours about whether or not I really wanted to go through with it. And I had divorced him. Still a good decision, but he was there for me in this instance when his replacement was acting like a bowl of mush. Old mush.

I don't think I'll ever get over having chosen to destroy that baby. I read about how other women have this experience too—this regret and guilt. I look at my existing children, and wonder how this one would have turned out. I hope I don't spend eternity in Hell because I killed somebody. I worry about that a lot. I've talked to my priest who is now a bishop, and he's said there are no sins that are unforgivable. He even told me to stay away from Mass for a couple of weeks because right after my abortion the Church was having its big "right to life" campaign and he thought that would be pretty tough for me to take.

There's another punch line to all of this. I stayed with Mark another year after the abortion—don't ask me why—I guess I felt he owed me something. Then out of the clear blue sky one day he told me he was never coming back— he had gotten a big promotion and had to give me up to get it. And he left. He's been gone now for four years, and I keep seeing in our local Catholic newspaper that he's on this committee and that committee, having received this award and that award—a real star.

They bought him. I think he's just like one of these sleazy characters in an Andrew Greeley novel—a better priest for having known a woman. Greeley has yet to address what happens to the women after the priest has cast them off and learned from them.

I wonder if Mark ever thinks about me or the baby. Or if I have been replaced by someone else. Or if he worries about going to Hell. He always used to say he felt like such a hypocrite when he slept with me and then celebrated Mass the next day.

I think he's a bigger hypocrite now.

After several years, I interviewed this woman again. She says that she deeply regrets the abortion and that, if she had to do it over, she would choose to raise the child herself.

The priest is now the pastor of a large parish and was made a Monsignor. He is still sexually active.

Dedicated religious women are increasingly vocal about their right to be heard—certainly when issues touch them directly and essentially. There is a theme of disregard of women—from gentle neglect to flagrant abuse—that runs through many accounts of the practice of priestly celibacy-sexuality. The words of Sister Margaret Ellen Traxler (1979) have to taken seriously:

Men of the church have yet to understand a basic principle, namely, that they have no right to tell women what to do with their bodies. That principle is already understood in the new and growing women's consciousness, and men of the Vatican will have to understand and respect it.

7

THE HOMOSEXUALITIES

Homosexuals have the same emotional and sexual needs as straights, only more dangerously and frustratingly.

—Fr. Joseph Gallagher

There is no area of sexuality more misunderstood, distorted, maligned, and actually feared than the homosexualities. The use of the plural is not accidental. Since we do not have a sophisticated moral and behavioral vocabulary with regard to homosexual development, orientation, and behavior—as we do with heterosexuality—the use of the plural is necessary to avoid glibness and to pursue accurate definition and delineation.

For instance, the man who loves his wife and is devoted to his daughters prides himself that he is "heterosexual" in orientation and behavior. But he hardly would put himself in the same category as the man who stands by the schoolyard eager to engage little girls in sexual activity, or as the man who lurks in dark corners looking to overpower some woman with his sexual passion. He would insist that one be identified as a pedophile and the other as a rapist. He would not be satisfied that all be described as heterosexual in orientation and behavior, but would demand more accurate definition and more precise categories. Heterosexual orientation or behavior is not necessarily a *good* in and of itself.

A firestorm against gays was unleashed in the wake of public attention to sexual abuse of minors by priests. Because many cases of abuse involve adolescent boys the uninformed cried "its all a homosexual problem—they are ruining the church!" This is a false conclusion and makes no sense. When a 30-year-old man—or priest—abuses a 13-year old girl it is not logical to excoriate heterosexuals. Orientation and pedophilia are two distinct entities. The latter is a disorder of sexual object attraction.

Of course there are both celibate *and* active homosexually oriented men in the Vatican. There are also high-ranking clerics who abuse minors. The Vatican, however, intends to put the sexual abuse problem in an "American and homosexual" context. This constitutes a real puzzle since informed sources within the Vatican paint a different picture of the Curia atmosphere and politics.

> In some Vatican circles, the phenomenon of homosexuality—a state of being that today is regarded with clemency and understanding—can help a hopeful candidate advance more quickly and cause a rival to lose the desire to present himself for promotion. The intrigues are cruel, and protagonists are even more so.
>
> In the list of hopefuls for promotion, the one who gives himself from the waist down has a better chance than the one who gives his heart and mind to the service of God and his brothers. In those cases, charm is worth more than merit.
>
> For many prelates in the Curia, the beautiful boy attracts more goodwill and favor that the intelligent one. (The Millenari, 2000, p. 110)

Homosexual Orientation

Generally speaking, the only distinction made about "homosexuality" is between orientation and behavior. Both are often labeled "bad" or "defective." Some moralists tolerate orientation more readily than behavior. There is little understanding of the place of the homosexualities in the developmental process, in spite of Freud's pioneering explorations in his *Three Essays on Sexuality* (1905). He distinguished three types of homosexuality. "Contrary sexual feelings": "absolute" (obligatory), "amphigenic" (bisexual), and "contingent" (situational) homosexuality. He also dealt with the questions of innate predisposition versus acquired character of the sexual instinct, and degeneracy.

Three shifts in awareness are needed to understand reality facets of the homosexual.

First, one must abandon the simplistic assumption that the distinction between homosexual orientation and behavior is sufficient to define reality, any more than merely distinguishing between heterosexual orientation and behavior tells the whole story.

The division between homosexual and heterosexual is a semiper-meable membrane. The Vatican in 2002 started an *inquisition* to ban homosexual candidates from seminaries. It is akin to a gay bar refus-ing service to homosexuals. The Roman Catholic church is a homo-social institution. Like a prison environment, if men are bound in it, a certain number, regardless of their orientation, will develop same sex affections.

If the Vatican acted honestly—i.e. followed through on their belief, it would eliminate a substantial portion of the hierarchy. This mis-guided effort ignores the fact that some of the most admirable churchmen of every rank have had a homosexual orientation.

Second, one must develop neutrality about the concepts *homosex-ual* and *heterosexual*. *Homosexual* is no more "bad" than *heterosexual* is "good." Just as the idea of *food* in and of itself tells us nothing about its being good or bad, since it can be applied to pheasant under glass in the most expensive restaurant, and to a carcass in the middle of the jungle.

Third, *homosexual* and *heterosexual* are not oppositional concepts, at least developmentally, as if being heterosexual or behaving hetero-sexually obviated or protected one against homosexual feelings or be-having homosexually. Psychic bisexuality is a safe assumption. Put in a homespun way: "We all have a father and a mother. It would be foolish to think that we inherited qualities only from the parent of our same sex. Boys are like their mothers and girls are like their fathers, just as much as being like the parent of the same sex."

Kinsey's work made me aware of the need to expand my own under-standing of the homosexualities. One passage jarred me at first: (Kinsey, Pomeroy, Martin, & Gebhard, 1953): "Heterosexual coitus is extolled in most cultures, but forbidden to Buddhist and Catholic priests. Homosexual activity is condemned in some cultures, tacitly accepted in others, honored as a religious rite in others, and allowed to Buddhist priests" (p. 320).

When I consulted Buddhists about Kinsey's statement, I quickly became aware that their frame of reference regarding the homosex-ual-heterosexual spectrum was distinct from the Western Judeo-Christian tradition of discontinuity and opposition. The Eastern view, as I understand it, sees sex as one, and homosexuality is part of a developmental phase or variation. One Buddhist monk said he was sure that homosexual activity was common. It would be seen as a failure of growth and detachment, but would be "smiled upon" much the same way one indulges a child involved in some naughtiness that must pass if he is to be promoted or grow up.

A visitor to a Tibetan monastery received a different response to his inquiry: "Celibacy is an important element in Tibetan Buddhist monasticism. It is taught as a value from the earliest years and is one of the four *musts* in terms of monastic vows. They are, not to steal, to kill, to have sexual relations, or to lie. Breaking any one of the four commandments is cause for immediate expulsion. As far as celibacy is concerned, any violation with another is a serious matter. I asked Kalsang about homosexuality. He said it is not a problem with Tibetans. If any incident between males did happen, it would mean the end of one's monastic life" (Kelly, 1986, p. 37).

These examples are not far removed from attitudes held by seminary officials. Both *expulsion* and *tolerance* exist. Limited homosexual experience in a candidate's background was better tolerated than an experience of heterosexual intercourse; the logic was that if one had experienced coitus, he was not likely to complete the course of studies. As a seminary professor put it: "Once they get a taste of *that*, it is very tough to keep the discipline"—meaning, of course, celibacy. The shame and guilt of an isolated homosexual encounter, plus the structure of the seminary schedule, were presumed to be positively motivational rather than a deterrent to celibacy.

Here again we see the split between the official teaching (homosexuality is bad) and the practical application (homosexual experience can be tolerated). The system of secrecy prevails here. Data from a total of 20,000 men and women led Kinsey and colleagues (1953) to say:

> The data indicate that the factors leading to homosexual behavior are (1) the basic physiologic capacity of every mammal to respond to any sufficient stimulus; (2) the accident which leads an individual into his or her first sexual experience with a person of the same sex; (3) the conditioning effects of such experience; and (4) the indirect but powerful conditioning which the opinions of other persons and the social codes

may have on an individual's decision to accept or reject this type of sexual contact. . . . In actuality, sexual contacts between individuals of the same sex are known to occur in practically every species of mammal which has been extensively studied. (pp. 447–8)

HOMOSEXUALITIES AND THE CLERGY

"People who mediate between different levels—between mankind and the gods in the case of priests, or between youth and adulthood in the case of initiates—are often made sexually ambiguous and, therefore, sacred. Indeed, part of their sacred quality results from this sexual ambiguity" (Hoffman, 1985, p. 32).

The problems involved in understanding the homosexualities are complex and not limited solely to questions of behavior or orientation. Developmental, situational, and stress factors influence both ideation and behavior—sometimes in the service of growth as well as of regression. The Roman Catholic clergy is an exclusive one-sex institution; that fact alone makes it a productive source of information about sexual functioning and orientation.

A brief review of Vatican documents from 1975 to 2002 shows clearly an organization struggling to come to terms with this sexual reality. The remarkable movement has been from pastoral understanding to witch-hunt.

A January 30, 1976, article appearing in the *Baltimore Sun* read as follows:

> The Vatican daily, *Osservatore Romano*, expanded yesterday on a papal document dealing with homosexuality, saying such behavior occasionally may not be "sinful" because of gays' psychological and physical factors.

It urged churchmen to adapt general rules to individuals.

A Vatican document released 2 weeks ago (*Declaration on Certain Questions Concerning Sexual Ethics* from the Sacred Congregation for the Doctrine of the Faith—S.C.D.F.) reasserted that homosexuality and sexual behavior outside marriage were "sinful" in principle. In a

4,000-word article *Osservatore* urged prudence and understanding in dealing with individuals.

Osservatore said homosexuals were suffering from "discrimination which is unjust except for some reservations—unjust because homosexuals often have a richer personality than those who discriminate against them."

One of the authors of the *Declaration*, Father Jan Visser (1976), was quoted in the *London Clergy Review*:

> When one is dealing with people who are so predominantly homosexual that they will be in serious personal and perhaps social trouble unless they attain a steady partnership within their homosexual lives, one can recommend them to seek such a partnership and one accepts this relationship as the best they can do in their present situation.

This tolerant pastoral attitude is in stark contrast to the October, 1986, *Letter to the Bishops of the Catholic Church on the Pastoral Care of Homosexual Persons* (1986), also from the S.C.D.F. Here, there is no pastoral encouragement for latitude, understanding of circumstances, or individual conscience. All homosexual acts are described as "intrinsically disordered," and under no circumstance are to be approved. Homosexual *orientation* is not called sinful, but strong condemnation follows: "It is a more or less strong tendency *ordered toward an intrinsic moral evil*; and thus the inclination itself must be seen as an *objective disorder*." Father Visser's earlier compassion is rejected: "Therefore special concern and pastoral attention should be directed toward those who have this condition, lest they be led to believe that living out this orientation in homosexual activity is a morally acceptable notion. It is not."

This shift in pastoral regulation coincides with an increase in the homosexualities among the clergy reported in our study. Generally, 30 to 50 percent of clergy (estimates are from 2002 and established from all sources) are either involved in homosexual relationships, have a conflict about periodic sexual activity, feel compelled toward homosexual involvement, identify themselves as homosexual, or at least have serious questions about their sexual orientation or differentiation. Not all of these men act out any sort of sexual behavior with others.

Between 1978 and 2002, reports of homosexual behaviors increased significantly and the reliable estimates almost doubled. Sexually active homosexual clergy tend to give higher estimates of homosexually oriented or active clergy. This phenomenon may be partly due to projection, but is also in part due to their greater awareness of and sensitivity to the cues to the secret life-style and to multiple shared sexual contacts—both verbal and physical. The highest estimates given were 75 percent.

Has the number of homosexually oriented and sexually active priests increased in the American church or is that merely a perception? (Cf. Hoge, 2002.) Some of the factors to be considered are the following:

First, it is increasingly acceptable to speak directly and openly about sexual matters—even the homosexualities. Men talk to each other—not merely in the privacy of the confessional or the consulting office—about their sexual fantasies, problems, and behaviors. This makes some questions seem more prevalent, when they merely were not voiced previously.

Second, proportionately more men left the clerical state to marry than to avail themselves of a homosexual partners. This gives an appearance of an increase in the numbers of homosexually oriented active priests, when in fact there has not been. It is merely an adjustment in the proportion of sexual orientations and behavior.

Third, the feminist movement and the gay liberation movement have made people conscious of the homosocial organization of clerical life (seminary, parish, and religious house)—that is, men are central and necessary to the organization, whereas women are adjunctive and dispensable. Also, the hierarchical structuring of the church is monosexual—that is, power is reserved to one sex. These are realities that have existed for centuries, but we have only recently gained an awareness of them and an ability to name them. This is an important shift, but only makes the reality more apparent.

Fourth, the gay liberation movement encouraged open expression of sexual affection. This movement has gained acceptance among a certain proportion of the clergy. Overt sexual activity *has* increased in a segment of the clergy, in spite of their profession of celibacy.

Lastly, several factors *have* increased the proportion of gays in the ministry—the open acceptance of the homosexual men in seminaries, greater tolerance of individual behaviors, and freedom of movement that makes various lifestyles possible. And the increasing need to recruit more priests has altered admission standards to seminaries and religious houses. The appeal of the priesthood to some who openly identify themselves as gay has increased.

These last two factors do represent a *real*, not merely an *apparent*, shift, which, if not redirected, will result in a shift in the total clergy population to a point at which the majority could be involved in the homosexualities over the next decades.

DENIAL OF THE
HOMOSOCIAL STRUCTURE

Although the Vatican has spoken more voluminously about heterosexual behavior than about the homosexualities, it is in this latter area that celibates have a great deal to teach about sexual development and homosexual reality. There is, however, an aura of psychological denial that surrounds questions of homosexualities and the clergy. Although the official pronouncements from Rome are consistent in condemning homosexual behavior the pastoral practice has become more tolerant with regard to lay persons. Vatican directives were usually addressed to the pastoral care of the laity. However, since *any* sexual activity for celibates is a violation of the "perfect chastity," the shift to stricter pastoral norms has only theoretically to do with lay persons.

Up until 2002 there has been no papal acknowledgment that there is a clerical problem with homosexuality. This is because all sexual activity of clerics—whether heterosexual or homosexual—is relegated to the secret forum. Any acknowledgment of sexual problems among clerics is invariably minimized while references to the vast majority of observant priests predominate.

Seminary life has changed over the last half-century. Many seminaries have closed. The enrollment in those that remain has diminished drastically. In the early 1960s, the pattern of seminary scheduling was such that every segment of the day was regulated. Most activities were monitored. Little chance was left for the serious and observant student to get into sexual trouble. Summer vacation could offer a period when sexual experimentation was possible. Some wealthier dioceses had summer villas or camps where attendance reduced the time spent out of a supervised daily regimen.

In 1966, a team of psychologists was invited to consult with the rector and faculty of a diocesan seminary with an enrolment of more than 500 students. A note from the consultation reads: "All of the seminarians were dressed in cassocks, several still wearing surplices and carrying birettas (three-cornered hats). The deacons proudly carried their breviaries. It was noon and this large group moved in an orderly and quiet fashion down the long arch-lined corridor from the chapel to the refectory."

This regimented and homogeneous procession was noteworthy in its contrast to other college-age groups. The cause of the upset within the halls of this institution in retrospect seems more amazing now than then. The reason the consultants were called in was the serious request by the students that a Coke machine be available to them in one of the corridors. The rector's response had been, "If we allow them a Coke machine now, soon there will be women in their rooms!"

The logic of the rector's comments made sense and demonstrated his knowledge of the structure of his institution, each part of which was intricately interwoven with and interdependent on the rest. The time schedule for rising and retiring, for meals, prayers, classes, recreation, and periods of silence were intended to make each boy into a disciplined man, and each man into a celibate. The regulation did in some small way acknowledge the danger of homosexual behavior or attraction, however, as evidenced by the periodic warnings to the students to avoid "particular friendships." The theory was that if one kept the *horarium* (the regular hours of activities) and did not become a friend of just one other man, one would naturally be celibate. This theory was built on the presumption that the world outside the seminary walls—that is, women—constituted the major temptation against celibacy.

As it turns out, the breakdown of the finely tuned seminary schedule did follow the introduction of the Coke machine. However the rector's fears of "women in the rooms" did not come about. But he was correct. The realignment in the structure did have sexual consequences. Subsequently the enrolment dropped to less than 100 and was dubbed the "Pink Palace." A lawyer taking a deposition was told: "Everybody in the gay community knows that you can pick up a trick there [the seminary] any time of day or night."

The shift in the social atmosphere of this seminary can be recorded as the history of the Coke machine that evolved into an in-house cocktail lounge. Both lay and clerical observers reported the open flaunting of behavior reminiscent of a gay bar. It was common for the students to call each other by girls' names. Some faculty and students frequented gay bars as part of their personal recreational program.

The question is: Has homosexual behavior among the faculty and students increased, or has it just become apparent? Both are true. There is no doubt that the reporting of homosexual behavior has doubled. However, it must be remembered that the clergy population itself did not remain stable in those years. More significantly, the homosocial organization of the seminary that was designed to keep women at bay and thereby secure celibacy revealed part of its essence as homosexual. It became apparent as pressure dissolved its protective facade.

Priests are set aside and given prestige. They are special—their very existence blesses families. They have a spiritual perspective, yet are assured honors and financial security. They supply ceremonial rites, moral instructions, and visionary leadership similar to berdaches, those sexually ambiguous figures revered to the Native American. Williams's *The Spirit and the Flesh* (1986) clarifies the role of the *berdache* in that culture:

> They are set apart as a kind of order of priests or teachers . . . [who] devote themselves to the instruction of the young by the narration of legends and moral tales . . . spending the whole time in rehearsing the tribal history in a sing-song monotone to all who choose to listen. (p. 55)

THE MALE MATRIX

The seminary is called a gay subculture when a large, visible, and vocal group of homosexual men seem to predominate. And it *is* homosexual in the sense that it lacks masculine and feminine definition that can come only from a system where men and women are tied together in an interdependent system of reciprocity. The development of the history of homosexuality in 20th century America has helped sensitize everyone to social and cultural constructs that formerly were ignored. (Cf. Loughery, 1998)

Since the Council of Trent, the seminary has been an extension of the hierarchical system of the church. It participates in its structure and its essence: only male figures have power; the ultimate justification for this power structure is that God is sexed. The Ideal for whom one gives one's life is Jesus Christ, masculine and divine. . . . A virginal mother is provided as an inspiring and loving support. All other women are disregarded as love objects, valued only in subservient roles. Spiritual functions are not complementary (male and female), but infused by one saving Spirit of God, also masculine.

Do seminaries attract men who are homosexually inclined, or do the homosocial structures of the clerical world foster and develop involvement in the homosexualities? Most men can tolerate a homo-*social* environment without becoming active sexually with each other. But some cannot.

I have scores of reports from priests about affectionate, sexual approaches from teachers during their training. One informant related a situation that occurred while he was in the philosophy phase of his training—equivalent to the last 2 years of college. There had been a series of student departures in the middle of the term—disruptive enough for the authorities to call in a consultant to ascertain the cause. Some of the students who departed were disgruntled and had muttered about a bunch "queers and fairies." The repercussion and nonspecific accusations impelled the investigation. The consultants were told nothing except that an unusually large number of the most promising candidates had left the program precipitously.

After interviewing a number of students and teachers, the consultants saw that the concern of those who left was "sexual." The authorities were looking for a culprit among the student body who was driving their students away. The conclusion was that one of the most popular professors, whom many seminarians sought out as a confessor, had a practice of embracing and even kissing certain penitents, especially after a particularly difficult spiritual unburdening. The confessor's conscious intent was to "show God's love, mercy, and acceptance." The isolation and the intimacy of the confessional sharing—and the unconscious affective strivings—were more than some of the students could tolerate.

The underlying assumptions that reinforce denial of the homosexualities in the priesthood are deeply ingrained in the clerical organization structure. After all, celibacy is taken up in the service of religion—"on account of the kingdom"—and it has to have religious and theological justification for its existence and continuance. Appreciation of the male matrix is *central* to the theological justification of celibacy (and to all the sexual teaching of the Catholic Church). The traditions of male exclusiveness and superiority are deep and central to the Old Testament even if personal celibacy was not.

THE SYSTEM OF SECRECY

The line between affectionate and frankly sexual interaction from priest to seminarian is not always clear. Reports of hugs and kisses in the public and open forum seem to be in the same category as the exuberant embraces after an athletic contest. They are generally easily absorbed psychically and pose no threat to celibate practice if other elements in the man's life are balanced and not energized by some particular developmental stage or internal crisis. Hidden, exclusive exchanges that threaten to break the defensive denial have to be preserved and shielded by the system of secrecy, are defended as "acts" rather than "relationships," and form the core of problematic homosexualities in priestly training.

Scores of priests report incidents of sexual approaches while in the seminary. Some incidents proved to be part of the priest's "growing up." But some have the force of sexual abuse. Betrayal of the generational and trust boundary can be severely traumatic to the subsequent development of the individual.

Each of three elements is essential to the preservation of the problematic system.

First, denial. This literally keeps any sexual problem out of consciousness. "It doesn't exist," or "It is not important." This defensive manner keeps at bay the reality implications of sexual incidents on the development of men who are challenged to work out their sexual identity not only in a homosocial setting, but in one that presumes sexlessness.

Second, a system of secrecy is employed to encapsulate any breakthrough either into conscious awareness or behavioral expression. Certainly the system of secrecy is partially in the service of confidentiality, necessary for the individual's growth, but it is also in the service of "not giving scandal," thus sealing institutionally the system into a mode of operation that perpetuates the very problems it is designed to eradicate. Secrecy obliterates accountability. There is no other single element so destructive to sexual responsibility among clergy as the system of secrecy that has both shielded behavior and reinforced denial.

The third element is the definition of any sexual problem as an "act" isolated from its developmental and relationship implications. Equating incidents with sin reinforces this element. The sin is submitted to the system of secrecy. It then is "forgiven" or "forgotten," with minimal awareness of the relationship of the behavior to the person and his responsibility. Some priests can continue the same sexual behavior for years, several times each year. If they confess at all at other times, they will do so to their regular confessor, but these special acts are confided to an anonymous priest. The reality of the sexual behavior simply does not break into consciousness because when one system of secrecy threatens self-exposure, a subsystem is added.

A 50-year-old priest was productive and well adapted to his celibate lifestyle every part of the year, with the exception of two or three periods he spent with a long-time priest friend. They would golf together, share their intellectual and social concerns, have a few good meals, attend some cultural event, and sleep together. Before parting for their respective assignments, they would pray together and return home refreshed. Neither ever confided this sexual activity to anyone

else. Nor did either have sex with anyone else. When one of the partners died, the other sank into a deep depression. During the course of
his psychotherapy for the depression, the priest for the first time asked
himself about the sexual implications of his relationship with his
friend. He had had no guilt while his friend lived and neither man
had ever identified himself as a homosexual.

Another example of how resistant the system of denial and secrecy
is to reality was revealed by the psychiatric treatment of a 45-year-old
man who had responsibility for the initial training period of candidates for his religious order. After his daily lecture, he would gather
the men in their recreation room. There they were instructed to form
an "elephant line"—each man facing the back of the man in front of
him holding onto the penis of the person behind him. This had been
explained carefully to the group as an exercise to "desensitize" them
and prepare them for their future ministry.

What struck the psychiatrist when the man was referred for treatment was not the psychotic process of the priest himself, who had
finally succumbed under prolonged, severe personal pressure, but the
fact that the situation had existed for several sessions before any of
the candidates reported the behavior to his superiors. Because the
priest was a genuinely good and conscientious man with a reputation
for liveliness and wisdom within the community, even such a frankly
bizarre psychotic episode could be for a time absorbed into the system of secrecy.

DEVELOPMENTAL QUESTIONS
AND VARIATIONS

Homosexual identity, then, evolves out of a clustering of self-images
that are linked together by the individual's idiosyncratic understanding of what characterized someone as a homosexual. . . . There is no
such thing as a single homosexual identity. Rather, its nature may
vary from person to person, from situation to situation, and from period to period (Cass, 1985, p. 105).

The illusion that the homosexualities constitute a single entity is
exposed with the slightest serious examination of the subject area.
Even the most commonly named factors in the formation of gender
identity—possible prenatal hormonal factors, biological predisposi-

tion, intra-psychic dynamics, parental sex assignment, environmental conditioning and imprinting—defy reductionism.

It is clear:

> Males do not represent two discrete populations, heterosexual and homosexual. The world is not to be divided into sheep and goats. Not all things are black or all things white. It is a fundamental of taxonomy that nature rarely deals with discrete categories. Only the human mind invents categories and tries to force facts into separated pigeon-holes. The living world is a continuum in each and every one of its aspects. The sooner we learn this concerning human sexual behavior, the sooner we shall reach a sound understanding of the realities of sex. (Kinsey et al. 1948, p. 639)

In evaluating Richard Ginder's *Sex and Sin in the Catholic Church*, reviewer Fr. John L. Thomas (1975) says:

> Finally [the book] assumes that homosexuality is a condition that pertains to the very essence of the individual and consequently designates a distinctive kind of being. But there is no such thing as a homosexual *being*.
>
> What exist are male and female beings who may experience same-sex desires or engage in same-sex activities. But neither desires nor acts constitute *being*. They are dynamic, learnable and unlearnable, mutable in quality and persistence, and always in a state of change and becoming. It is a serious mistake to ignore all the evidence that men and women are amazingly sexually malleable creatures.

The developing body ego is also important in forming sexual identity, which includes a host of sensations, their quality and quantity, and specifically the sensations that come from the genitals. These define the physical and psychic dimensions of the self.

Prenatal and Early Influences

Animal studies have demonstrated that demasculinization of mating behavior is governed by the hypothalamus on the right side. This is accomplished prenatally by using brain implants of steroidal sex hormone (Nordeen & Yahr, 1982). John Money (1984), along with many others, points out the obvious profound implications of this and other prenatal experiments for adult sexual development. "If someone is prenatally programmed so that conformity to either male or female stereotype is difficult, then learning experiences may lead them to develop either a role of trans-sexual gender identity or one of [obligatory] homosexual gender identity" (p. 24).

Bisexuality and the celibate clergy is also a very important area for examination. A career dominated exclusively by male power and the masculine address "Father," while enjoying the refinement of female nurturance and vestment makes sense for one who is endowed with both a homosexual and heterosexual psychic disposition. Freud assumed that the human animal is endowed with a bisexual constitution. Although prenatal and biochemical studies are in their infancy, we cannot minimize their import for sexual programming and disposition.

Infantile Sexuality and Identity

Infants experience sexual excitement, boys have erections, and girls lubricate from birth. They discover their own bodies, including their genitals. At about 18 months of age, the toddler usually increases his masturbatory activity. Children commonly experiment in some sort of sexual play with each other and expose themselves. The reactions of parents to all of these activities have lasting effects on the child's body image and sense of self. Excessive parental shame, accompanied by revulsion and rejection, enforces a sense of extreme embarrassment and self-consciousness. A parent's sense of self and each parent's image of his or her partner, and of the complementary sex in general, are transmitted and cued to the child and incorporated into his or her own sense of self and gender identity—all within the first 5 years of life. Obviously, gender identity influences sexual object choice later on.

The Negative Oedipal

Freud's oedipal theory is too well known to belabor here. It is generally accepted that the resolution of the early relationships with father and mother has to be accomplished in order to broaden one's social interaction, leave home for school, form a conscience, and generally progress to maturity. For a boy, the impulse to love the mother and reject the father must give way to the need to become like the father and find a love object of his own.

But every child goes through a positive and a negative oedipal. For the boy, the mother becomes the love object, the father the object of fear and rejection. However, the father also alternately becomes the loved one and the mother becomes the feared and rejected one. Both experiences can lead to development or regression.

A Necessary Homosexual Phase of Development

There is another stage of development that is relevant here—the surge of oedipal strivings that recur at the prepubertal stage of development. In fact, at this time occurs an upsurge of all infantile sexuality. In the face of the challenges of approaching adolescence, boys turn to each other and to adult males for masculine reinforcement—often idealized teachers, sports figures, coaches, or ministers. Their fear of women leads them to denigrate anything associated with women or girls as ridiculous or "yucky."

In 1905, Freud recorded this phenomenon in his *Three Essays on Sexuality* (1953a):

> One of the tasks implicit in object-choice is that it should find its way to the opposite sex. This, as we know, is not accomplished without a certain amount of fumbling. Often enough the first impulses after puberty go astray, though without any permanent harm resulting. Dessoir [1894] has justly remarked upon the regularity with which adolescent boys and girls form sentimental friendships with others of their own sex. No doubt the strongest force working against a permanent inversion of the sexual object is the attraction which the opposing sexual characters exercise upon one another. (p. 229)

This is an age when girls and boys are vulnerable to grooming and sexual advances of an adult, such as a priest, who is trusted by the family.

Both the negative oedipal and this stage of puberty can broadly be called "homosexual" in that they constitute a turning toward the object of the same sex and away from the opposite sex through devaluation or denigration. It is necessary to pass through these stages on the way to adult heterosexual adjustment. This is why I call it the "necessary homosexual phase of development."

This latter phase is particularly important for understanding celibate practice and development in the church organization and structure. Much of the homosocial organization of clerical culture is *fixed* at this stage. It is the culture's natural protection. The power structure of the Roman Catholic hierarchy can be seen psychically only in the context of encapsulating, solidifying, and protecting this stage of development; in this sense, it can rightfully be called homosexual. If it moved to any other level of psychosexual development, it could not maintain itself in its present structure. These steps of psychosexual development are common to all boys in some variation or other preceding adolescence, when psychosexual identity and object choice is usually solidified.

Of the priests in our study, twenty percent (20 percent) expressed concern about their sexual identity or reported homosexual behavior. However, half of that group (8 to 10 percent of the clergy) tentatively identified themselves as having a homosexual orientation or at least seriously questioned their orientation or sexual differentiation, although they based their judgment on little and oftentimes no homosexual experience in their adult life. As a rule, this second group did not act out any sexual behavior with others.

One priest, a psychologist, said that he did not know whether he was homosexual or just underdeveloped. He felt that many of the clergy he dealt with were similarly underdeveloped in their sexual identity. Like many in this category, he tended to be sensitive, productive, and conscientious. Some in this group were highly disciplined and had well developed spiritual lives and consciences. Others supported their celibate resolve and disciplined lifestyle with psychotherapy. Needless to say, this group with its idealism and sense of sacrifice forms an important core of dedicated religious servants.

Episcopal Bishop Paul Moore said what many Roman Catholics would be afraid to verbalize. It is true of Roman clergy: "Historically many of the finest clergy in our church have had this [homosexual] personality structure, but only recently has the social climate made it possible for some to be open about it" (1976).

The institutional church had been perceptive in soliciting candidates for the celibate priesthood at an early age. Ensuring a better fit into the ecclesiastical, organizational, and structural reality, it recruited candidates while they were in their "necessary homosexual phase" of development, when male idealization is high and sexual activity more childlike than adult. Recruiting older candidates does not shift the organizational fit. Men, of any chronological age, can maintain this psychosexual mind-set that *fits* the church structure. (Cf. Jordan, 2000.)

Dozens of examples of informants who reported various sexual behaviors—or only masturbation—could be relegated to this stage of psychosexual identity formation. They would not, however, identify themselves as homosexual or have any question about their own identity.

Pseudohomosexuality

An interesting subgroup emerged among the informants. They were marked by the *fear* that they might be homosexual. They were conscientious and would identify themselves as "gay" if that would resolve their internal conflict. But they could not. They might have had no adult homosexual experience and were relying on their memories of childhood or adolescent sexual play with friends or family. Some had experimented briefly in adult life with both sexes. They were not caught in preadolescent development. They were more like the college student who fearfully asks, "Am I normal?" They wished to be priests, still held celibacy as an ideal, but wanted to be "like everybody else."

A 36-year-old priest who was an informant for 11 years of the study demonstrates the point. He joined the seminary at 13 and found the atmosphere supportive and warm, in contrast with his home where his mother had died 2 years earlier and his father was becoming more and more aggressively and frequently alcoholic. He fit into the seminary program well. The athletic program met his needs and he became first academically. He was sent to Rome for his theological studies, and it was in his first year there that he experienced his first real questioning of celibacy and his vocation. After a brief depressive episode, he regained his enthusiasm for his studies and life.

When he obtained his graduate degree, he was assigned to the chancery office staff and over the next 8 years became increasingly involved in the administrative decisions of the diocese. Then a policy dispute over a financial crisis abruptly ended the personal and political support necessary for him to keep his job. The bishop—a man he admired as a friend and father figure—suddenly dismissed him.

For the first time since he had taken his vow of celibacy 12 years earlier, he began to masturbate. His new assignment in a parish afforded him time to "escape"—as he put it—to a large city some distance from his home for several days every few months. It was there that he began to experiment sexually, awkwardly asking bartenders where the "action" was. These adolescent-like ventures brought him both his first heterosexual and his first homosexual contacts (mutual masturbation). His native sensitivity and training combined to make him "Holden Caulfield–like," in his approach to sexuality. He could not tolerate the pain of his conflicted conscience and curtailed his experimentation after four or five episodes. He did not feel he could leave the priesthood; similarly, he did not feel he could continue to pursue either heterosexual or homosexual liaisons or activity.

Later a second parish assignment brought him professional success. An administrative position recognized and utilized his talents. At 47, he was practicing celibacy, but still feared he was homosexual, although most of his fantasy and ideation was heterosexual.

Some feel we are seeing basic *bisexuality* in this man and in this group. A pertinent observation by Money (1984) is:

> If one travels the manifest path of bisexuality, then, by the age of sexual maturity, one will almost certainly label oneself as homosexual. The explanation of this error is historical. Homosexuality has been considered as a sin on a par with heresy and treason. Sinners are still labeled for their vices and not their virtues. Thus, bisexuals are still singled out, not for their heterosexual but their homosexual actions.

However, I am convinced that Lionel Ovesey (1969) describes accurately the situation we see frequently among priest celibates:

> The great majority of so-called homosexual anxieties are motivated by strivings for dependency and power. These anxieties . . . stem from pseudohomosexual fantasies that are misinterpreted by the patient as being evidences of frank homosexuality. In reality, the sexual component, if present at all, is very much in abeyance. More often it appears to be entirely absent. (p. 31)

The uncertainty of this group persists in the face of little or no sexual experience. Their fear seems to be the salient element. It is difficult to say whether they are truly bisexual and would become oriented to both sexes no matter what the circumstances or environment, or if they are simply a subgroup fostered and held in place by the celibate organization and structure.

Defensive Homosexuality

Many men fear the idea that they may be homosexual. Others are so homophobic that they cannot tolerate the idea of being close to or friendly with a homosexual person. But there are also a few men who can more easily accept the idea of being homosexual than the idea of being heterosexual; they find the latter threatening and fearsome. There are "reactive forms of homosexuality also, namely, identification with the other sex, for the purpose of denying fear of the other sex" (Fenichel, 1953, p. 310).

A 30-year-old priest was productive in his parish and as a part-time high school teacher. He had had a few homosexual encounters, but no pattern of sexual activity, and did not feel compelled to act out his sexual impulses. He was well regulated in his lifestyle and talked about his desire to be celibate. He could not see himself being anything but a priest. He was comfortable about identifying himself as a homosexual, in private, but did not openly claim "being gay"—a stance that would have been uncommon and incongruous at that time.

His trouble began when one of the women teachers at the school took a particular liking to him. When she declared her feelings and made a move to hug and kiss him—a response he had no awareness of inviting or provoking—he went into a panic state. The acuteness and vehemence of his physiological responses frightened him. He had a genuine *heterosexual* panic. His response is hard to explain, but was observed and recorded in 1927.

> Probably no male human being is spared the fright of castration at the sight of a female genital. Why some people become homosexual as a consequence of that impression, while others fend it off by creating a fetish, and the great majority surmount it, we are frankly not able to explain. It is possible that, among all the factors at work, we do not yet know those which are decisive for the rare pathological results. (Freud, 1961b, p. 154)

Over the course of the study I have interviewed a sufficient number of priests with this dynamic to know that it forms one subgroup within the celibate band. This phenomenon does not need sexual activity to keep it in force; it can exist with brief episodic heterosexual experimentation.

In a paradoxical way, defensive homosexuality keeps the priests bound to their vocation and celibacy. They know that sexual activity with another person is a violation of their vow. They cannot rationalize or split sexual behavior from their consciousness; they feel guilt about any sexual activity in which they may become involved. The idea of homosexuality does not interfere with their life choice. As one priest put it, "The Church demands celibacy of homosexuals anyway. If I'm homosexual and I have to be celibate, I might as well be a priest and be useful to the Church." Therefore, to maintain their equilibrium, these men reason that prayer, humility, and reasonable vigilance of their lifestyle will keep them safe and save their souls. The idea of being heterosexual, with the possibility of a legitimate sexual relationship with an available woman, threatens their equilibrium since it destabilizes their whole life.

Regressive Homosexuality

There are kinds of regressions that serve growth, development, and social stability. Play remains one of these situations throughout life. Men hunt and fish together, have their beer and bowling nights to refresh themselves, and return invigorated to their families and work. This homosocial regression is accepted in society. The men don't do anything overtly homosexual, but their orientation for this brief period is "men only." Only men count, understand each other, and bond together, and they exclude women. Behavior and humor here are very much like the adolescent boys' clubs.

Freud had a close friend to whom he confided: "The company of the friend, which a special—perhaps feminine—side demands, . . . no one can replace for me. . . ." And "I do not share your contempt for friendship between men, probably because I am to a high degree party to it. In my life, as you well know, woman has never replaced the comrade, the friend." Freud wrote this self-appraisal when his intimacy with Fliess had declined and he could afford to be clear-sighted. In 1910, looking back on the whole fateful attachment, Freud bluntly told several of his closest disciples that his attachment to Fliess had contained a homosexual element. (Gay, 1988, p. 86.)

What happens when men live in a *homosocial* existence? How do they regress? After the male bonding and the intense feelings of friendship, they have no wife and family to ease the sexual tension increased by male competition and exchange. Under tension and pressure, or perhaps under the weight of depressive feelings, some priests regress to a homosexual stage of development—to the prepubertal *sexual* as well as *social* exchange. This kind of situation can lead outside the clerical circle into the anonymous and tenuous world of furtive sexual encounters in bars, restrooms, baths, or massage parlors. Many priests make a complete psychic split between their sexual behavior and their professional clerical life; this is also true of those who involve themselves in heterosexual behavior. The maturity, judgment, and values lived and expressed in their professional life are entirely abandoned in their "play" world, where they operate almost wholly apart from those values.

A responsible priest, aged 42, reported that over the previous 7 years he had periodically searched for homosexual partners in a series of bars and peep shows, usually after spending time with his good priest friends. Another priest went twice a month to a hotel for a massage. Although the masseur never touched the priest's genitals, the priest always ejaculated during the massage; it was important to him to have the touch of a male and to avoid the idea of a masseuse.

Although it is most common for the regressive behavior to be split from the clerical life, some priests reported being approached by other priests for sexual contact within the clerical setting—while visiting their parish house, helping with some special function, or on vacation.

Alcohol can be a factor in this regression. Two priest informants took an annual vacation together at a posh beach resort some distance from their homes. Long-time friends, they enjoyed many common interests. At least one night of each vacation, they would drink to the point of drunkenness, come back to their hotel, and masturbate each other—something they did not do at any other time of the year in their association. They never spoke of it with each other. One of the parties in no way considered himself homosexual; the other man felt he had homosexual tendencies, and wanted to be more involved with his friend, but was afraid of being rejected if he broached the subject in any other circumstance.

There can be a compulsive quality to sexual regression. Men reporting this dimension to their homosexual activity describe the inner force that drives them to seek sexual involvement regardless of (or possibly because of) the danger or possibility of damage. A typical example is the priest who reported returning compulsively to the restroom of a highway interchange, seeking a sexual contact when he knew intellectually that the police were keeping that exact spot under surveillance. Another priest repeatedly picked up sexual partners from among the young men who paraded on the local "meat rack" of his city, in spite of having read in the local newspaper that multiple arrests had been made there for sexual solicitation.

Situational Homosexuality

Doctor Lewis Hill, former medical director of Sheppard and Enoch Pratt Hospital in Maryland, used to tell his resident psychiatrists, "Man is a loving animal, and he is going to love whatever he is near." The sexual histories of farm boys frequently recorded passing involvements with animals. Sucking calves respond equally to their mother's teat, a finger, or a little boy's penis. This is usually a situational phenomenon dependent on sexual development, social isolation, loneliness, and positive loving feelings for a friend.

What happens to the average man when he is isolated for long periods of time, with restricted affective (social) outlets and limited positive sexual development? One of the early psychological studies NASA commissioned was to project the effect of prolonged periods in space on astronauts. Dependent on one another, one set of factors to be taken into account would be the positive effect that would or could mutually develop when no other loving objects were near. The logical question then became whether homosexual feelings would be aroused eventually after a long time in sexual isolation. Kinsey and colleagues noted the frequency of homosexual contact "among ranchers, cattlemen, prospectors, lumbermen and farming groups in general" (1948, p. 457). All of these virile and active groups tend to face the perils of nature in a practical way and approach sex the same way.

Navy men at sea are assured, "If you're under way it's not gay," to allay the fears about feelings between them that might be aroused during long periods of isolation. "What happens aboard, stays aboard," is an assurance that missteps are situational.

However, priests faced with homosocial isolation for long periods of their life are not allowed to accept sex in the way the groups above do. One expects and finds more restraint of sexual activity among clergy when compared to other groups of men. But the homosocial situation *does* stimulate feelings. Although only 20 percent of clergy report homosexual behavior or identity, 40 percent report having homosexual ideation at some point during their training or later.

At times the situation rather than the core sexual orientation of the priest dictates his sexual choice. Many reports in this category are similar. A long-time friendship and isolation in a learning or living circumstance lead to a sexual exchange between friends. Subsequent history and development can reveal an essentially heterosexual orientation and choice.

Obligatory Homosexuality

This homosexuality is a state and not necessarily a behavior. It is determined either by genetic endowment or by environmental factors so compelling that the affective orientation toward one's own sex as the primary relational object is irreversible by any known psychological or physical means. In this sense it is determined by nature. More and more biochemical research is examining the influence of hormones on prenatal development.

In its essence, obligatory homosexuality has nothing to do with behavior or sin. There is nothing immoral about it as a state—a declaration that can be equally valid for heterosexuality. Of course, it is not the norm in any culture, but is a variation of nature and development.

As Nash and Hayes (1965) say: "Awareness of a homosexual orientation does not imply identity; identity does not imply acceptance; acceptance does not imply commitment" (p. 35). A person who aspires to celibacy will sooner or later have to come to grips with the question of his sexual identity, even in spite of limited or no sexual experience. In fact, sexual activity can be indulged in with less thought than sexual restraint. The latter forces one to rely on inner resources having moorings in one's past and lying deep in one's unconscious, as well as on conscious relatedness to transcendent love objects that can encompass a world.

Since sexual activity of any stripe is forbidden to the celibate, the protected and homosocial environment of the priesthood—where male association dominates, but sexual activity is taboo—can be a haven of peace as well as an arena for productive and loving service. Some who have professed celibacy and practiced it for prolonged periods of time have difficulty identifying themselves as obligatory homosexuals in spite of tremendous inner honesty and self-awareness. Those who do not act out may not be sure of their sexual identity, but use their sexual ambiguity to advantage in the understanding of and ministry to a wide range of persons, both male and female.

Sexual Addiction

There are, of course, those who are aware of their obligatory orientation and have acted on their sexual attractions, before or after taking a vow. Of special concern here is *addictive* sexual behavior. Addiction is troublesome whether the sexual object is male or female, adult or child. In one who professes celibacy, it violates a trust of office. The priest has entrée to and the confidence of another person precisely because he is a priest and presumed celibate. This is the case in instances of sex with minors. However, even in the cases of anonymous sex, addiction violates self-trust at the deepest level of one's ego. One literally cannot trust himself.

Sexual addiction among the clergy is described by both the tortured addict and by his victims. The system of secrecy surrounding the sexual behavior only compounds the problem and interferes with breaking the cycle of addiction. The behavior is not dealt with in the confessional. At times, confession becomes part of a cycle of denial. It facilitates the split of sex from the rest of one's conscious functioning. In confession, sex is treated as an "act," and not acknowledged as a pattern of addiction. The "sin" is forgiven, but the state remains.

A priest reported that while he was on temporary assignment at a parish, another priest came to his room, and begged to be held. He offered to fellate him. When the first priest declined, the second told him that at times he could not control himself and that he would get into his car and "cruise" the streets of the city looking for a sexual contact. This behavior had led him to some bizarre and dangerous situations. But he could not stop himself, nor could he predict when the impulse would seize him. This confrontation did eventually lead him to psychiatric treatment and subsequent control of his addiction.

The addictive state is different from compulsive behavior. Addiction can be controlled, but not cured; in the above example, it rested on an obligatory homosexual orientation. A person with an obligatory orientation can go through periods of compulsive behavior which are usually due to stress, depression, or some transient developmental crisis.

A 40-year-old priest who accepted his homosexual orientation and who had had a sexual encounter in the army prior to entering the seminary had had no sexual contact with any other person until the death of his mother. He experienced then a resurgence of his sexual drive and sought out sexual contact with a parishioner whom he knew to be actively homosexual. As he described it, there was a real *compulsion* to his behavior. When his mourning for his mother was completed, the compulsion was more easily absorbed and he returned to celibate practice.

The death of a parent, especially a mother, has been reported a number of times as the trigger for either accepting one's obligatory orientation or for acting on the impulses one had either suspected or known.

Committed Homosexuality

There is a group among priests who can be called "committed homosexuals." Their sexual attraction, fantasy, emotional and social preference, and their self-identification or awareness are all congruent. They may or may not practice celibacy, but if they do choose sexual activity, it is invariably homosexual. This can change over time, since all of these factors are interactive and open to development and alteration (cf. Klein, Sepekoff, & Wolf, 1985).

A priest who had contact with our study for 17 years is an example. During part of that time he was assigned to be the superior of the candidates entering his religious community. Situated geographically in an isolated area and separated even from other members of the larger community, he formed strong and affective bonds with his subjects. As the years went on, he developed noticeably feminine characteristics that had not been observed previously, although he was 50 years old.

In his reporting, it became clear that his sexual awareness had been intensified by his isolation and emotional stimulation by successive groups of young men who passed exclusively under his tutelage. He became comfortable with what he termed his "mother" role and demonstrated a tenderness and warmth that had been lacking earlier in his life. This was not unattractive, but it was noticeable to those who had known him in his 30s, when he had given the impression of "macho stoicism." He admitted to one period of sexual crisis that threatened his celibate practice, but was generally observant and developed no pattern of sexual activity with others, although his fantasies were consistently homoerotic.

Among this group are the most observant of religious celibates, self-aware and self-restrained, dedicated to their ideals and selfless in their service to others. They genuinely love humanity and are honest in their internal and external lives. This group represents the "silent current within the ministerial mainstream."

Another group is men who have more or less long-term sexual relationships (from 3 to 20 years) sometimes with other priests, or single or married laymen.

The wife of a choir director became concerned when she found out that her husband had had a long-term sexual liaison with their priest. Prior to that point, she had not been aware of her husband's bisexuality or the priest's homosexuality. After her initial shock, she remained tolerant of the friendship and chose not to pay attention to sexual activity between the priest and her husband.

Other sexual friendships begin in the seminary and continue through periodic contact over the years. I did not find that priests living in the same small groups or parish house ordinarily have a sexual liaison with each other. More common is a situation where two men living in a house suspect each other of being an active homosexual, while each knows that he, himself, is. They socialize well and have many friends in common, but they are not sexual with each other.

Most often, some distance is preferable for both priests to maintain a guilt free ministry and relationship. Sexual activity between these men is ego-syntonic; they experience no guilt. They do not confess, or do so only in the very beginning of their relationship. Their partners tend to be appropriate in terms of age, mutual consent, and circumstance. They do not come to the attention of civil authorities. Because the activity is not disruptive to their work or to the group immediately around them, these men do not command attention.

The sexual activity is integrated with their lives and religious goals and ideals; or it is rationalized as natural and even necessary for them to carry on their service to the church. They frame their homosexual activity in much the same mold that they do masturbation—as necessary and inconsequential. They do not experience it as a threat to their vocation.

One priest in the study did not intend to take the vow of celibacy. He consciously and audibly said "no" when he went through the ceremony preceding his ordination to the subdiaconate. He also wrote clearly in the necessary documents that he did "not" promise celibacy. He has lived a productive ministry over a period of 35 years. He says, "I wanted to be a priest; I never wanted to marry, but I had no inclination to be celibate either. I decided to live my life as a responsible Christian gentleman. And I have." He has had several sexual friendships over the years, but has never been promiscuous or compulsive in his behavior.

Public exposure is uncommon in this group, but when it happens, it has particular force. An American archbishop was confronted in the press with a letter he had written to a close male friend years earlier. It was a "love letter" explaining the rupture in the relationship and specifying his intention of returning to a celibate way of life. The incident was compounded when it was revealed that money was paid to the recipient. It appeared to be a cover-up.

The important issue is not any particular churchman's sexual practice, but the fact that sexual activity that is proscribed by church teaching, and disavowed by men who profess celibacy, can take place at the highest levels of power. There is nothing I could or would say that would detract from the good Archbishop Weakland did in office. There is also nothing I could omit that will alter the truth about sexual practice among the hierarchy. Cardinal O'Connor said: "The Holy Father demands that the Truth, whole and unvarnished, be made available to everyone."(*Time*, October 13, 1986.) This, of course, runs counter to the operation of the secret system.

The sexual practice of clergy is part of the important teaching truth of the Catholic Church. Example is as much as, or even more than, the word, a powerful and effective means of teaching. Celibacy in religious tradition is meant, among other goals, to be a lived example of how to regulate the sexual drive in accord with Christian principles. In the estimation of the general public, celibacy is not merely a legal state of nonmarriage, but a way of life sexually in conformity with church teaching. It is legitimate to ask not only what is the church's teaching on sexuality but how it is lived by church teachers and leaders.

Especially in the area of the homosexualities, the time has passed when simple denunciation and condemnation can be satisfactory. To label homosexuality a "sin" or "essentially disordered" does not aid understanding, responsible sexual practice, or abstinence.

In my study, I have made no distinction between priests with or without hierarchical power. But one cannot assume that station and power are guaranties of sexual orthodoxy in practice or proof of consistency between word and behavior. In fact, there is ample evidence that clergymen can publicly and vehemently denounce sin in others while quietly and repeatedly indulging in it themselves.

Some people assume that *guilt* is an adequate controller or regulator of behavior. It is not. The ego with the sum total of its integrative capacities and object relatedness is the agency that determines behavior (cf. Hartmann, 1958). Too little attention is paid to this reality in the education and formation of men who would be celibate.

There is another subgroup among the committed homosexual population of priests. They are the growing and articulate group who are generally allied with gay rights and who talk freely about their sympathies. They find support more outside the clergy population than within it. But they also are vocal and often seek out clergy for understanding and support. This group does not split their behavior and their celibate ideal. They frankly disregard celibacy as not possible or desirable. The dichotomy in their lives is more between who knows and who does not know their orientation or sexual preference. One wag among this group said that "the unmentionable vice, now mentioned, can't keep its mouth shut."

There are priests championing the cause of justice for homosexuals who believe in celibacy where appropriate. Pioneers like John J. McNeill and Father Robert Nugent faced squarely the theological questions posed by the reality of the homosexualities and church teaching and were silenced. Some priests have declared their own obligatory homosexual orientation; other supporters are heterosexual. There is a movement of gay priests who band together to support each other in their celibate strivings. The membership is guarded; they operate according to the principles of Alcoholics Anonymous.

Latent Homosexuality

A simple definition of latent homosexuality describes it as a true homosexual impulse that can be conscious but is mostly unconscious, and is not overtly acted out. It is beyond the scope or intent of this study to speculate on the number of priests who do not admit a homosexual orientation or who genuinely may not be aware that unresolved homosexual tendencies may indeed motivate their lives and behaviors.

In 1910, Freud made some creative observations about Leonardo da Vinci and his psychic structure, especially the preservation of his relationship with, and fidelity to, his mother (1953a, p. 78). In 1928, he observed of Dostoevsky that "a strong innate bisexual disposition becomes one of the preconditions or reinforcements of neurosis . . . and it shows itself in a viable form (as latent homosexuality) in the important part played by male friendships in his life, in his strangely tender attitude toward rivals in love and in his remarkable understanding of situations which are explicable only by repressed homosexuality" (1961b, p. 184).

Those observations about Dostoevsky's novels could be applied to the lives of a number of priests, just as Leonardo's homosexual attachment to his mother has echoes in the lives of many priests. In his *Three Essays on Sexuality*, Freud does not equivocate. He says: "The unconscious mental life of all neurotics (without exception) shows inverted impulses, fixation of their libido upon persons of their own sex" (1953a, p. 166). Likewise, in his *General Theory of Neurosis* of 1917 he says:

> Neurotic symptoms are substitutes for sexual satisfaction . . . , and I indicated to you that the confirmation of this assertion by the analysis of symptoms would come up against a number of difficulties. For it can only be justified if under "sexual satisfaction" we include the satisfaction of what are called perverse sexual needs, since an interpretation of symptoms of that kind is forced upon us with surprising frequency. The claim made by homosexuals or inverts to being exceptions collapses at once when we learn that homosexual impulses are invariably discovered in every single neurotic, and that a fair number of symptoms give expression to this latent inversion. Those who call themselves homosexuals are only conscious and manifest inverts, whose number is nothing compared to that of the *latent* homosexuals. (1963, p. 307)

If, according to Freud, some type of latent homosexuality is generally related to all neurosis, it is the specific and core dynamic conflict of male paranoia: "the wishful phantasy of *loving a man*" (1958, p. 62). I have not observed, nor have I ever heard it said that there is any greater number of paranoids among the celibate clergy than among any other segment of the male population (cf. Meissner, 1978). But anyone who has worked extensively with priests in intensive psychotherapy will resonate with Freud's case history, *An Infantile Neurosis*

(1961a, pp. 7–122). Because the roots of a celibate vocation are of necessity laid down early in life, they will be entangled with early developmental conflicts and relationships. Neurosis is not the inevitable outcome of celibate striving, but there is not one recorded life of a celibate saint that does not include deep self-searching, dark nights of self-awareness, and agonizing struggles for maturity and integrity.

In limiting my observations to the conscious behaviors and orientations of priests, I am not side-stepping the question of latent homosexuality. It is simply immeasurable. I think that the spiritual life many priests pursue faithfully leads them to an intense self-awareness. Meditation makes them conscious of their inner psychic dynamic and this in turn gives them the direction and strength to transcend neurosis, whatever its origin. True celibates transform their energies into the loving service of their fellow human beings.

ALCOHOLISM

There was a time when psychological theory branded severe alcoholism as having an underlying latent homosexual personality structure. That is an oversimplification. Invariably, however, alcohol addiction interferes with sexual function. Many priests report that they come to grips with their sexual behavior and identity once they've dealt with their alcohol addiction. Over 50 percent of clergy who are treated for severe alcohol problems have some homosexual concerns. This is an important minority to consider when one approaches the sexual practices of clergy.

There is an Irish bias that was reported several times: "If Father is an alcoholic, he must be celibate." A drinking problem is seen as a proof of fidelity to the celibate vow and lack of sexual involvement. Studies correlating alcohol use and sexual practice among the clergy are yet to be done.

ACQUIRED IMMUNE DEFICIENCY SYNDROME

It is obvious that clergy are emerging as a clear subgroup of the homosexual population that has so far contracted AIDS. Judy Thomas of the *Kansas City Star* published a study of priests with HIV/AIDS.

She concluded that priests die of the virus in twice the numbers as men in the general population (2000). All of the reasons are not yet clear.

> Health officials who deal with sexually transmitted diseases have long been aware of the frequency of homosexuality among Catholic priests. In the words of one such official, "I and most of the public-health directors I've talked to about this subject estimate that in our communities at least a third of Catholic priests under forty-five are homosexuals, and most are sexually active. They almost always engage in anonymous encounters, the highest-risk sex of all, and when they want help they don't come to clinics. I've met with priests in some of the strangest places." (Leishman, 1987, p. 48)

The Task Force on Gay/Lesbian Issues in San Francisco estimates that the homosexual population among the Roman Catholic clergy is also at 30 percent.

One of the men in Thomas's study population who died was actively homosexual. By preference he sought out black sexual partners and contracted syphilis once and anal gonorrhea twice. Although he considered himself homosexual from his early years, he was not active sexually while at the seminary. Two years after his ordination and the subsequent death of his father, he felt himself overwhelmed with loneliness and isolation in his remote rural parish. He planned vacations to large urban areas specifically to experience sex where he found himself feeling accepted and safe with black men. His period of promiscuity lasted about 3 years.

With a reassignment to a more socially stimulating environment, he altered his sexual behavior somewhat and found a group of compatible priests with whom he did not engage in sexual activity, even though he felt they were homosexual. Fellow priests supported him during his long illness until his death from AIDS.

AIDS is a worldwide problem with medical dimensions like cancer and social dimensions like world hunger. That it is a disease that can be sexually transmitted thrusts it into the moral arena. The danger is that glib moralizing and homespun theology—*AIDS is God's curse for sexual sin*—will foster intolerable fears in the name of religion. Worse still is the possibility for illness to be used as an excuse to hate. Father Joseph Gallagher (1987) wrote a perceptive and balanced Christian response to AIDS. The temptation to abandon a priest patient or for the priest to isolate himself in shame or fear should not be tolerated. Likewise, cover-ups in the name of avoiding scandal only increase the problems and encourage irresponsibility rather than accountability.

HOMOSEXUALITY AND MENTAL HEALTH

Homosexual priests are not willing to accept a psychiatric diagnosis because of their orientation. Some are vocal and radically active; they feel honesty about their sexual orientation is part of their vocation, and sexual activity is their God-given right. There is a kind of consistency about their internal logic—they refuse to lead a double life. This small but growing faction is truly part of the gay subculture that has been incorporated into clerical life.

Some homosexual behavior is part of a basic mental health problem. Character disorders that involve poor impulse control, excessive narcissism, and depressions are prominent. These disorders are frequently complicated by the use of alcohol. Some of this group come to the attention of church authorities or the legal system because of their choice of inappropriate partners or circumstances for their sexual activity. Sexual abuse of minors and child pornography are prominent here.

An example of a character disorder involving homosexual activity was a priest who maintained an active and prominent life in ecclesiastical circles. He died suddenly at the age 45 of a heart attack. The priest assigned to put his affairs in order found in the deceased priest's apartment a cache of illegal drugs (including cocaine), and a library of pornographic homosexual videotapes. The priest had recorded the names, addresses, and descriptions of the sexual preferences of dozens of young men. It was obvious that he was as well known in the homosexual subculture as he was in church circles.

A chronically depressed priest, who was conscientious about his clerical duties, periodically sought anonymous, dangerous sexual contacts. His bouts with sexual acting out coincided with his episodic depressions. The event that brought him to treatment was a frightening encounter in which he submitted for the first time to anal intercourse. On his way to his residence at 2:00 A.M., after a particularly hard period of work, he entered an all-night pornographic movie house. In the washroom, he propositioned a man; the violence of his own sexual response, including the ripping off of clothing, motivated him to seek psychiatric treatment. In curing his depression, he was also able to choose to modify his sexual behavior. The tragedy is that many people do not seek treatment for their depression, but self-medicate with sex.

The narcissistic personality whose relations remain superficial and self-centered can abuse people. A priest who was a university professor had an inflated view of himself and his importance built on a base of genuine popularity. He repeatedly selected a male student as a companion and cultivated him as a protégé. Once established in the bond, he became envious and demanding, and felt he was entitled to whatever he requested or needed, including sexual exchanges. These seemingly intimate relationships were interchangeable with anyone who could better fill the priest's needs. The academic setting made the transient quality of these relationships seem logical. In truth, the setting was a convenient cover for a superficial and self-serving life-style. A student who had taken the offer of friendship as genuine brought the priest to the attention of superiors.

As in all segments of society, the borderline personality inhabits the ranks of the clergy. Their tendency to overidealize (and/or devalue) can be mistaken for religious enthusiasm. Their basic rage can find worthy objects in the enemies of religion—sin, degradation, abortion, contraception, and even homosexuality. Their tendency to projective identification can be read as good assimilation into the religious mind-set. Even their proficiency at splitting—setting different members of a group against each other—can be rewarded if they succeed in allying themselves with the winning party. It is the poor impulse control and the unhealed scars of separation that lead them to homosexual activity. Their impulsiveness and infantile rage sometimes bring them to the attention of authorities.

Some clergy behave homosexually episodically due to situational stress or as a part of a transitional adjustment reaction. These men have severe or at least moderate guilt feelings in association with their homosexual activities. They really try to control their behavior, mostly because they see it as a contradiction to the ideal they have set for themselves. They are the first to call themselves hypocrites. Men in this group tend to seek spiritual or professional help with what they clearly define as a problem. Some of this group come to the attention of authorities more because of their naïveté and ineptness at seeking a sexual outlet. They are easy victims for traps and hustlers. This group does not tend to be impulsive, but can experience transitory compulsions. Some seem to have an unconscious desire to "get caught" or to atone for their "sins" by exposure.

One middle-aged priest remained persistently immature sexually in spite of heroic efforts to grow. He sought out young men who were hustlers or call boys, using his real name and address. However, he tried seriously to alter this pattern when one of the young men threatened to blackmail him.

Other priests get caught in the trap of making an appointment to "meet" someone they originally encountered in a bar. Later, at the arranged time and place, the priest will find not simply his intended sexual companion, but one or two others who proceed to threaten, assault, or rob him.

Some of these priests get caught in police traps at highway rest stops or other centers of anonymous homosexual exchange. They differ from the other priests who may or may not get caught as they do not have an established pattern of homosexual behavior or fixed sexual identity, and as the behavior occurs under some transitional stress or growth phase.

This group faces a tremendous growth challenge. They set a high, lifelong ideal sometimes at a young age. They exist in a unique environment that supports them socially and economically at the same time it makes them dependent. Sexual maturity is an elusive goal, not necessarily achieved under the most favorable of circumstances. But sexuality is relentless, natural hankering fueled by a persistent normal curiosity. Although many priests succeed at celibacy, sex is a difficult drive to fight or to conquer even with highly refined methods of sublimation. This is as true for the man of homosexual orientation as it is for the heterosexually oriented.

Within this group of *immature* priests are some who may or may not be obligatory homosexuals. They literally do not have enough sexual experience to resolve for themselves their sexual identity. Their fantasy life is ambiguous, as are their friendships. Their limited sexual play may be heterosexual as well as homosexual. They generally are capable of solid relationships and seek supportive friendships. Their immaturity may lead them to occasional homosexual behavior within the context of these friendships; that behavior in turn is confusing, ego-dystonic, and spiritually unsettling.

Frequently, a sexually more experienced layman or sometimes a fellow priest who is committed to homosexuality picks up the unconscious sexual cues of the person and acts as his teacher or leader. This liaison may exist briefly or may recur several times.

Many in this group are pained by their sense of loneliness, and they desire most of all simply "to be held," or to "have someone accept me as I am." They naïvely look for a relationship among these contacts and some have even recounted a humorous result when they assumed friendship where there had actually been only a "business" deal. One priest's gifts and sentiments sent the hustler into a panic—he thought he was being set up by a government agent.

This immature group differs from others who lack a capacity for relationship, and from those so deeply scarred by separation and early deprivation that every relationship futilely seeks the primitive mother.

Some find in a transient homosexual experience the psychic push to complete their adolescent development, thereby resulting in a decent adult heterosexual orientation. They literally complete their adolescent development in their 30s or 40s.

The whole range of homosexualities is difficult for both individual clergy and the church as a whole to deal with. The influence and power the church has to teach, to heal, and to save persons from unnecessary suffering and injustice are curtailed when homosexual orientation and behavior are approached from an exclusively moralistic point of view. The reality of nature exists—people *do* behave thus-and-so. To be a moral leader, the church must deal with the realities of nature.

There have always been a substantial number of homosexually oriented men who have given themselves to the service of the church. There are, of course, some who do not either practice or even care to achieve celibacy. But some find the practice of celibacy possible within the homosocial organization of the church. Some men achieve celibacy in the monosexual hierarchical structure just as some heterosexually or bisexually oriented men do. A growing number of homosexually oriented and/or sexually active men among the clergy are gaining a voice and visibility—often unwanted—that must be reckoned with.

8

SEXUAL COMPROMISES

I am not at all optimistic that celibacy is in fact being observed.

—Franjo Cardinal Seper

Priests are part of that segment of the male population who "cannot marry." The church presumes that this is a self-limitation. The vocation is a call to sacrifice everything to follow Christ. That *everything* includes heart, mind, and will. Marriage and any directly sought sexual pleasure are forbidden. *Everything* includes a rejection of over-dependence on material things (some form of religious poverty). A *weltanschauung* of obedience presumes the will of God is the supreme law and it is expressed through legitimate authority.

For some priests these ideals are formalized in vows. However, with or without vows, the histories of all clerics—saints and sinners alike—are ultimately measured against these gospel ideals. It can be most accurately stated that the approach to the ideal is a history of the compromises made in reaching them. Acknowledging honest failures proves success.

Sublimation of the sexual instinct makes celibacy possible. I have observed areas of failure in achieving that sublimation—areas that are essentially victimless. The most common modes of sexual expression involve pornography, transvestism, exhibitionism, and bestiality.

WHAT IS NORMAL?

Celibacy, because it depends on a "grace," is a supernatural vocation. Certainly it is not *natural* for the average man to remain celibate. Celibacy is not the norm for society; in that sense it is not normal. Priests have a difficult time getting an education in sexuality. This can lead some to explore various avenues to satisfy their normal curiosity. Is it normal for the priest to view pornography? The *Report of the Commission on Obscenity and Pornography* stated:

> Approximately 85% of adult men and 70% of women in the U.S. have been exposed at some time during their lives to depictions of explicate sexual material in either visual or textual form. Most of this exposure has apparently been voluntary, and pictorial and textual depictions are seen about equally often. Recent experience with erotic materials is not as extensive as total experience, e.g., only about 40% of adult males and 26% of adult females report having seen pictorial depictions of sexual intercourse during the past two years. (1970, p. 19)

According to these figures, regardless of the *morality* of viewing pornography, it cannot in itself be called *abnormal* adult behavior. The priest who rejects marriage and sexual contact may find himself in the position that Dr. Benjamin Karpman (1954) called "the normal pervert." This appellation will not be welcomed by clergy or psychiatrists, but can be instructive for one who is trying to understand the sexual behaviors of men vowed to celibacy. Karpman thinks that behaviors that are essentially pathological in their extreme form are acceptable. "In milder forms and degrees, especially if they are indulged in as a subsidiary part of normal relations; as a sort of preliminary, they should be regarded as falling within the framework of the normal" (p. 416).

He also pointed out that "children indulge in all sorts of sexual experimentations which include perversion" (p. 416). One of the problems of celibate education is a propensity to leave childhood sexual orientation unexamined. If one dismisses celibacy as a form of pathology, he or she will not be interested in struggling for an understanding of the dilemmas, behaviors, and vagaries of one who is striving for sexual maturity without the benefit of the mating and marital experiences. The observer needs tolerance and empathy with the educational and growth struggles of that minority whose "*handicap*" is a supremely high spiritual ideal. A priest attempting celibacy does not develop psychosexually in the same way or at the same rate as the average man. Can priests be considered the *normal pervert*? Such is

. . . one who, despite the handicap imposed by an unorthodox and socially unacceptable sexual orientation, does manage to live an otherwise normal life according to general standards of ordinary behavior. He is really no different from the individual who suffers from a physical handicap and who nevertheless contrives to make for himself a way of life that is generally useful and attended with more than an ordinary amount of satisfaction. But while the victim of a physical handicap is praised for his efforts, the victim of a psychosexual handicap is condemned. The principal reason is because the victim of a physical handicap is regarded as having suffered a misfortune, while the victim of a psychosexual handicap is labeled a pervert as though his psychosexual handicap were a matter of voluntary choice and deliberate selection. . . . (Karpman, 1954, p. 417)

This is a humane stance, but it fails to take into account elements of behavior that may be criminal and debilitating. The priest who is crippled should be in a transient state. In this sense he deserves understanding, and help to find healthier means of sexual growth.

THE PLACE OF WOMEN

A question related to celibate compromises is that of the place of women in the life of a priest who does not want to be sexually or affectively involved. The place of the priest's mother is often enhanced by devotion to the "Blessed Virgin Mother Mary." This spiritual emulation tends to fixate the priest in the role of a son who is affiliated with a male-centered "idolatry." The structure of the church justifies men's right to dominate all women. The man, whose mother becomes the center of his affective universe, becomes himself very special in a real or imagined reciprocity.

The Christian feminist contention is that the Churches are hung up on a sort of male-centered idolatry that in turn justifies a belief that men are superior with right to dominate women (there are other tragic assumptions around all this—the right to dominate nature, for one). Yet no true mutuality is possible within a framework of domination and subordination, attractive as it is to those who find intimacy difficult. (Furlong, 1987, p. 1084)

By revising the view of Christian womanhood, women are challenging the traditional structure of power that has become inextricably interwoven with celibacy. Celibacy that is dependent on immature sexual identity will be threatening to women and, equally as important, will be frightened of them (cf. Karl Stern, *The Flight from Women*, 1965). Women's experience of the church and their articulation of it are helping the priest to experience his own gender conflicts and to have them exposed in bold relief. Questions of sexual identity can be manifest in behaviors involving pornography, transvestism, and exhibitionism, among other things.

Gender identity—the sense that one is male or female—is laid down very early in life. Sexual identity—the sense of *how* masculine or feminine one is—also begins to develop in the first year of life, a development that becomes increasingly focused from the 3rd year of life through adolescence, building on gender identity. The place of the mother and her expressions play major roles in forming these identities. The mother's response to her baby and her facial cues of approval or displeasure are crucial to identity formation.

If sexual development does not mature, sexual identity is stifled or delayed. Untimely "childhood" behavior becomes overly attractive. The priest is stuck in an attempt to solve his immaturity in ways more appropriate to the development of childhood sexuality, for instance, using vision as a source of excitation.

> Looking at the naked body, particularly at the genitals or buttocks of others, produces, from a very early age, intense pleasure satisfaction. Even with adults, the sight of the loved object is frequently the first source of excitation. In the case of perversion, the erotogenic pleasure in looking leads to scoptophilia. Being looked at when naked also often excites intense, even ecstatic pleasure of an undoubtedly sensual nature in children. (Sterba, 1968, p. 55)

The knowledge that seeing erotic material can be sexually stimulating was recognized in ancient ascetic tradition, which counseled "custody of the eyes" as a protection against sensual temptations. Today it is accepted that both the desire to see pornography (voyeurism, certainly) and the desire to be seen (exhibitionism) have their roots deep in infancy.

FEAR OF WOMEN

If the use of pornography is coupled with the fear of women the probability of fixation at immature levels of psychosexual development becomes more likely. Devotion to the idealized Blessed Virgin enhances early concepts of other less idealized women as dangerous and inaccessible. Fear inhibits development. The fear of women is generalized; they become "the most dangerous enemy."

The sexual flame of curiosity is actually fanned by some priests' fear. Their attempt to overcome it and their sexual inexperience leads them to pornography. Like other patrons of adult bookstores and movie houses priests have had less sexually related experiences in adolescence than the average male. Their pastoral work confronts them with the sexual concerns of others; this in turn challenges them, leading to a high degree of sexual orientation in adulthood.

Many people would question the value of pornography as an educational element in any man's life, let alone that of a dedicated celibate. Pornography, however, is a fact, an ancient fact and in some cultures, but not in Christian tradition, is considered an art form. "An erotic art," Foucault said (in *The History of Sexuality*, 1978, p. 67), "is the usual way for a civilization to make sense of its knowledge about sex." He pointed to the existence of such artistic expression in Etruscan, Roman, Arabic, Persian, Indian, Chinese, Japanese, and many other civilizations but not, alas, in the Christian.

There is no question that women are exploited in heterosexual pornography. But the implications are far more extensive for the priest who has difficulties establishing his sexual identity.

In *Presentations of Gender* (1985), Robert J. Stoller discussed some of the manifestations of gender disorders and their impact:

When we look closely at the behavior that makes up a man's perversion— when we get an in-depth subjective description of the erotic behavior— we find, regardless of the overt form of the behavior, that he is under pressure from envy and anger toward women. . . . The evidence is found in the fantasies these men have that they are degrading women. Examples are rape, coprolalia (dirty language as an erotic stimulant), voyeurism, fetishism, exhibitionism, pedophilia, necrophilia. In all these you will find evidence of uncertain manliness. And so, though there may be no desire to put on clothes of the opposite sex or otherwise to behave (or fantasize behaving) as a member of the opposite sex, in the perversions is nonetheless buried unsureness of gender identity. (p. 18)

The feminist arguments hold some special significance for the priest whose sexual experience and education are limited, and who is, therefore, unduly influenced by what he does see and hear. A priest's unresolved fear of women often manifests itself in a harsh and denigrating attitude toward them that has multiple pastoral and even theological ramifications.

WHAT IS PORNOGRAPHY?

Sexually explicit writings, drawings, paintings, sculpture, ceramics; private performances, recorded or spoken recitations, plays, dance, and religious rites, can all be pornographic and have existed in every culture. They stimulate fantasy. Oftentimes these materials are banned or circulated "underground."

> The best empirical definition of pornography is that it is explicitly depicted erotic and sexual material that generates in a viewer, reader, or listener who has access to it, a sense of being sneaky, surreptitious, and illicit, provided access to the same material by the same person at a younger age would have been prohibited, prevented, and punished. (Money, 1986, p. 167)

Supreme Court Justice Potter Stewart defined hard-core pornography, "perhaps I could never succeed in intelligibly [defining it]. But I know it when I see it."

Sigmund Freud's wife Martha "thought her husband's psychoanalytic ideas 'a form of pornography'" (Gay, 1988, p. 61). Others may see the psychiatrist as a kind of voyeur. Indeed, probably all the helping professions, including medicine and ministry, demand a quality of character that can tolerate an intimate view of other persons' sexual problems and lives. At times, there may be a very fine line dividing pastoral concern from prurient interest. It is simply an occupational hazard that each professional must deal with responsibly.

Priests deprived of a sexual outlet can turn to pornography and in that broad sense exhibit voyeurism—behavior limited to men, encouraged by deficient heterosocial skills, and usually associated with masturbation. Many priests report exploring both visual and literary pornography. For most of these priests, the incidents were part of their attempt to supplement faulty sex education or represented immature forays.

Pornography is available to everyone, including priests. Adult bookshops with their bright signs have proliferated across the United States landscape with a familiarity similar to the markings of the interstate road system.

Legal, familiar, and accessible hard-core pornography has become almost stylish. Computer Web sites and videos make every form of sexual activity available to interested persons in the comfort and privacy of their homes. A number of priests have responded just like the public in general with curiosity and experimentation. Some report that by "seeing" some sexual activity they were, for the first time, confronted with their own sexual interest and orientation.

For example, a 32-year-old priest who had entered the seminary in his teens and whose sexual experience was limited to occasional masturbation, observed one night from his rectory window a teenaged couple "making out" in a parked car. This couple sneaked past the chaperons at a parish dance to their rendezvous. The angle of view and the lighting favored the priest's observation and he stood in the dark of his room transfixed by the thrashings and passion of the young couple. He found himself more sexually stimulated than he had ever been in his life and he masturbated. After this experience, he went through a phase of visiting pornographic bookshops and peep shows. He was fascinated with the female body and became aware of how much he wanted to make love with a woman. Although this period lasted several years and was distressing and confusing to the priest, it finally was incorporated into his sexual maturation.

The use of pornography is often accompanied or followed by masturbation. Sometimes it is a prelude to or reinforcement of other sexual activities, including homosexuality and pedophilia.

In *The Psychoanalytic Theory of Neurosis*, Otto Fenichel (1945) said the following:

In lovers of pornography one frequently meets two contradictory, reassuring attitudes: (1) The fact that sexual details are described in print proves the objective existence of sexuality; by the mechanism of "sharing guilt" it relieves guilt feelings by making sexual fantasies more "objective." (2) Nevertheless the feared sexuality is not quite real; it is enjoyed in empathy by reading about it in a book, not by experiencing it actually, and thus it is less dangerous.

Masturbation with the help of pornographic literature is nearer, in one respect, to normal sexuality than is masturbation without it, the book being a medium between sexual fantasy and sexual reality. In adolescents or persons with perverse inclinations who are ashamed of admitting their wishes, the book or picture may simply represent a substitute for a sexual partner. (p. 351)

An accurate first-person description of the use of pornography by a priest is profoundly illustrative. He used the pen name "Father Augustine" in "Help and Hope for the Sex Addict."

I first began to "act out" sexually about 20 years ago. That was in the late 1960s when the so-called sexual revolution was just getting under way and when pornography became widely and easily available. It was with pornography that my addiction first manifested itself, and my addiction has continued to center on it, although it has developed other manifestations.

I had been ordained about 10 years, felt happy in my vocation as a priest and a member of a religious order and had received my first permanent assignment. I went about that assignment in a large Midwestern city with all the zeal I could muster "for the kingdom of God." I now understand that my zeal contained within it the core of what I consider my primary addiction: workaholism.

I soon began to subordinate in practice (though not in theory, of course) all my time and energies to achievement in my ministry. Just why I *had* to achieve, I now see, goes back to my childhood and adolescence, but at the time, I was not even aware that it was a problem. I, in fact, thought of it as a virtue.

I shaved time off my prayer and fitted God into my schedule in the few moments I could spare. Friends and recreation suffered in the same way. I, in effect, was shutting down on the affective, humane side of my vocation. The fact that I was attaining immense success in my ministry only fed the ills concealed in my zeal. I had time for everybody and everything except myself.

My prurient interest in pornographic magazines and movies grew accordingly, and I found myself with some frequency in the bookstores and cinemas that fed it. Even at this early stage of addiction, my denial had sufficiently developed to allow me to walk out of these situations with a relatively clean conscience. What devastated me in those early years, however, was that two or three times a year I would go on a binge—spending hours in the cinemas, buying the literature, bringing it home where I consumed it and masturbated over it.

This led on the "mornings after" to thoughts of suicide and to anguished visits to confessionals where I prayed I would find a priest who would not recognize me. Every confession brought the firmest resolutions that I would never, never do it again. But within a few months the pattern repeated itself, resulting in the same self-hate and the same firm but utterly ineffective resolutions. By this time I had, for obvious reasons, given up the practice of a "regular confessor."

One year during a retreat I became painfully aware of the pattern and of the fact that my resolutions were getting me nowhere. I needed help, and God gave me the strength to talk to another priest about what was going on in my life. The priest could not have been more surprised, for my life gave absolutely no evidence on the outside that anything was wrong. I was, in fact, admired by him and by many others as a colleague who "had it all together."

I have to admit that as I told my story I surprised myself. The person I described did not seem to be *me*. Although like most human beings I had struggles with my sexuality while I was growing up and even during my years in the seminary, neither I nor others saw any cause for particular alarm. I believed all along—and continue to believe—that I had a genuine call from God to serve in the priesthood and religious life. But things were happening in my life to make it seem to be the worst of hypocrisy. The image of Dr. Jekyll and Mr. Hyde often flashed through my mind.

The priest was kind and compassionate. He suggested a number of standard spiritual remedies, and especially insisted that I be open with him about everything that was going on. I count that interview as the beginning of my recovery, for I had become an expert at keeping secret even from myself the deep and dark forces that were at work in me. Nonetheless, my acting out did not cease. In fact, its frequency and intensity increased, especially after I was transferred to another large city where I once again could not bring myself to talk about my problem to those who might help me. The shame was overpowering.

I began to have some physical contact with others who sought the same sexual thrills as I did, but the real center of my disease continued to situate itself in various forms of pornography and masturbation. I occasionally had several weeks during which I felt I had everything under control, but as time went on my binges became more frequent, more prolonged, more devastating, more reckless. Alcohol became one of my preferred "props" to help me get the sexual highs that were gradually becoming more elusive.

By this time I had mastered the art of hiding my secret activities, but I could at least vaguely see what others could not. My life was careening out of control. I began to miss work and to feel obsessed for days on end. I could not, however, stop doing what I so much hated. Given the places that I frequented unremittingly, it is a miracle that I was not mugged, knifed, or arrested.

After a particularly frightening experience one night when I thought I was recognized by someone at a pornographic movie, I told one of my superiors about it—and about everything else. As the months passed I continued to try to keep in touch with him, wrenching though these interviews were. I remember weeping bitterly in his presence on several occasions; but despite the compassion and good advice I received, I still could not stop. (*America*, Oct. 1, 1988, pp. 190–1)

This priest demonstrated the pattern and progress of a growing absorption with pornography. First he confided the incident, as sin, to his confessor. Quickly he moved to the second phase where he sought out an anonymous confessor to whom he told isolated transgressions of his conscience. Third, he indulged his interest and avoided telling any priest about his activities. At this point, the problem had moved deeper and deeper into the system of secrecy, more and more isolated from the priest's religious ideals or perhaps completely split off from them. The visual stimulation led not only to masturbation but also to sexual contact with other men or with women.

Frequently there are men or boys around adult bookshops and peep shows who are willing or eager to exchange sexual activity. If the store is in an area of bars, prostitutes are often also available. It does not take long for even the shy inexperienced clergyman who is seeking pornography to find people who are ready to enact what the books describe and the movies depict.

One 55-year-old priest came to my attention not in his lifetime, but in death. He had a heart attack in a pornographic movie theater. His church superiors were anxious to keep the site of his death out of the newspapers, which they were able to do. The facts of his sexual pattern were revealed in the aftermath. He had kept a complete record of all the foreign ships that docked at a seaport near his home. Certain foreign seamen frequented the pornographic theater that he visited; his visit always coincided with the shore leave of a foreign ship. All of his sexual activity had involved pornographic films in conjunction with homosexual contact with sailors in the theater. This methodical priest kept a meticulous accounting of his adventures. The rest of his life was productive and well regulated.

Although pornography can lead a priest to sexual contact with others, it may also follow or substitute for contact. A priest who had had a prolonged sexual affair with a woman when he was in his 30s renewed his vow of celibacy when she died; he subsequently refrained from sexual activity. But he began to collect pornographic literature after her death. Since he was a teacher and scholar, he incorporated his hobby into his intellectual interests—he became an authority on Henry Miller.

There are a number of priests who practice celibacy and even eventually achieve the state who use modern cinema and literature very well. Literally, they learn to mature from it. They are rarely interested in pornography because of its paucity of person and event. In pornography, the only object is a penis or a vagina; the only event is the orgasm. Persons of spiritual and intellectual depth and maturity are fascinated by life and are usually bored quickly by pornography.

For some priests, pornography is an occasional or passing interest as a victimless outlet for their sexual tension. Some do become addicted. There are a few who relish their role as censors and crusaders against pornography. A layman reported his aversion to the enthusiastic cleric who was trying to elicit his help on a church committee to stamp out pornography for the protection of the youth of the area. With a wild gleam in his eye, the priest had said to the layman, "You should *see* what they *show!*" The layman noted also that many of the committee members spent a disproportionate amount of time reviewing and riling against the material to be stamped out.

For the average priest or the average religious layperson, pornography is not the object of prolonged or undue interest. The most apt similarity to the interested priest is the adolescent—curious and afraid of sex, relatively inexperienced, yet eager to learn about it and not quite certain of an avenue that is both safe and acceptable to his conscience.

Because so many priests have been exposed to some pornography and yet it so rarely persists in isolation without masturbation, or even homosexual or pedophilic activity, we make no estimate of pornography as an isolated sexual outlet. Suffice it to say that many have been exposed, but only a few become addicted. Certainly pornography is not a preferred method of teaching priests about human sexuality. Some priests use it along with alcohol in the seduction and abuse of minors.

EXHIBITIONISTIC BEHAVIOR

In contrast to voyeurism, where sexual pleasure is achieved by seeing, exhibitionism is a mode of deriving sexual pleasure from *being* seen. Technically, it is the exposure of the sexual organs in situations in which exposure is socially defined as inappropriate, and is carried out, at least in part, for the purpose of sexual arousal and gratification.

It is safe to say that as an unvarnished disorder it is rare among priests vowed to celibacy. Other researchers have pointed out that in the population generally, exhibitionism is age related; "the peak of exhibitionism is in the 20s, and it decreases rapidly in the 30s; over the age of 40 the symptom occurs only in rare instances. Although the peak of the exhibitionist's behavior is around age 25, the onset of symptoms has two major periods, one in midpuberty, and the other in the early 20s. Exhibitionists as a group are young; offenses occur-

ring at an older age frequently indicate other factors, such as alcoholism, organic deterioration, or another sexual deviation, especially
pedophilia" (Mohr, Turner, & Jerry, 1964, p. 127).

There was one priest who took great delight in walking nude from
the bathroom to the bedroom in his parish house when he felt the
housekeeper, whom he disliked, had invaded his upstairs domain. Although it was mean-spirited, the housekeeper was intrigued as well
as frightened, but it lacked real sexual excitement on his part. He had
other problems.

Several reports of incidents where priests who were drunk exposed
themselves inappropriately were reported; control of the alcoholism
seemed to eliminate these incidents. Exhibitionism that is a factor in
pedophilia proves troublesome to the offender and his treatment, and
to the victim.

Since celibacy is dependent on the more or less successful sublimation of the sexual instinct, one has to be aware of the partial and derivative ways in which a person seeks to be celibate. We learn from the
spectrum and not merely from the extremes of success and failure.

Clinical exhibitionism "also differs somewhat from the more general usage of the word . . . [which denotes] anyone who enjoys showing off his or her body and being admired and desired for his physical
attractiveness" (Tollison & Adams, 1979, p. 237). The clerical office
puts men on exhibit; they become public figures and command the
attention of throngs of sometimes adulatory people. Some men exploit this aspect of their vocation. Other men who were exquisitely
aware of the inner workings of their hearts and minds (by way of long-
term daily meditation) humbly acknowledged the part played in their
ministry by their love of attention.

The traditional way of understanding exhibitionistic behavior was
to see it as a result of psychosexual immaturity.

Three ways in which exhibitionistic expression serves a man with
an underdeveloped sexual personality:

1. It calls upon the reactions of others to reassure him in the face
   of his own inner doubts about his masculinity.
2. Inspiring fear in the other, he does not have to be afraid of
   himself. One priest who had exhibitionistic fantasies when

he masturbated was a remarkably dramatic preacher. He had been a popular retreat master at one time in his career. In his parish he carefully arranged the lighting to focus only on a large crucifix and himself in the pulpit. In one of his favorite presentations, he would prostrate himself before the crucifix, "casting himself at the feet of Christ." The whole of his drama would reach a crescendo when he would speak about sin and God's response. "He will hate you! He will hate you! He will hate you!" he would shout at the top of his voice, pounding the pulpit with his closed fist (a surprisingly clear masturbatory gesture) before a rapt and terrified audience. This particular presentation would always give him a great sense of relief and reassurance.

3. An imagined element of magic exists in exhibitionistic fantasy. The distinction between male and female disappears. The exhibitionist acts like the transvestite; he "acts" the girl who shows her penis. He reassures himself that he is sexually OK, without the fear of harming himself by physical contact. (Cf. Fenichel, 1945, p. 346).

The elements of unconsolidated and ill-resolved *gender* and *sexual identities* are eminently important to the understanding of some aspects of celibacy. The fantasy lives of some priests who degrade women reveal that they struggle under pressure from envy and anger toward women. In the case of priests committed to celibacy in whom direct sexual behavior may be minimal, it is in fantasy that their relative levels of sexual anxiety are revealed. The psychiatric diagnosis takes into account not only a man who acts on his urges, but also the man who is "markedly distressed by them" or who masturbates while "fantasizing exposing himself" (*DSM-IV*, 1994, p. 525).

TRANSVESTISM

Clothing does have meaning. Clergy do wear fancy clothes. The higher the ecclesiastical rank the more colorful and elaborate. The silks, satins, brocades, laces, and ermines required for some ceremonies are no more than a uniform to the vast majority of clergy. The clothing—from the cassock to the cope—is of another time. It is vestry that is sexually ambiguous in present day culture. And it can be a symbol of the lack of sexual differentiation so common in the priesthood.

A sufficient number of priests report behavior strictly defined as transvestism to conclude that 1 percent of Catholic clergy make this sexual compromise. An understanding of the clerical transvestite—as in understanding other manifestations of sexual compromise—requires an examination of transvestism in its strictest clinical sense and a look at the psychosexual developmental dynamics underlying it.

One strict definition follows:

> The term *transvestism* has been used for any cross-dressing. I restrict it, however, to those, again biologically normal, who put on clothes of the opposite sex because the clothes are sexually exciting to them. Though this fetishism can occur in childhood, usually it is first manifested at puberty or later in adolescence. It is almost always found in men who are overtly heterosexual, of masculine demeanor, in occupations dominated by males; and it occurs only intermittently, most of the subject's life being spent in unremarkably masculine behavior and appearance. (Stoller, 1985, p. 21)

A priest who fits this definition had collected a series of costumes throughout his career. Sometimes he used them in his teaching and sometimes in his role as a host for both private and parish-related parties. The clothes were not exclusively feminine, but often were ambiguous, including King Solomon–like flowing robes or the garb and earring of a pirate, or occasionally the dress of some Shakespearean character. However, he never exhibited his most exotic outfits in public, reserving them instead for himself while relaxing in the privacy of his room. He enjoyed wearing very tight corset-like garments, especially those that held his genitals firmly, under every costume.

His parents had died when he was a child, and he had spent some time in an orphanage prior to his placement with an older couple whom he described as attentive and loving. He was conscientious about his work in all regards; he entertained many and offended no one. His insecurity about his own masculinity and his attitudes toward women were his private crosses.

Another priest of similar age was the product of an unhappy home. He spoke of his father as harsh but ineffective and his mother as overprotective and frowning. He entered the seminary in high school in part as a way out of his family's conflicts. He was an excellent athlete with an unquestionably masculine face and form, so much so that it was nearly impossible to conjure the mental image of him dressed in any of what he described as a "closet full" of women's clothing. No one had ever seen him dressed up. His living arrangement allowed him complete privacy. He would return to his home at night, put on feminine finery, have his meal, and relax before the television or with a book.

Although he had no desire to change his behavior, two fears brought him to psychiatric care. The first was that he might be involved in an accident and someone would discover his secret wardrobe; the second was his growing urge to steal women's lingerie. He had been able to assemble his other clothes on buying trips out of town, but even there he could not bring himself to purchase undergarments, the very items he found most sexually exciting. They held a direct fetishist quality for him and conflicted most with his vow of celibacy.

A third example is that of a hardworking priest who was concerned about his masturbation. He was very troubled and felt tremendous guilt; no confessor had been able to console him, even those who told him that masturbation was "natural" or that he had too delicate a conscience. Because the priest's episodes were relatively infrequent, it was difficult for a confessor to fathom the depth of the anxiety and remorse each incident caused this tortured man.

However, what this priest failed to confide was the mode of his sexual activity. He would sustain long periods of sexual abstinence and then would be overcome by an urge to put on women's clothing, especially pantyhose, a corset, or any other tight-fitting undergarment, being careful not to touch his penis with his hand. When he was younger he had thought that such touching was the essence of the sin of masturbation, and that if he could avoid touching himself he would not be guilty. Nevertheless, in struggling against the binding undergarment, he would have an erection and ejaculate. He had been the product of a broken home and had always felt that his mother would have been happier if he had been a girl, a thought he found abhorrent. He reasoned that as a priest he could at least take care of her.

Another priest, with a flair for the dramatic, coached drama students, sustained a long-term involvement with amateur theater productions. He had an early awareness of his desire to dress in women's clothes. His mother was a seamstress and would get him to play the dressmaker's dummy when she was exercising her craft. At first he had not wanted to work with her, but recounted that eventually he experienced a closeness, warmth, and sense of fun with her that he had never had before. His sexual fantasies always revolved around those moments, and his behavior was an attempt to relive them. The childhood of a fetishist cross-dresser differs from the experience of very feminine boys.

St. Jerome, who died in 420, was one of the most colorful Fathers of the Church. He was a staunch and implacable proponent of clerical celibacy. His stature is established as a scholar who spent a half-century translating the Scriptures. His sexual life found no autobiographical witness like his contemporary, St. Augustine, but there are provocative intimations that are worthy of a psychohistory. A thousand years after his death, part of Jerome's life was immortalized in the incomparably beautiful illustrations in *The Belles Heures of Jean, Duke of Berry*. Jerome was a learned man versed in the pagan philosophies. The story goes that he had a dream in which he promised to give up his secular studies. In that dream two whip-wielding angels scourged him in the sight of God on His throne. The manuscript reads:

> Then the Judge ordered a severe beating. Jerome cried out: Lord have mercy on me, if I read these [profane] books again I shall have denied Thee. Then, dismissed, he suddenly regained consciousness in streams of tears and found terrible scars on his shoulders. (Meiss & Beatson, 1974, Fol. 183v)

The commentators remarked that:

> Jerome made public his resolution taken in a dream, and many years later it was used against him by Rufinus, who ridiculed him for his classical quotations. The saint was not, however, seriously troubled; his

attitude to dreams had changed. "Can dreams," he asks, "be used in evidence? . . . How often have I dreamed that I was dead and in the grave . . . How often have I flown over mountains and crossed the seas! Does that mean that I am dead or that wings grow from my sides?" (Meiss & Beatson, 1974, Fol. 183v)

In the same source is recorded and depicted the famous incident where Jerome appeared in the monks' choir wearing a woman's dress. Biographers have called the occurrence a mistake on Jerome's part, saying that he fell into a trap set by monks who were jealous of his popularity with rich Roman women—friendships that were the subject of much gossip. According to biographers, an evil monk substituted a woman's dress for Jerome's habit, and in the dark Jerome put it on, not realizing what it was. Whatever the motives or facts of the incident, it propelled Jerome to leave Rome, never to return. He subsequently spent 4 years in the desert and was known to wear a hair shirt rather than soft garments. Under a miniature of Jerome in the desert reads an inscription taken from one of his letters to his student, Eustochium:

> How often as I dwelt in that waste, in that vast solitude burnt away by the heat of the sun, which provides a terrible abode for monks, I imagined myself among the delights of Rome. My twisted limbs shuddered in a garment of sackcloth. (Fol. 185v)

In another of Jerome's letters, he described being tempted by dancing girls:

> Daily I wept, daily I groaned, and when overcome by sleep I resisted, my bones, scarcely holding together, were bruised by the ground. Although my only companions were scorpions I often imagined I was surrounded by dancing girls, who kindled the fires of lust. (Meiss & Beatson, 1974, Fol. 186)

The miniature showing Jerome translating the Bible indicates accurately that his life's work did not really begin until he had extricated from himself some thorn of the flesh. Metaphorically, he removed a thorn from the paw of a lion, who subsequently became his docile companion. The text under this miniature reads:

Having, therefore, done penance in the wilderness for four years,
Jerome went to dwell like a domestic animal at the manger of the Lord
in Bethlehem where, remaining chaste, he labored for fifty-five years
and six months at the translation of the Bible and the Holy Scriptures.
(Meiss & Beatson, 1974, Fol. 187v)

Jerome's life makes sense if we understand his episode of cross-
dressing not simply as a trick of wicked monks, but as a manifesta-
tion of his sexual development that must be reconciled with his
brilliance and later sanctity. His asceticism and hair shirt, although
not entirely uncommon practices at that time in Christianity, can be
seen as a reaction to having been caught in behavior that was little
understood in religious form at that time.

It is not idle speculation to search the lives and writings of saintly
celibates to reconstruct their psychosexual development. I believe
that sound scholarship can verify from Jerome's own writings a far
clearer picture of his sexuality and celibacy than has been painted
thus far.

Homosexuality can also play a part in cross-dressing: The homosexual man replaces his love for his mother by an identification with
her . . . not by imitating her object choice but by imitating her "being
a woman" (Fenichel, 1945, p. 344). The essence of transvestism is
"identification with the woman, as a substitute for, or side by side
with, love for her" (Fenichel 1953, p. 169).

The challenge to establish one's masculinity and the struggle then
to remain celibate is not a simple matter. Freud believed in the inherent bisexuality of humans, but he did not espouse gender equality.
He, with most thinkers of his time, held the male gender to be the
superior biological and psychological sex. The persistence of this
stance is indispensable, for understanding the celibate structure of
the church.

The idea of male superiority is necessary to keep the male matrix
in place—to preserve male exclusivity, hierarchical structure, and the
homosocial organization of the clergy.

Celibacy grapples with the demands of consolidating masculinity
while foregoing sexual activity. The history of celibacy demonstrates
some failure in achieving gender and sexual identities. Transvestism

is a compromise that helps explain some priests' dilemmas and their unconscious attempts to be men but not too sexual. He can "get inside the skin" of a woman (her clothes) and yet experience himself as a man (his erection).

Celibacy holds some priests safely in a stage of development where it is not necessary for them to define their sexuality. They can be close to a woman (inside her skin) without running the risks of rejection; they can maintain a sense of masculinity without indulging in the external aggression needed for sexual activity with another person. For these men, things, not persons, reassure them that they are all right and give them gratification. Their sense that they are not involved sexually with anyone else saves the appearance of celibacy or maintains abstinence for relatively long periods of time, even if this security comes from the "cloth."

The questions about transvestism are more important than the answer. How is transvestism related to celibacy? How do celibates consolidate their sense of masculinity? What meanings do the robes of office play? Is there an element in clerical reality that gives credence to the cliché "Clothes make the man"?

PRIESTS AND ANIMALS

Among our informants were three cases of patterned sexual behavior with animals. They can be classified as paraphilia because each priest demonstrated persistent and exclusive sexual urgings and activity with animals. These examples came to light because each of the priests was troubled enough about his behavior to seek help. One history was traced to early experiences on a farm. No projection of estimates of this kind of sexual activity is attempted from the information here, but the question of bestiality among celibates should remain open.

SUFFERING AND SEXUAL VIOLENCE

Catholic tradition forges a close link between suffering/martyrdom and sex/celibacy. This is deeply instilled in average Catholics and taken seriously by some boys aspiring to the priesthood. One priest told of being encouraged to take scalding baths to temper his passions. He was to endure water as hot as he could possibly stand and was not to tell anyone of his ascetic practice lest it lose its value.

David Plante (1986) opened the preface to his novel, *The Catholic*, with this image:

> A young nun told us one morning during catechism class how missionaries from France had been captured and tortured by the Indians in America. The Indians stripped the missionaries naked, tied them to stakes, then pressed red hot tomahawks to their flesh. This was done to them because they were Catholic and loved God. The nun's face, in her fluted wimple, was flushed. My knees were shaking.

Plante concluded the preface with the confrontation of his childhood sexual identity on the eve of his first communion.

> My brother and I concentrated, with bright halos of attention, on one another's prepubescent members, and I said, suddenly, "Ainque les Peaux Rouges ont cela" ("Only Red Skins have this"). My brother didn't deny it. We were different from anyone else.

Celibacy is an ascetic practice of the first order, and its relationship to love and suffering is extraordinary. The interplay between the beauty of the ascetic ideal and the gruesomeness of the fleshly reality is graphically portrayed in the artistic and literary renditions of celibate martyrs. St. Bartholomew was skinned alive. St. Stephen was stoned. St. Sebastian was transfixed with arrows. St. Francis was marked with the bloody wounds of Christ. St. John, St. Paul, and St. Denis were all gloriously and adeptly beheaded. St. Lawrence was grilled like a piece of meat.

Women were depicted in even more grisly detail as they defended their virginity. St. Ursula and her companions were slaughtered. St. Lucy and St. Catherine were beheaded. St. Cecilia was beheaded after being boiled in oil. St. Agatha had her breasts cut off with large pincers.

The psychological implications of these examples are clear. Celibacy—the avoidance of sex—in the service of the love of God is worth any amount of suffering. There is a real and mysterious connection between suffering and sexual excitement.

> Sadomasochism is, I think, a central feature of most sexual excitement. My hunch is that the desire to hurt others in retaliation for having been

hurt is essential for most people's sexual excitement all the time but not for all people's excitement all the time. (Stoller, 1979, p. 113)

The potential ramifications of Stoller's hunch are tremendous. It causes one to pause at St. Augustine's insistence that no sexual excitement could be wholly separated from all trace of sin. Suffice it to say here that there is some connection between violence and sex, as well as some sense of "doing violence" to oneself in the service of celibacy. Both are mysteries yet to be explored.

Murder

Priests at times put themselves in harm's way in search of sex. Several priests, in recounting their histories remarked, "I'm lucky I didn't get myself killed." Two priests did not live to be able to say that. Both murders were reported to the press simply as random robberies; both victims, however, were well known to informants—one a psychiatrist and the other a parish pastor.

The first victim was a priest in his mid-30s who, for a period of 5 years, periodically sought out casual sex, usually in public restrooms. He would suffer a paroxysm of severe guilt after each encounter and would vow never to seek another. His resolve would last for several weeks or months. He described to a friend, how his tension and a growing preoccupation built to a breaking point. He imagined the meeting place, white-tiled walls and floor, the memory of the mixed smells of disinfectant and human bodies, and the thrill of the danger.

Upon reflection, he could see that the desire was several days in the building, but the final thrust to action always took him by surprise. He would "find" himself in the area rather than "plan" to be there. His heart would pound; he would salivate; the place itself took on great significance—something akin to Hemingway's Nick Adams in his search for clean, well-lighted places. Ironically the priest's search led to his senseless murder.

In other regards, this man's life as a priest was unremarkable. He was responsible enough and sociable enough, and in no obvious way did his proclivity interfere with his work. He was perceived as the kind and conscientious priest he was.

The other priest who was murdered was noticeably successful in his ministry, if judged by the prestige and regard he enjoyed. He had entered therapy a few months prior to his death, consumed with a feeling of loneliness that no association or friendship within his priesthood could assuage. In fact, the more success he achieved and the more generally popular he became among his peers, the more his feelings of loneliness and desperation grew. At times in the depths of his despair he would cruise the streets for a companion, and would occasionally invite a stranger into his living quarters. These exploits were sexually motivated. When he was found murdered in his office, the crime was attributed to robbery, as the priest was fully clothed and some cash was missing. However, the priest's pattern had been known by his psychiatrist and suspected by a few of his priest friends.

Suicide

Generally, the idea of suicide is not associated with priests and no data exists on their rate of suicide compared with that of dentists and psychiatrists. In the 1950s Dr. Francis Braceland, an eminent Catholic psychiatrist, said that early in his life he had mistakenly believed that nuns and priests were immune from the act of self-destruction. Bitter experience had taught him otherwise.

The refinement of understanding between religion and psychiatry over the past decades has made representatives of both professions more realistic about the mental health of religious people (McAllister, 1986). Depression, for instance, knows no religious boundaries. In fact, there seems to be a strong depressive component to the psyches of seriously religious people. Certainly, a depressive-like encounter is necessary to the pursuit of celibacy.

Over two dozen reports of clergy suicide have been reported in the past decade related to the sexual abuse of minors. Other reports of suicide we reviewed were intrinsically bound up with the sexual conflicts in pursuing the celibate ideal. Suicide is always a tragedy, and no less so among the clergy; however, among them it probably also has some special symbolic power, contradicting the message of hope inherently implied by ministry.

A priest in his mid-30s sought the help of a Catholic psychiatrist specifically because of his doubts about celibacy. He was successful in his priesthood and was considered an "exciting intellectual" by those who knew him. He had entered the seminary in college after some brief periods of dating. He was genuinely popular wherever he studied or served. After a decade in the priesthood, he still found himself questioning his sexual identity and had a tremendous desire to experience dating again.

His choice of a psychiatrist was truly unfortunate. This psychiatrist was not only unaware of the depth and complexity of the priest's celibate struggle, but also had the monumentally poor judgment to encourage the priest simply to date. He arranged a meeting with a woman. She would supposedly help the priest sort things out. Occasionally the psychiatrist and his wife would even accompany the priest on his outings. Rather than helping, the escapades only led to a deeper feeling of desperation and confusion on the priest's part.

When the priest consulted a second psychiatrist, he was even more convinced that there was no way out of his dilemma and was terrified that he was "going crazy." The second psychiatrist was able to see beyond the smiling and even jaunty manner, in which the priest presented himself, to the tortured soul within. However, the priest's manner did fool most of his friends and some other professionals into thinking that his confusion was temporary, superficial, or merely intellectual. Most missed the agony, which, in this case, certainly did not look like ordinary depression. One priest friend who talked with him the week before he died reported that he had been greeted by the laughing remark, "You're only welcome today if you have brought a gun."

The day before the priest died, another priest friend encouraged him to "forget the guilt and just get involved with a woman; that's what I do." He could not have known that it was exactly the wrong kind of support for his friend, who by this time had become so entangled in his despair that he feared the prospect of hospitalization. Terrified of the possibility of ending up as a chronic mental patient, he killed himself. One who knew this man's struggle intimately found him a heroic religious figure, "who struggled manfully and fought the good fight. He served and saved many others, but could not save himself."

Another priest was hospitalized for severe depression, torn between his love affair with a young woman and his religious family who were counting on his continuing priesthood. During his hospi-talization, the woman sent him passionate letters declaring her love for him and encouraging him to leave the ministry, a move he knew he could not make. His best priest friend advised him to incorporate the relationship into his priest life, as he himself was doing with an-other woman. After his release from the hospital, the priest tried to do just that, struggling with the relationship while hopelessly trying to maintain celibacy. When he began to experience another severe de-pressive episode, he swallowed an overdose of medication and died.

A priest in his early 40s became increasingly distressed by his sex-ual fantasies, and suspected for the first time in his life that he might be homosexual—a prospect so abominable to him that he began hav-ing panic attacks that crippled his work and life. He had always been a sensitive man, described as "high strung" by those who knew him well. He was also a very active, prolific worker. He never gave anyone a chance to know the dynamic behind his fear, but he apparently killed himself because of it. No one could find any evidence that he had ever acted out sexually.

On the other hand, a priest who was involved in sexual liaisons that were about to become public and cause a considerable scandal in his area drove his car into an abutment, killing himself. He had left a note to a priest friend telling him exactly what he intended to do. In contrast to the first two priests described above who could not recon-cile their celibate vows with what they saw as the hypocrisy of their sexual activity, this priest very comfortably incorporated it into his ministry over a long period of time. It was finally the threat of dis-covery that destroyed his ability to deny and to split his sexual func-tioning off from the rest of his life.

Another incident of a priest's suicide presented itself more vaguely as a vocational problem. The priest could neither leave the priest-hood nor dedicate himself to it. His family and friends experienced him as nervous but not self-destructive. He appeared to be a spiritual man and a loner who took no one into his confidence. He hanged himself.

Celibacy has martyrdom as its historical antecedent. The ideal that one should be willing to sacrifice everything—life itself—in the service of one's fellow humans is in the imitation of Christ. It is difficult to see this ideal at work where suffering is glorified for its own sake or where self-abnegation leads not to service and love but to waste and death by one's own hand.

The mystery of the priesthood is not merely the history of individuals, but a reality that transcends persons and times. To what extent individuals may be sacrificed or may sacrifice themselves for the preservation of discipline or structure is not clear in individual circumstances, even if an ascetic or theological ideal were clear. An ideal may be measured by those who fail to achieve it, but the idea that suffering in and of itself is good or salvific is a misrepresentation of the life of Christ as well as of those who blazed the trail for a celibate lifestyle.

PART III

THE HEART OF
THE CRISIS

9

PRIESTS AND MINORS

He remembered the smell of incense in the churches of his boyhood, the candles and the laciness and the self-esteem, the immense demands made from the altar steps by men who didn't know the meaning of sacrifice.

—Graham Greene

The question of sexual abuse of minors by Catholic priests had been brewing for the better part of last half of the 20th century. Church authorities denied, minimized, blamed the media, the victims, their families, the culture, and "a few bad apples" for the problem. A public relations response was intermittently effective with a Catholic population that was reluctant to dethrone their parish priest from a position of trust and regard. Most priests, indeed, were not guilty of sexually abusing minors.

But court cases filtered into the press. In 1983 a young journalist in Louisiana—Jason Berry—led the attack into hither-to forbidden territory of church sexual scandal by reporting a case of abuse in the Lafayette Louisiana Diocese (Berry, 1993). A bold editor of *The National Catholic Reporter*, Tom Fox, ran the stories—a first for the Catholic press.

Reports of cases of abuse by priests proliferated across the country, but mostly gained only local attention. The Father James Porter case centered in Fall River, Massachusetts, in 1992 was the exception. Porter admitted privately that he had probably abused 200 minors while he was active in the priesthood. The affair grabbed national attention and focused the local stories into a national and international context.

A series of reports on abuse by the Searchlight Team of *The Boston Globe* began publication on January 6, 2002. The name of the offending priest—John Geoghen—is almost incidental, as were the number of his victims—over 150. The effects of the reports were cataclysmic. Like the Boston Tea Party of 1773 that roused a nation by galvanizing a series of local discontents but led to a fundamental confrontation with authority, so the *Globe*'s exposure of abuse took a quantum leap in the controversy about sex abuse by priests (The Investigative Staff of *The Boston Globe*, 2002).

By exposing the dynamic that supported, and conspired to keep secret the individual priest abusers they tapped into the lifeblood of Boston Catholic power—the pope's representative—Cardinal Law. They unfolded the *pattern*—almost a template—that was being used generally in American dioceses to hide abusing priests, and silence victims.

The repercussions of the series can hardly be overestimated. Within 10 months the highest levels of power in the American church and Rome were mobilized. Meetings in Rome, Dallas, and Washington, DC exposed the depth of the power conflict. They also focused the hostility of the victims/survivors, and symbolized the worldwide dimensions of the problem. Four hundred and twenty-five American priests were removed from active duty because of allegations. Several bishops were forced to resign from their posts because of allegations of their own sexual activity. And this is only the beginning.

Sexual abuse of minors is the most threatening crisis to the American Catholic church's stability in its history. No one has yet measured the eventual reverberations. But a poll from September 2002 claimed that 80 percent of Americans favor criminal charges for offending priests and for bishops who cover up clergy crimes.

The present conditions are very similar to periods that led to major church reformations. I predict that this intrusion into the secret world will culminate in reformation.

The sexual abuse of minors by clergy and the involvement of the American hierarchy in its protection, cover-up, intimidation of victims and decades of organized resistance to real reform has been an abomination. Forced to the wall by incontrovertible evidence of complicity in dioceses nationwide, the United States Conference of Catholic Bishops and the Vatican began to deal seriously with the problem in 2002. The crisis is only at its beginning. Once the systemic elements of the phenomenon are exposed, the secret system of celibate violation begins to unravel. Abuse is the symptom of a secret and corrupt mode of operation.

Priests have traditionally cared for the education and protection of children. They can appeal to the example of Christ who "took a little child, stood him in their midst, and putting his arms around him, said, " 'Whoever welcomes a child such as this for my sake welcomes me. And whoever welcomes me welcomes, not me, but him who sent me'" (Mark 9:36–7).

For many priests, work with children and young people is a healthy and productive sublimation of their generative drive. They perform a parental function and become "father" in the best spiritual sense. Saints of the early church exhorted priests and laity to tend to the care of children: "The corruption of the world remains unchecked because nobody guards his children, nobody speaks to them of chastity, of despising riches and glory, of the commandments of God" (Quasten, 1960, p. 465).

Monastic and cathedral schools had centuries of experience in teaching young boys prior to the existence of medieval universities. The Jesuits, founded in the 16th century, took upon themselves the mission of educating the masses, not merely the sons of the noblemen and the wealthy. As a result, they had a profound influence on the popular attitudes toward children. "They stressed the notion of childhood innocence, shame, modesty, the need to protect children from adult secrets, and the schooling of children. The Jesuits began to view children with compassion, urged speaking decently to them, ended the practice of children and adults sleeping together and prohibited familiarity between servants and children" (Schetky & Green, 1988, p. 25).

Concern, sexual protection, and restraint is expected from the clergy. Parents who entrust their children—both boys and girls—to the care of priests as teachers, coaches, club directors, counselors, pastors, or advocates presume that the contact will foster good character and growth in self-confidence, moral values, and spiritual and mental health. Those priests who use their positions of trust and the presumption of moral integrity as a cover for their sexual activity with children present a formidable challenge to celibacy.

Christ's tenderness with children is a unique and prophetic stance in early literature. Powerful is the admonition against giving scandal to the young. "Anyone who is an obstacle to bring down one of these little ones who have faith in me would be better drowned in the depths of the sea with a great millstone around his neck" (Matt. 18:5–7). There is no equivocation about the inappropriateness of an adult's sexual activity with a child.

It is clear that the U.S. Bishops—and bishops worldwide—have not taken the sexual violation of children seriously. The behavior has been known and recorded for centuries in church documents. Public exposure and scandal are the gravest threat to them. The harm done to victims and the violation of celibacy has, in practice, been treated secondarily. Secrecy and avoidance of scandal have been the primary concerns of the church.

WHAT IS PEDOPHILIA?

The media has caused a lot of confusion by labeling all sexual activity of an adult with a minor *pedophilia*. It is not so. Sexual activity of an adult with any minor (a person under 18 years of age) is illegal. Pedophilia is a medical term.

The *Diagnostic and Statistical Manual of Mental Disorders* (4th ed.) (American Psychiatric Association, 1994) says that "pedophilia involves recurrent, intense, sexual urges and sexually arousing fantasies, of at least 6 months' duration, involving sexual activity with a prepubescent child. The person has either acted on these urges, or is markedly distressed by them. The age of the child is generally 13 or younger. The pedophile is 16 years or older and at least 5 years older than the child" (p. 527–8). Pedophilia can be either *homosexual* or *heterosexual*, but attraction to girls, among offenders in the general population, is more common than attraction to boys. Both young boys and girls sexually arouse many pedophiles.

Fred S. Berlin, M.D. (1985), of Johns Hopkins University, claims that pedophilia occurs almost exclusively in men. He also notes that because people do not decide voluntarily what will arouse them sexually, there are great differences among pedophiles as to which partners and behaviors will appeal to them. Pedophiles experience differences in the intensity of their sexual drive and their ability to resist sexual temptation. Some simply decide that no temptation *should* be resisted.

The pedophile impulse can either be *fixated* or *regressed* (Groth & Burgess, 1979; Groth, 1982). Fixated sexual offenders experience no erotic attraction toward adults and "manifest an arrest in their psychosexual development and maintain a primary psychological and sexual interest in young children who are prepubertal" (Schetky & Green, 1988). They are more likely to victimize boys than girls, and generally first act on their impulses during their adolescence.

Regressed pedophiles are men who find both adults and children erotically appealing, and tend to select female victims. Their tendencies emerge when they are adults and are usually triggered by a stressful sexual situation with an age-peer.

In the United States, the law makes no criminal distinction in its broad category of child molestation between the victim who is an adolescent and the victim who is younger. Pedophilia, on the other hand, is a specific psychiatric term, referring strictly to the sexual abuse of a prepubertal child. Similar criteria are used to evaluate sexual activity with adolescents, but the term ephebophilia is used to describe it.

Two percent of Catholic priests could be called pedophiles in the strict sense of the definition. Of this number, three-quarters are homosexual or bisexual, and the remaining quarter heterosexual, in contrast to the general population, where heterosexual abuses outnumber homosexual abuses by two to one.

I also found that an additional 4 percent of priests are sexually preoccupied with adolescent boys or girls. The behavior can be occasional, compulsive, or developmental—the last being those instances where the priest will act out with a child once or twice as part of his (the priest's) developmental experimentation. The behavior is not part of a pattern, but is nevertheless troublesome and a crime. The perpetrators can be either heterosexual or homosexual in orientation. Homosexual contacts are four times more likely to come to the attention of parents or authorities.

FREQUENCY OF OCCURRENCE

The abuse of minors is a highly underreported crime. The majority of victims never reveal what has happened to them. "Careful studies have indicated . . . that child molesters commit an average of 60 offenses for every incident that comes to public attention. These must not be thought of as situational or hidden in some other disorder . . . if they are to be understood completely and treated successfully." (Reid, 1988.)

According to one study "24% of a population of 4,441 women had experienced sexual abuse during childhood" (Schetkey & Green 1988, p. 30). Early studies of female college students reported a 19 percent incidence of abuse during childhood and adolescence, and 9 percent among male students. Other more recent studies put the percentages at 50 percent for women and 20 percent for men.

The percentage of *offenders* in the general population is unknown and will probably remain so. "Older persons are the teachers of younger people in all matters, including the sexual. The record [of 2,749 cases of preadolescent sex play] includes some cases of preadolescent boys involved in sexual contacts with adult females, and still more cases of preadolescent boys involved with adult males. Data on this point were not systematically gathered from all histories, and consequently the frequency of contacts with adults cannot be calculated with precision." (Kinsey, et al., 1948, p. 167.)

In 1974 the first state laws were passed requiring professionals to report child abuse. This law and a nationwide program encouraging children to speak up when they are sexually touched or assaulted have produced results.

The laws requiring reporting had a dramatic effect. In 1976 there were 6,000 cases of child abuse confirmed in the United States. In 1985, there were 113,000. At the dawn of the new millennium 300,000 incidents are reported annually. Experts estimate that 8 percent of reported cases are false accusations; about 22 percent cannot be corroborated.

Since the early 1980s *public* awareness of priests' sexual involvement with minors has changed dramatically. During a 7-year period extending into the 90s, one psychiatric facility alone treated 300 priests for "serious sexual behavior problems."

Lawsuits and investigative reporting have highlighted the problem in the American Church. The *Washington Post* reported (September 16, 1989) that between 1983 and 1987 200 priests or religious brothers were reported to church authorities, an average of one case per week. Following the reports of minor abuse in the *Boston Globe* over 400 priests were either dismissed from the priesthood by a bishop or restricted by a religious superior, between January and October 2002.

SOCIAL RAMIFICATIONS OF ABUSE

Sexual abuse of a minor impacts three interrelated social systems. The legal system considers sexual activity with a minor of any age a *crime*. The religious system views it as *sinful*. The psychiatric/medical system labels it irresponsible, a perversion, or *illness*. Each system deserves examination.

Legal

Sexual abuse of a minor is a crime. Who is to be held accountable when a priest commits abuse—the crime? Thousands of civil cases have been filed against priests, bishops, dioceses, and religious superiors in the last decades of the century. They are increasing in the 1st decade of the 21st century. Bishops are no longer immune from examination or prosecution.

This question relates to clergy malpractice.

> For a period of many years, charitable groups and organizations including non-profit groups such as churches were immune from liability. . . . Many claims against churches and church personnel are met with the defense that under the doctrine of separation of church and state, the Church cannot be sued or held liable in a civil court. (McMenamin, 1985, p. 3)

Already in 1985, the insurance industry adopted an exclusion of coverage for members of the psychiatric and psychological professions for claims arising as the result of sexual contact between the patient and his or her therapist. The exclusion was a reaction to many large payments of such claims by insurance companies in the years

immediately preceding the policy. Most dioceses can no longer purchase liability insurance to cover the sexual offenses of clergy. Molestation lawsuits and their related expense have cost the U.S. church
over 1 billion dollars from 1985 to 2002. In some dioceses costs
threaten the economic viability of the church.

Who is liable—an issue apart from *who* is responsible—when a
priest commits a crime? Current litigation does pursue dioceses and
their officials in lawsuits that allege negligence in educating, hiring,
and supervising clergy, and failure to protect victims or report abuse.
In 2002 there are 12 jurisdictions that have convened grand juries to
determine the culpability of church officials.

Canon law has the effect of law over the clergy, but how its rele-
vance will be interpreted with respect to civil law in a specific case will
be tested by the Vatican's interaction with the American bishops over
the guidelines they proposed in their June 2002 meeting in Dallas.

Although sex with any minor is illegal, sometimes there is nothing
that the legal system can do to intervene. Girls and boys 15, 16, and
17 years old often have minds of their own about their sexual practices, even with adult partners. The questions of responsibility or
guilt are not simple.

A 47-year-old priest had a long-standing friendship with a
Catholic family who were not his parishioners. He was a warm and
physically demonstrative person who was accepted "as one of the
family" even on family holidays and vacations. One of the sons, 17
years old, announced that he was going to "live with Father" and did.
He was accepted in the parish as "Father's nephew," but he had told
his parents that he had been the priest's lover for 2 years.

The boy insisted that he had had a great deal of sexual experience
prior to introducing the priest to sexual activity. The priest insisted
that this boy was his first sexual partner. Psychosexually, they were
well matched when the boy was 15 to 18 years old. The young man
was the one who outgrew the relationship and subsequently developed an interest in girls his own age. In this instance, it is difficult to
say who is the victim. Certainly it is not an attempt to exonerate a
47-year-old priest to say that the teenaged boy was the "older and
wiser" person in this relationship. The priest's naïveté and his psy-

chosexual arrest were hidden behind the facade of his administrative and pastoral skills and his pleasant personality.

It took a sexually precocious youngster to expose a dimension of the priest's character that was hidden from everyone, including the priest himself. The mother of this boy revealed that she herself was more than casually interested in the priest. Although she had found some of his signs of affection stimulating, she had not talked about them nor offered any sexual response. She held herself responsible for the "sexual" dimension of the relationship that she felt. She presumed the invulnerability of the priest's celibate commitment and presumed his sexual innocence until confronted with her son's announcement and confession of his seduction. In fact, if this priest had been more developed psychosexually, he might very well have been able to respond to the mother's unexpressed feelings.

Likewise, I have dozens of examples of teenaged girls who have taken the lead willingly and with a certain amount of pride in a sexual relationship with a priest. The ignorance or neurosis of the priest is *no* excuse. The priest poses a criminal problem that must be dealt with. The priest must always be held responsible because of his position of power.

These situations do not prohibit the victim from bringing criminal or civil charges against the priest even years after the abuse. Sexual activity of an adult with a minor *is* a crime. This reality has not changed from 50 years ago and before. Bishops have not held themselves or their priests legally accountable for abusive behavior. If fact, it is clear that most church officials have denied, covered up, and been involved in varying degrees of conspiracy to avoid legal responsibility.

Moral

The Catholic Church considers any sex outside marriage to be gravely sinful. Because priests are, by definition anyway, celibate, the church is reluctant to make official statements about priests' sexual activity. Papal statements on Catholic sexuality are intended to govern the laymen, not the clergy. Thus far, the church has chosen not to address directly the underlying human sexuality issues of its called servants, and until it does, their moral development will remain un-defined and unsupported.

Eugene Kennedy said "[United States bishops] have chosen to take the advice of lawyers on issues that cannot be resolved merely by making the Church legally defensible. It is a very narrow vision of life. Lawyers are not intrinsically interested in morality, but in making their small area no wider than a ledge on which to balance themselves and their clients. Nationally, responsible journalists are beginning to interpret it as a cover-up story, which has a terribly negative potential for the Church. It has failed to examine the con-flicts about the human sexuality that throb within it." (*Los Angeles Times*. March 20, 1988.)

Bishops and religious superiors have indulged a double standard in addressing sexual issues when priests were involved. Their blatant be-havior has aroused an unprecedented reaction among lay Catholics.

Psychological/Pastoral

The Doyle-Mouton-Peterson Report, presented to every American bishop in 1985 warned:

> We are approximately at the same point in time with pedophilia in the medical/psychiatric world as we were with alcoholism in the late 1950s. Then the American Medical Association finally agreed that alcoholism was a disease in its own right and not a "moral weakness" or a "personal-ity disorder" or "personality defect." (p. 4)

Bishops did not take the problem seriously from the point of view of the harm done to victims. Because some bishops and numerous priests were involved in this behavior the issue was considered one that they "could handle" without outside interference. The motiva-tion was clearly to avoid scandal. The scandal is that they covered up the problem.

The church has often misused psychiatry by referring offending priests for treatment without supplying all of the information about the priest's past. Psychiatry has also failed the system by giving priests a wide birth, covering their aberrant behavior with diagnosis of a "drinking problem." The logic being, if father doesn't drink he will not behave in this way. Both missed for a long time the addictive component in much sexual abuse.

CAUSES

"It appears that some men become vulnerable to the development of this type of sexual orientation [toward minors] by virtue of having been sexually active with an adult when they were children, or by virtue of manifesting certain biological abnormalities" (Berlin, 1986).

Many experts feel strongly that biology is a cause of sexual attraction to minors. "It is highly likely that *in utero* a type of programming of the brains of all persons takes place that contributes to the later expression of sexual behaviors in humans. This includes sexual orientation (heterosexual, homosexual, bisexual), sexual energy level (libido), and perhaps even erotic age preference (pedophilia *versus* preference for age-appropriate partners)."

Premature childhood experiences and other environmental factors can enhance biological endowment. But there is no question that biological factors are significant and determinant in the development and functioning of human sexuality generally.

> Biological factors in animals significantly influence sexually related activities. In some species of birds, normally only males sing, but if a female zebra finch that has been administered estradiol while just an embryo is given androgen hormones as an adult, she will do so also, and will have an increased number of cells in the nucleus robustus archistraitalis and other brain areas (Miller, 1980).
>
> She will also display distinctly male courtship behavior. Adult female rats that were exposed to testosterone at a specific time *in utero* will show sexual mounting behavior that normally predominates in male rats. (Money, 1971)

Discussions on the relative importance of heredity and environment in determining behavior are age-old. The same discussion arises when attempting to assess the etiology of sexual attraction to minors.

Classic studies indicate that by the time boys are 12 years old, 38 percent have been involved in some form of sexual play, of which 23 percent is heterosexual and 30 percent homosexual. Most of these boys do not grow up to be abusers. A certain amount of *childhood experimentation* is normal.

But when sexual activity of a minor involves an adult, different dynamics come into play. Environment and life experiences do play a role in the development of gender identity, sexual orientation, and interest. Many adult men who experience erotic urges toward minors were sexually abused when they were children. In these cases the former victim sometimes becomes the abuser. His biological constitution, circumstances, and childhood experiences combine to determine his psychological urges. No one knows why, as adults, *only some* victims of childhood sexual involvements with an adult experience sexual urges toward minors. There is some indication sexual abuse of minors is found more frequently in some families than in others, and there may be specificity in the familial transmission (Gaffney, Lurie, & Berlin, 1984, p. 546). A large proportion of priests who become either pedophiles or sexually active with adolescents were themselves victims of sexual abuse—sometimes by priests—as children or adolescents.

Some priests who were sexually abused as children, and do not abuse, find that the choice of vocation is determined by the need to reject the overwhelming and confusing realities of sex. One celibate who kept his vow with great mental anguish reported in the course of his psychotherapy that he had been sexually abused by an uncle who lived in his home, when he was about 5 years old. The uncle would take him into the bathroom and set the child on his lap, with the boy's bare legs wrapped around the uncle's erect penis; he would play with his uncle's genitals. The priest recognized what a large part these early experiences had in his choice of vocation.

Another priest was introduced to sexual play at the age of 8 by a cousin who was 16. The younger boy was intrigued and flattered by his inclusion into a secret world and by the special affection of an older boy he idolized. The older youth would persuade the younger to help him with his chores and would then "reward" him with mutual masturbation. The younger boy curtailed his sexual activity, even masturbation, in midadolescence when he entered the minor seminary. He said it was then that he "vowed" never to do that with another child when he grew up. And he did not. He was, however, bothered for many years of his priesthood by the images of the genitals of adolescent boys. He remembered his cousin's "huge" phallus. He did not act out his fantasies, but was tormented by his feelings of sexual inadequacy.

A third priest, when he was a 15-year-old seminarian, experienced anal intercourse with a priest. He, along with others, was on a summer pilgrimage to a religious shrine. The sleeping arrangements were haphazard and he was assigned to a bed with the older man. Years later he recalled with both excitement and regret his one and only sexual contact with another person. With no other sexual experience with which to compare the contact, it remained a vibrant and troublesome thorn in his flesh. For a brief time in his adult life he became phobic that he would repeat the behavior with some other adolescent.

The adolescent sexual experiences of priests, or the memory of an intense sexual episode takes on a particular significance. Latter celibate deprivation enhances the memory or firmly fixates the priest's psychosexual development at a preadolescent or adolescent level. Some priests mature slowly and finally resolve their identification at age-appropriate levels. Others are impelled to act out with individuals who are essentially on their same level of immaturity. The immaturity of some priests accounts for the fact that not every homosexual contact between a priest and an adolescent proves the priest's orientation. Some behavior is experimental in the adolescent sense, not compulsive or exclusive. However, it is always problematic, certainly for the adolescent who is the victim of a generational transgression and a serious betrayal of trust.

Social *isolation* and physical *deprivation* can contribute to sexual excitation. These factors come together in the following example.

A 30-year-old priest completing his doctoral studies was on vacation with his married sister and her family. His two nephews, 4 and 6 years old, were typically energetic youngsters and enthusiastic about the visit of their very important uncle. They demanded his time and attention, which he willingly accorded them. He genuinely liked them, but became increasingly aware of his own sexual excitement as they hung on him and showered him with their affection. Because he had been so immersed in his studies and socially deprived for the preceding 3 years, he attributed his reaction to his recent sense of isolation. He did not act on his impulse to play with his nephews sexually, but grew more and more concerned when his masturbatory fantasies began to include images of children.

His concern drew him to a psychiatrist, and during his treatment he recalled some memories of having been sexually molested when he was 8 years old by a neighbor boy, 6 years his senior. In therapy he worked through other sexual issues. He never acted out any of his fantasies. On follow-up 10 years after the disturbing vacation, he was active in his ministry and content with his celibate life, feeling very fortunate to have sought treatment before establishing a pattern of sexual activity. This man's superior intellect and well-disciplined lifestyle were important supportive factors as he grappled with his sexual identity and conscious attraction for children.

AVENUES OF ACCESS

Priests have natural access to children. They are teachers, pastors, confessors, coaches, and the traditionally honored and trusted members of the family and community. The school, rectory, or church can be settings for abuse. These settings form a privileged environment for the priest, where he has control. The priest abuser cultivates the family; he becomes a friend and sometimes forges an alliance with a child's mother. When he is trusted he can take youngsters on trips or have other extended associations with parental consent.

His place of honor and trust becomes the cover and the occasion for the sexual abuse. One woman reported that as a young teenager she would be sent by her widowed mother to ask their parish priest to come to her mother's bedside. Before accompanying the girl home, the priest would fondle her. When they arrived at her house, the girl would always be given some other errand to run while the priest visited with her mother. Although she was very uncomfortable with the priest's advances, the girl could not easily talk to her mother about them, since she became aware that her mother's indisposition was a cover for her own sexual liaison with the priest.

Another priest used his prowess in sports to attract young boys to himself. In the process of "horsing around"—usually after a ball game or while skinny-dipping with the boys—the priest would engage in touches that became progressively more sexually explicit. Several times in his career he had misinterpreted the admiration he sensed from children as sexual responsiveness and comfort, when of course it had been neither. As a result, he had been the subject of a series of complaints that marked his frequent changes of parish assignments.

Altar boys' activities are a common arena for a priest to associate with children. Thousands of Catholic men recall fondly their childish heroism in trekking through the snow or rain to serve at a 6:00 A.M. mass. They frequently report having experienced a sense of pride and honor at being close to something sacred—the altar, consecrated bread and wine, dressing like a priest. They could hold the golden paten, carry the cross or chalice, and perform services that were off-limits, even to the nuns who taught them in school. Some memories are humorous and constitute a Catholic boy's rite of passage—sneaking a taste of altar wine or communion wafers, or even a smoke in the sacristy under the cover of the smell of burning incense. But for some, the experience of being an altar boy was stripped of its sense of the sacred and deprived of a memory of real fun and community with the other altar boys because these boys were selected by a certain kind of priest for his private sexual service.

Occasionally, the priest does not have to go out looking for his victims. One priest who was not himself sexually attracted to children became aware of the sexual activity of some of his fellow priests when he was sent to a new area to replace a young man of his order. As far as he knew, the move was a routine one. Consequently, he was quite surprised when, within the first few weeks of his new assignment, young boys approached him. They made clear their sexual interest in him. When it happened a third time, the priest quizzed the boy. Why were they making these advances? The boy replied that the "other Father gave us five bucks if we'd pull his nail" [fellate him]. When the priest inquired further, he discovered that there had been a succession of priests who had used the local boys in this way. These particular preadolescents were not associated with the church, but the street tradition in this area was that they could earn money by selling sex, and some priests were easy marks.

BEHAVIORS

Records exist of priests involved in every known type of sexual abuse from fondling to rape. A few priests have been the prime suspects in unsolved murders. Priests have fewer total victims (an average of 2 to 50) than abusers in the general population (average over 200). Priests tend to cultivate or groom their victims, playing on the trust and admiration of their office. Direct physical force is rarely used, but the full psychic duress of religion is common both in initiating the act and in demanding its secrecy.

The range of abuse, were it not well documented, seems unbelievable. More than one priest "anointed" his victim with semen, telling the victim the act had been sacred. Frequently the priest assures his victim that the behavior is holy and a special God-given gift. A frequently asked question is—how can a priest behave this way and still carry on as a minister? Rationalization, denial, depersonalization, regression, and splitting are common.

Rationalization

Some *rationalize*: the activity is educational or helpful to the child. A 60-year-old priest was arrested for child molestation based on incriminating evidence found in his home. No prior complaints were lodged against him; his detection had been accidental. The police had been searching for another suspect and were mistakenly given the priest's address by a young boy who was their informant.

The priest had had sexual liaisons with young boys all of the years of his priesthood. Consistently selecting children who were physically or emotionally deprived, he felt that by his friendship and association with them he was offering them genuine love, protection, and guidance along the lines of the Greek ideal, and a chance for a better life adjustment. He did not feel any guilt. Some of the boys would engage in the sexual activity very willingly, sometimes even initiating it. The priest would never hold onto the boys once they reached adolescence, instead encouraging them to participate in school and social activities, and trying to direct them to a level of sexual and emotional maturity that he himself could not attain.

> When a person desires sex or falls in love, it is often easy to become convinced that the relationship is good and healthy and not harmful or wrong. Such self-deception may at times be easy for the pedophilic individual in light of the fact that sex with children, though wrong, may not in every instance be damaging. Some children may enjoy certain aspects of their sexual relationships with an adult, thus facilitating self-deception. (Berlin, 1986)

Denial

Some priests are generous and caring to their victims and attend to their needs in many ways to gain the child's affection, interest, loyalty, and to keep the child from reporting the sexual activity. The priest acts *as if* it never happened.

Each year a pastor who was in his 60s selected three 8th-grade girls from his school to help around the parish house, performing such duties as stuffing envelopes, running errands, and doing light cleaning tasks. For these services, the girls would receive tuition reduction and a small salary; it was also well known that there were extra treats to be had, such as candy, ice cream, and occasional trips, all of which made the parish house duty a coveted assignment. From some parents' perspectives, the generous tuition reduction plus the honor of being so closely associated with the pastor made them eager to have their daughters chosen.

In the beginning, the girls would do their work in groups of two or three, but as time went on, a pattern of singularity developed—one of the girls would emerge each year as the most sensitive (or loving, needy, or vulnerable, as the case might be). She would become Father's special companion and would be able to lie on the couch with him as he took his afternoon nap, exchange kisses and hugs with him, and comfort him with back rubs when his arthritis acted up. The pattern was honed to perfection.

Little by little, the genuine affection between the priest was focused on the most suitable candidate, and the subsequent sexual dimension of the relationship receded into a secret area shared only by that girl and the priest. Because the priest did not expose his genitals and did not "deliberately" touch the girl's (although there was playful wrestling during which some contact was made), the victim was left with the conviction that any inappropriate thoughts or feelings were *her* fault, not his. When the priest would ejaculate spontaneously while having the girl's body close to his, he would feign sleep, and if the girl was aware of what had happened, she would believe that "Father hadn't done anything." The priest experienced no guilt about his behavior. He genuinely liked the children, and in his mind, "What happened, happened."

Depersonalization

A 40-year-old priest who had a long history of sexual activity with preadolescent and teenaged boys described in detail his method of seduction, and how he learned it. As a 12-year-old orphaned boy living with relatives, his parish priest befriended him. The priest included him in outings with groups of other youngsters his age. On occasion, the priest would take one or another of the boys to a movie by himself. During the movie, the priest would hold his leg close to the boy's, testing the youngster's comfort with "accidental physical closeness." If the boy responded positively to the gesture, the priest would place his hand on the child's knee, being very careful not to advance too quickly. The process was one of conditioning the physical familiarity. If the priest sensed that the boy was comfortable, on the next outing he might "accidentally" brush his hand against the boy's genitals while passing him a box of popcorn. Through testing the child's sexual excitement, the priest would know when to proceed to more direct and prolonged sexual fondling. Under the cover of darkness in the theater where no words or looks had to be exchanged, the sex could take place "as if it never happened." It was the pattern used on the priest when he was a child and one that he perpetuated as an adult.

These are examples of the *denied* and *depersonalized* way the abuse is carried out—what happened, happened as if it never happened.

The priest doesn't experience guilt. The child carries the burden of the silent sin and the task of incorporating it into reality.

Regression

Many priests employ a technique of initiation into a secret boys club—they become *one of the boys*. When the friendship is ripe the priest supplies the minor with alcohol, tobacco, marijuana, pornographic magazines, or movies. This is part of the seduction. All manner of sexual activity follows. The youngster is chained to secrecy because he has indulged in a whole series of "forbidden" things, not just sex.

Some victims do experience abuse that can only be labeled *sadistic*. Some severe physical punishment—usually "paddling"—masked the priest's sexual excitement. Some priests report masturbating after completing the punishment, while others experience an ejaculation during it. Some priests, appealing to the martyrs as examples, single out a young protégé and under the guise of ascetic or athletic challenge direct him through a series of intricate maneuvers to train him in discipline and manliness. Within the context of these activities, the priest gets sexual satisfaction. The sexual activity is posed as a final "initiation." One priest reported that he masturbated while his protégé endured boot-camp–like paces wearing an athletic supporter.

There tends to be a strong sexual exhibitionistic component in some priests—the more immature the stronger that component seems to be. However, exhibitionism is not necessarily a precursor to pedophilia.

Splitting

It is well known that highly placed churchmen—cardinals, archbishops, bishops, and priests—have been sexual abusers. They demonstrate a mechanism that many abusing priests use to maintain their equilibrium. They are often rigidly conscientious. They live the rules and excel in the organization. This is their *social conformity* that assures their status, employment, and economic security, and identity as an honored man of the cloth. They keep this life consciously separated from their *inner sexual needs*. Sometimes they assume posed identity—a businessman or salesman—to seek sex. At other times they simply use the ploy within clerical circles.

VICTIMS—THE AFTERMATH

A minor victim of abuse can sustain physical harm especially in a sexual encounter that involves vaginal or anal penetration. Victims in addition, however, consistently suffer serious and long-term emotional damage from the sexual betrayal of a priest. Adults who report having been touched, fondled, or otherwise sexually violated by a priest when they were children recall the overwhelming *guilt* they experienced about any sexual feelings. They blame themselves.

Imagine the violated preadolescent struggling with his sexual development, sitting at mass on Sunday with the symbol of the community's moral authority before him. Like other children at age 11, 12, or 13, this child is unable to absorb completely his or her changing body image, sexual feelings, or relationships. The young person is deprived. The adult world that should foster growth, support, protection, moral guidance, and example instead complicated and impeded his or her development.

Younger children are more trusting, less suspicious, and less sexually experienced than their adolescent brothers and sisters, all of which make them more vulnerable to a priest's sexual play.

> The overwhelming power and authority of the adults render them silent: often they are deprived of their senses. Yet that very fear, when it reaches its zenith, forces them automatically to surrender to the will of the aggressor, to anticipate each of his wishes and to submit to them, forgetting themselves entirely to identify totally with the aggressor. (Schetky & Green, 1988, p. 28)

The priest who abuses transgresses the *generational* barrier and violates a sacred *trust,* and traps a minor into an *incestuous liaison.* The "Father" whom they think is safe, with whom a spiritual involvement would be a protection from the dangers of family love turns out to be more sexually available and dangerous than the males at home.

Many nuns who reported early sexual abuse by a priest came from large families and poor circumstances. In their eyes, the church had great stature and power. Early involvement with parochial school activity and church work with the parish priests were seen by them as ways out of poverty and a legitimate distancing from their chaotic home environments.

Typical of this history is that of a woman who was one of 12 children in her family. From her early years until puberty she slept in one bed with four of her siblings—both boys and girls, since her parents made no effort to segregate the sexes. She became increasingly uncomfortable not only with this situation, but also with the drunkenness and harshness of her father.

At 10 years of age, she gained a measure of distance from the rest of her family by declaring that she was going to join the convent. Thereafter, she was allowed to spend time working in the church sacristy instead of doing chores at home. Later on, she was permitted to sleep alone on a couch on the porch; the explanation that it was part of her ascetic preparation for life in the convent became an acceptable rationalization for all parties. Her brothers, who had been sexually assertive with her and her sisters, now left her alone. Apparently the threat of violating someone intended for the church was stronger than any incest taboo. A future nun in the family became an honor for all of them.

The girl was a sweet child, and quickly endeared herself to the church staff. She was conscientious in her sacristy work and partook in daily mass and communion. The parish priest often spent time talking with her after she had completed her tasks, presented her with gifts of a rosary and a daily missal, and sent fruit and candy home with her for her whole family. So when the priest first hugged her, she accepted it as a gesture of his genuine and appropriate affection. She did not associate it with the drunken groping of her father or the adolescent intensity of her brothers, which had frightened her and which she had rejected. The contrast between the poverty of affection in her turbulent home and the warm, peaceful glow of the church made the gentle advances of the priest seem not wrong to her.

Her contact with the priest eventually became sexual and continued regularly until she left home for a convent boarding school at age 14. Despite this, her affection for the church, her vocation, and the priest remained intertwined until she became an adult nun. Only with great pain was she eventually able to separate her sense of viola-tion from the elements of support the priest had extended to her.

Many women report grade-school experiences of having been touched or kissed by a priest. The sexual element that becomes so ap-parent to them from their adult perspectives had not been evident to them as children. Under the guise of playfulness and obscured by the children's expectation of the priest's celibacy, he could, as one woman put it, "cop a feel that I would have slapped a boy's face for."

Adult men, abused as minors, tell the same tale. They describe the same dynamic and are burdened with a horrific weight of anger that they often turn inward by drinking, drugging, inept social relationships, and sometimes suicide.

The effects of sexual abuse are *serious* and *long-lasting* and some-times the results of are irrevocably *tragic*. Abuse does interfere with subsequent sexual adjustment; it contributes to identity confusion, to a loss of educational and employment opportunities, and frequently leads to a complete loss of trust in religion. A high incidence of anti-social behavior from drugs to repeated abuse is common (Finkelhor, 1979). Churchmen have failed to recognize this reality. Only under the barrage of court cases and press revelations have they begun to pay attention to victims and their plight.

Some victims become priests in the hope of avoiding sex in the future. Some of them like other victims become abusers themselves.

Victims—survivors of clergy sexual abuse—have had a profound effect on the church in America and the world. They have brought the bishops and even the pope to their knees—belatedly acknowl-edging the problem and asking forgiveness. SNAP (Survivors Net-work of Those Abused by Priests) and The LINKUP have been major groups who fought for recognition, supported victims, pursued per-petrators, and publicized incidents. They pleaded with bishops for a hearing. They were the first to encourage timid lawyers to take up their cause and a reluctant press to report their stories.

TREATMENT

Victims do not object to perpetrators receiving treatment for their sexual problems, but they do resent the attention, time, and money spent on priests versus the neglect of victims. And priest perpetrators do receive the best psychiatric treatment available. St. Luke's Institute in Maryland treated 306 pedophile priests between 1985 and 2002. According to their count only 14 have reoffended.

Treatment of pedophilia, especially among the clergy, is a long and difficult process. Often the priest does not recognize his behavior is inappropriate. He lacks empathy for his victims.

No clear personality profile of offending priests has emerged yet from clinical studies. But from talking with 69 abusers I have the impression that priest abusers tend to be self-centered (narcissistic), socially isolated (schizoid); and psychosexually immature, and to have poor impulse control.

Alcohol or substance addiction, depression, chronic anxiety, or a host of personality disorders can complicate their condition. This does not mean that abusers cannot be charming, energetic, and effective ministers. Many friends of abusing priests refuse to believe the offence even after it is admitted. Their experience of the priest is positive and free of any hint of malice.

Not all priests who experience attraction to children act on their feelings. I have interviewed 60 such men. A priest was in his mid 30s and assigned as a chaplain of an orphanage. He had been in delicate health. The nuns who staffed the institution were enthusiastic about this younger man who would be saying their Mass, hearing confessions, and generally enlivening the atmosphere. They willingly supplied him with every comfort they could afford to insure "Father's health."

As the priest regained his physical strength, he grew increasingly nervous, complaining to his superiors that he was bothered by all the "female attention," and that he missed the "man's world" he had known in the seminary and in his prior assignments. However, he confided to his closest priest friend that he found himself sexually excited by the children who were always eager to hold his hand, sit on his lap, or hug him whenever he had any association with them. Eventually his anxiety escalated to such a degree that he had to be reassigned. Subsequently, he cultivated the reputation of not liking children, a reputation reinforced by his avoidance of any contact or activity with them or with young people.

The victim, who is in a powerless position of course, knows about the abusive activity. That activity comes to the attention of other priests through the confessional, or of psychiatrists through psychotherapy, either by way of the offender or the victim. Others—through observation or confidence—also know. Abuse is frequently an "open secret." Multiple reports are made to bishops and their officers with minimal investigation or reaction. Threat of scandal has been the most consistent motivator for some reaction.

Occasionally, a priest will seek help prior to acting out his desires, like the priest who found himself attracted to his young nephews on a vacation with his family. More often, however, fits of guilt are all too fleeting, and the abuser who desperately wants a relationship cannot sustain the adult demands of either psychotherapy or spiritual direction. Either might offer him a modicum of insight or help in working through his problem. Most active abusers do not "turn themselves in." Some seek anonymity by limiting their partners to persons who have no connection with their work or ministry. Others simply do not experience any guilt in connection with it. Most weave the abusive relationships into the fiber of their ministerial duties.

It is not true that every priest abuser is untreatable. But those who do seek help must stop rationalizing and develop strategies for resisting sexual and affective temptation. The compulsion of a confirmed pedophile requires a multifaceted mode of intervention to control him. I have found that—even in the best of circumstances—psychotherapy or spiritual direction, by themselves are inadequate treatment modalities. One transient incident of an adult-child sexual contact—although criminal—can be resolved through spiritual direction or psychotherapy if it is genuinely an incident only, and not part of a process. This does not take care of the victim's needs, however.

Drugs that lower an abuser's testosterone level have been successful in helping to control behavior. Most abusers are encouraged to attend group sessions similar to Alcoholics Anonymous where men have to report their behavior and impulses, and their temptations to act out. The recidivism of men attracted to young boys is twice that of men who prefer girls.

Basic to all treatment modalities for pedophilia is that the abuser must *acknowledge* his problem and *seek help*. A much more finely tuned assessment of the priest's total developmental history and his personality structure is needed to intervene effectively and help him come to grips with his sexual behavior.

There is a clerical myth that sexual corruption comes from outside the corps of priests—that is from the candidates entering seminaries. Not so. It comes from above, from superiors and the culture of the priesthood. The trouble with most of the sexual activity of celibates is that it is seen by both the perpetrator and the church authorities as an "act" (or sin) that can be resolved by confession and a firm purpose of amendment. They have come to rely on psychological intervention, but *without* a careful examination of the system that selects, educates, nurtures, and supervises its priests. Who are the men entrusted with these tasks? What is *their* celibate commitment? Many priests are introduced to a sexual subsystem within a supposedly celibate culture.

AWARENESS OF THE PROBLEM

Catholic parents are now alert to the possibility of sexual abuse by a priest—once unthinkable or at least unmentionable. A nun related the experience of grade school children lined up in church for confession. The line was long on one side and short on the other. When she encouraged some of the children to shift to the line in front of the other priest's confessional, they were reluctant. Finally one of the boys spoke up loudly, "My mom told me not to go to him. He's a wimp." That kind of awareness and response would not have happened 20 years earlier.

Why has the church not assumed a more active role in dealing with its clergy who abuse children? I used to think that church authorities were not aware of the magnitude of the problem until recently. In reviewing thousands of pages of documents, in over 100 cases of clergy abuse of minors, I have found that there is a long-standing awareness of the problem in bishops' ranks. What has surprised them is their inability to keep it secret—and the public reaction. Certainly the medical community, and the population as a whole, has become far more sophisticated about abuse, its symptoms, and means of intervention in the past half-century.

The church and bishops, who were confronted with the issue of illicit sexual relationships between priests and minors deserve some credit. They responded in a manner they thought to be responsible. They made an effort to aid the offending priest, and avoid scandal. To a degree they tried to protect the injured child. It is now clear that those actions that aided, comforted, or enabled the sex offender to continue his secret life were irresponsible and injurious to the sex offender and to past and future victims. Though psychological study is still in its infancy, the long- and short-term traumatic injury inflicted on the victim are known to be serious.

But one thing *everybody* has known is that it is criminal, and the church has gone to great lengths to keep knowledge of abusing priests from the police. Bishops have always known that the behavior was noncelibate. The church's tendency to stick its head in the sand on matters sexual when it concerns clergy is in stark contrast to its outspoken and harsh judgment on lay sexual mores—contraception, abortion, masturbation, sex before marriage, and so on.

The system of secrecy runs deep throughout the Catholic Church when it is faced with the choices of recognizing and confronting the sexuality of clergy or covering it, ignoring it, and hoping it will go away. Again, there are several reasons for the existence of the secret system.

The saga of sexual abuse of minors is a partly told tale. It has developed and will continue to be told in headlines around the world. The church authority has gone to great lengths to avoid "scandal." They seriously miscalculated the tolerance of lay Catholics for dissimulation. Lay people are responding to the financial out-lay without accountability by reducing donations. Bishops have lost their moral credibility particularly in—but not limited to—sexual matters.

THE FUTURE

There are some basic tasks that loom large on the horizon of the celibate church. We already know open disclosure and discussion of problems is preferable to secrecy. Immediate help should be offered to any damaged individual perpetrator or victim. Preventive measures have to be instituted on all levels of the clergy. No cleric, whatever his power position, is exempt.

Certain facts that the crisis of sexual abuse reveal must be faced:

1. The deficiencies of the seminary structure and failure of integration of sex and celibacy create a situation where adolescence is protected or postponed, or where the celibate priesthood becomes a hiding place for unresolved sexual conflicts.
2. The atmosphere and power structure of the church tolerates and in some cases encourages sexual regression and fixation.
3. Preference for secrecy obviates accountability on the part of the priest and his superiors.
4. The lack of credibility in the church's teaching on sex fosters primitive mental defenses such as denial, rationalization, and splitting.

The church of the future must examine carefully its current positions in moral theology and reassess its basic statements, many of which have been codified and accepted without question for years—or perhaps centuries. To survive, it must engage in such a reassessment.

10

WHO ABUSES?

The Church is my mother. She sometimes acts like a whore, but she is still my mother.

—Dorthy Day

Evil and ignorance are like shadows. They have no substance; they simply lack light.

—Jeffrey Anderson

Research conducted and published by Laurie Goldstein (*New York Times*, January 12, 2003) concluded that the full *extent* of clergy abuse remains hidden. But they could say the following:

> In dioceses that have divulged what they say are complete lists of abusive priests—under court orders or voluntarily—the percentages are Baltimore—6.2%; Manchester, N.H.—7.7%; Boston—5.3%. The *NYT* survey was based on the analysis of data on 1,205 priests accused of abuse.

At that time a validated list of over 2,100 abuser priests was in the process of compilation and categorization by Dallas lawyer Sylvia Demerest. Even this most authoritative directory will not record the full extent of abuse by priests.

Arguments exist about the number of priest abusers compared with Protestant ministers, and compared with the incidence of abuses in the general male population. So far comparative studies are not available. But protests that priests are "no worse" than other groups or than men in general is a dire indictment of the profession. It is surprising that this attitude is championed by church authorities. Although the *extent* of the problem will continue to be debated, sexual abuse by Catholic priests is a *fact*.

The reason *why* priests, publicly dedicated to celibate service, abuse is a question that cries out for explanation. Sexual activity of any adult with a minor is a criminal offense. By virtue of the requirement of celibacy, sexual activity with anyone is proscribed for priests. These factors have been constant and well known by all church authorities.

PSYCHOLOGICAL PROFILE

A preliminary *psychological* profile of priest sexual abusers is slowly emerging from therapists and from centers that specialize in treating abusive priests. A tentative and overgeneralized picture would be of a man who is self-centered, in need of reassurance or adulation, insecure about his sexual identity, somewhat isolated in adult relationships, poor at controlling impulses, dependent, and inept at handling his anger.

The portrait of the priest abuser is not a "paint by numbers" project. It would be foolhardy and irresponsible to give this profile more weight than it deserves. It is a preliminary sketch of what in truth is a vast panorama of personality typographies, complex developmental and situational vistas, and moral colorations. Our challenge, however, to paint a portrait of the priest sexual abuser, does have some perimeters and preliminary guidelines.

Four broad categories of priests who strongly tend to cross the appropriate psychic and physical boundaries between a religious minister and a minor are emerging. Some are priests who are genetically predisposed to a sexual attraction to minors. Others are dominated psychodynamically; their psychosexual immaturity or mal-development makes them vulnerable. Still other priests abuse in response to their clerical cultural and social situation. And finally the behavior of some priests is principally morally determined.

The church seldom talks about the last two categories of causation, those that specifically involve the church's celibate/sexual system and evil.

Not every priest who matches the psychological profile or is predisposed to a category of vulnerability crosses appropriate boundaries. I have treated a number of priests in long-term psychotherapy whose attraction for minors was clear and constant. They did not act out. Their vulnerability was mitigated by other factors of character or circumstance. However, mental or physical illness, trauma, or substance dependence influence personality regression and can activate and intensify latent potentials for abuse. Also, the four factors mentioned above may be interactive and may reinforce or exacerbate each other.

CATEGORIES OF VULNERABILITY

Genetic Predisposition

In 1960 I believed, along with many of my contemporaries, that psychosexual maturity was an approachable norm that would inevitably follow birth and growth unless some factors of nurture or environment derailed, delayed, *or* "perverted" that process. Experience has convinced me that some of the priests I have observed fit a category of offenders observed and recorded in the general population among pedophiles. The object of these priests' sexual attraction is genetically determined, much as their gender sexual orientation and level or sexual drive is.

Ongoing genetic, endocrine, and biochemical research will greatly refine our understanding of these men and their development and behavior. An understanding of sexual behavior will always have to consider biogenetic factors. A simple way to grasp the reality that certain people are genetically predisposed or preordained to sexual attraction to a certain age group is by way of analogy. We know almost from the time of some children's birth that they will never function at "normal" adult intellectual levels. In the most fortuitous of circumstances, the greatest care and attention can only assist them to function at their optimal intellectual capacity, which may be that of a 6- or 9-year-old. Unfortunately, in a less than *ideal* environment or worse, negative physical or psychological factors usually exacerbate the genetic limitation.

At first it may be hard to believe that certain persons are genetically determined and confined to a level of sexual development less than that usually attained by a child or an adolescent. We would like to think that everyone has the capacity for a satisfying adult-to-adult sexual relationship—physically, psychically, spiritually, and reproductively satisfying. It is not so. Human nature has programmed into itself a biosexual diversity, the scope and object of which we are only beginning to fathom.

There are a certain number of men with a genetically predisposed attraction to minors who either consciously or intuitively select the priesthood as the best place to live out their lives. At best they seek control for their impulse. At worst they seek a socially acceptable cover for sexual access to minors. Ideally, if they can embrace celibate development, their sexual drive will be redirected and their energies can be used in socially productive ways. I know priests who almost miraculously (certainly by special grace) have achieved celibate function when they are clearly locked at a level of sexual development, which, were they to be sexually active, would cause them to be true pedophiles or ephebophiles.

Young men who entered seminary training in their teens were generally unaware of the meaning and scope of their sexual impulses. Their sexuality remained undifferentiated for some time after their ordination. Accepting older candidates for the priesthood is not a guarantee that they have developed a mature or integrated sexuality. In fact, older candidates can hide their sexual proclivities under a slick and well-developed character "disorder."

If the genetically locked priest becomes sexually active, as is often the case, he will inevitably gravitate to minors who are the age level of his own predetermination. His choice of sexual object will be further influenced by two other separate factors that are also genetically determined or influenced: sexual orientation and level of sexual desire. At the extreme, these factors conspire to develop a driven and exploitative person. These priests are the sexual predators of minors.

A host of these priests have already come to public attention. Names like Fr. James Porter, Fr. David Holly, Fr. John Geoghan, and Msgr. Robert Trupia are now notorious. Each (and many others) deserves an in-depth case study to help discriminate this particular dynamic in the culture of the priesthood.

Psychodynamic Considerations

There is another group of priests who seem to have been treated more evenhandedly by nature. Their genetic endowment does not seem to be the over-determining factor of their choice of sexual object. Rather, they are men who follow most closely Freud's observation of male psychosexual development. In these cases factors within early object relationships, often coupled with early sexual over-stimulation and experiences, conspire to lock the person at one level of psychosexual development or to make him extremely vulnerable to regression to sexual attraction to minors.

Boys are affectively attracted to their own sex at a prepubertal stage of development. Part of normal development proceeds through the "gang age," a stage at which boys are more focused on each other than on girls. Hero worship is common.

It is normal for adolescent boys to be sexually attracted to adolescent girls and boys. But these attractions most commonly mature, more or less evenly, and are integrated with intellectual, physical, and social growth over time. Nevertheless, the path of integrated psychosexual development is not open to everyone equally. Psychic factors can be powerful enough to arrest or lock someone into a particular stage of development or may make persons of a certain age over-valued and over-invested as sexual objects. This may be coupled with over-inhibition or denigration of adult women—who are most commonly thought of by other males as desirable love objects.

This age period typically precedes 11, a time at which boys prefer association with their own sex. Girls are avoided and held in disdain, often as a cover for their fear of women. They also are loath to expose their own as-yet unsolidified sexuality to their buddies. Sex generally is rigidly denied while secretly explored. The rigidity extends to strict rules of inclusion *and* exclusion. Control and avoidance are of primary concern.

Psychodynamic theories of development are too well known to belabor here. I am convinced that the biogenetic and the psychogenetic factors that influence sexual behavior (nature and nurture) do not act in isolation or exclusion of each other, and they, along with cognitive factors (learning) account for what we observe psychiatrically in men who sexually abuse minors.

Psychiatric Observations

Church superiors have turned increasingly to psychiatry over the past 50 years to help them treat scandal-prone clerics. Some have earnestly tried to learn more about the psychological dimensions of life and even of spirituality. However, psychiatry can be misused or overused, and I have seen both happen in my career of studying the interface between religion and psychiatry.

All dioceses in the United States now have written policies to address complaints of sexual abuse by clergy. The implied rational goes like this: "A small fraction of priests (no larger than any other segment of the population) sexually abuses children because they are psychiatrically ill, either because of genetic (biological) or psychogenetic (psychological) forces. Such behavior is illegal and harmful to minors. Offenders will be treated psychiatrically. Bishops pledge full cooperation with civil authorities investigating abuse. Victims of abuse will be given comfort and offered counseling."

Of course these policies and understandings are a leap forward from the way priest abusers and especially victims were treated until recently. I wish to detract nothing away from this progress or the credit due to churchmen and women who are assuming some leadership in these advances. But I would be remiss if I did not point out that we know a great deal more about sexual abuse by Catholic priests than any policy implies. No policy has provided a satisfactory understanding of why some priests abuse children. And written policies are frequently not implemented.

Psychiatry has made great progress in the past 50 years in understanding the dynamics and treatment of the paraphilias. We used to call them perversions. Much of psychiatric (bio-psychosocial) theory is useful and applicable to clergy offenders. Understanding the addictive nature of sexual abuse is a big step forward in diagnosis and treatment. The church is wise to draw from psychiatric knowledge and research to understand and treat priest offenders. That knowledge can aid in preventing and combating this serious problem.

Psychiatry is particularly clear about the dire and long-lasting consequences of the sexual abuse of a minor. The trauma is compounded by the fact that the abuser is a trusted and revered person. However, psychiatry does not cover the whole truth. If it did, the task would be simple—identify the sick among us (or even the potentially sick) and make them known so the public can be protected. Therapy could be initiated to heal the offender and the victim; prosecution and incarceration could be effected where indicated and the law demanded. If psychiatry were the whole truth we could rid ourselves of this plague. In addition, we could guard the entry gates to ministry with sophisticated psychological testing.

Unfortunately, the problem extends beyond the psychiatric dilemma of sexual abuse by men who happen to be Catholic priests. The realities of the social situation and moral climate of the Roman Catholic priesthood are also significant factors in the perpetuation of child sexual abuse as are the genetic and psychodynamic factors. And many churchmen know exactly what I am talking about. The "clerical cultural" aspects of abuse must be confronted with a vigor equal to that of the psychiatric aspect. But there is a strong institutional resistance to attacking the cultural forces in the church's control because the culture of abuse extends high up in the system and takes many sexual forms.

Sexual abuse of minors opens up the whole system of Catholic sexual teaching and practice for examination. All agree that sexual activity between a priest and a minor is reprehensible and intolerable. A majority of Catholics, however, disagree with formal church teachings about sex. They do not believe the church's teaching on birth control. More than half believe that abortion is admissible under some circumstances. Most believe that condoms should be used to avoid contracting or transmitting HIV. Most do not believe that non-marriage is necessary for the priesthood. Sex prior to marriage and after divorce are considered morally permissible—and certainly not worthy of excommunication. Masturbation is rarely seen as sinful.

There are firm but fine lines between what is sexually abusive and what represents dissent from church discipline on sex and celibacy. The amazing question is this: Why has the church been so aggressive, sensitive, and proactive in response to dissent about church teaching, yet so blind, defensive, and reactive when it comes to questions of sexual abuse by their own? I will address this matter in the next chapter.

Psychiatry must not pretend that it can answer that question! Priests may be "ordinary men," as stated in the 1972 Kennedy-Heckler study of the priesthood, but they do not exist in an "ordinary" social-moral culture. Theirs is a culture apart, bounded by mandatory celibacy. It is exclusively male—power, control, employment, and even financial reward are dependent on the exclusion of women and the *appearance* of a sex-free existence. No one can say that this culture has nothing to do with the problem of child sexual abuse. In some instances it does induce sexual abusers.

The Social Situation

This third group of priests who abuse children do not fit simply into the standard psychiatric categories despite their having had sex with minors. This category is specifically clerical; it may have analogies in other populations, but the predominant lock is social-situational. These men may be basically healthy. They fit well into clerical culture. To do so, of course, they have had to sacrifice their sexuality or suspend their psychosexual development. The celibate process that is meant to redirect sexual energy is not engaged.

What is this social-situational setting like? Intellectually, conformity to set answers rather than openness to free inquiry is rewarded. Theologically, it is a man's world where God is Father, Son, and masculine spirit. The ideal and only woman venerated is mother or virginal (forbidden objects of sexual fantasy). Emotionally it is a world in which men are revered and powerful (pope, bishop, rector), and boys are treasured as the future of the church.

I have clearly posed that the institutional church exists in an adolescent stage of development. The culture it forms favors adolescent responses. This institutional structure, although it surely includes individuals who have matured beyond it, is dominated and entrenched in a level of functioning that cannot face the sexual realities of adolescence, let alone mature male and female equality and sexuality. This is an atmosphere and culture in which some men who are not genetically or psychodynamically determined, and who otherwise would not do so, do get sexually involved with minors. It has parallels to the forces that determine sexual activity in a prison situation.

Those priests who are socially-situationally influenced are usually devoted to the institution. They play by the church's rules. They conform to ecclesiastical expectations. They don't question authority; they need its approval. In some instances they are "loving" to their victims. In my years in studying the celibate/sexual adjustment of priests, I found that not all of the victims were equally regretful or resentful of the experience. Neither could all of the priests extricate themselves from this sexual pattern. These men may not be overly narcissistic or exploitative, but they do fail to move either celibately or psychologically beyond the social-situational limits of their religious institution.

Some of these priests do not come to public or legal attention; certainly not in as great a number as those who are compulsively driven. This behavior is often a passing phase of their celibate/sexual growth. I have consulted in scores of abuse cases where the priest's behavior was limited to one or two minor victims prior to a personal sexual reconstitution. These men are not able to be screened out of the ministry as candidates. They are products of the system. The celibate/sexual culture they so willingly absorb forms a psychological and moral field that makes affective exchanges and love between adult male (often the hero) and the boy or girl admirer "natural" in their minds. However, the behavior of these priests remains destructive. It is criminal. I judge that this phenomenon is specific to priests because it is culturally determined and supported. Abuse, even at its most horrifying, has been easily forgiven and overlooked in clerical culture. Some men in authority have themselves been involved in this pattern of behavior. They have greater empathy with the perpetrator than for the victim.

Moral Corruption

I have observed another group of priests who sexually abuse minors. They do not deserve the mitigating benefit of psychiatric diagnosis. Nor do they merit understanding as simple products of social-situational conditioning. They go beyond the limits of any institutional inadequacy. The category that defines them is clearly a moral one. They coldly, calculatingly, and by design involve themselves sexually with minors because they want to; they choose it, rather than act compulsively, indiscriminately, or impulsively. They divorce what they teach, what they require of others, from what they stand for in the eyes of others. In short, what they do is make a moral choice—they commit sin.

Let me say it even more clearly: What we are talking about is the category of evil, not illness. Psychiatric diagnosis does not make sin obsolete. This group of priests is not the most likely to be found in a psychiatric clinic for treatment. The priest in this category is not likely to come to the attention of legal authorities. He is too calculating; he picks his partners carefully, often from within the celibate system or from those groups of youth least likely to complain. These men are satisfied with this life and adjustment.

These priests can be found in the halls of power, in positions of responsibility. They are not victims of the system; they sometimes run the system. Examples from this group are available, though rarely diverted or prosecuted.

Because men who represent these last two categories may also have character flaws and personality deficiencies, they should not be subsumed within the psychiatric pale any more than men who have genuine psychiatric illness be ignored medically merely because their behavior also has significant moral implications. The core cause of each group's "abusive" behavior must be kept in focus and addressed appropriately.

Men from each category are liable for criminal and civil litigation. The legal system has been persuasive in forcing some response from church authority to the problem of sexual abuse by priests. In fact, the law and the survivors movement have been the only forces so far that have moved the church to any serious consideration of reform. However, neither the law nor psychiatry can reform the celibate/sexual system of the church or address fundamentally the evil that exists within it and the corruption it generates.

Child abuse by clergy is the tip of an iceberg. It does not stand on its own. Removing it from view will not solve the crisis of celibacy. Difficult as it is to accept, the hierarchical and power structures beneath the surface are part of a secret world that supports abuse. These hidden forces are far more dangerous to the sexual health and welfare of religion than those that we can already see. This is the face of a morally corrupt system.

Bishops have repeatedly said that sexual abuse within the clergy is "no worse" than in the general population. What a sad admission that priests have no better track record than the general population in this matter. What a moral indictment! Clergy—selected, trained, publicly acknowledged moral leaders, official representatives of Jesus Christ—

are not more moral, dependable, honest, and integrated than the general population.

Bishops should lead this reform. By analyzing the defenses and resistances employed so far against change we may understand the problem in greater depth and offer some hope for serious transformation. The next chapter will focus on these aspects of the crisis of celibacy.

FOUR CASE STUDIES

Sexual abuse of minors by Roman Catholic clergy is a long-standing problem. Abundant historical accounts of sexual violations by clergy exist from 177 C.E. on through the early church councils and the Middle Ages. In the United States there are records of abuse from the early 1900s until the present.

The phenomenon is a worldwide problem among Roman Catholic clergy. Europe, Canada, and Australia are being active in bringing the problem to public focus. Other countries are even more resistant to exposing the facts of clergy abuse. I, with others, have interviewed victims from the Philippines, India, Africa, and Central and South America. It is erroneous to think that the problem of abuse is the result of the Second Vatican Council or the "sexual revolution." The crisis is more long-standing than any recent events and when the whole story of sexual abuse by presumed celibate clergy is told, it will lead to the highest corridors of Vatican City.

Sexual abuse of children is part of a larger pattern of sexual involvement by priests with others—adult women and men. Although the latter is not illegal, it is still marked in many cases by moral negligence and abuse, and is tolerated by ecclesiastical authority. The hierarchy cannot claim *ignorance of* the sexual practices of their own—of themselves and their fellow priests—and at the same time expect to be credible and authoritative sources of leadership in sexual morality for the laity.

Celibacy is a culture unique to priests. The four categories discussed below—predispositions of genes, psychodynamics, situational nature, and outright evil—are not meant to be rigid slots into which abusers can be stored for reference. They are areas for consideration that deal more specifically with priest abusers than with other clergy or with men in the general population.

There are hundreds of case histories that illustrate the categories of vulnerability listed above. I have chosen bishops or chancery officials to make the point because this is the natural course of discovery. The current situation is of crisis proportions precisely because the discovery of clergy abuse cannot be confined to low level "operatives" or candidates for the priesthood.

Genetic Predisposition

High profile priests who have histories of hundreds of victims are well known. Often they have been treated in numerous psychiatric facilities, given multiple pastoral assignments within their own diocese or another, even in a foreign country. They continue to re-offend, some even after incarceration.

Fourteen of 325 American bishops have come under a cloud of public sexual allegations only since 1990. Several have resigned acknowledging transgressions against minors, or adult men or women. None of these so far can be relegated to a category of genetic compulsive behavior toward minors. However, Joseph Green, now deceased, but former bishop of Reno, Nevada, seemed to be plagued with this pattern of compulsivity. His earlier life and history as auxiliary bishop of Lansing, Michigan, are still unclear, however, but allegations of abuse and threats of arrest marked his time in Nevada. One allegation still stood in another state at the time of his death in 1982.

Certainly there are other bishops who are genetically determined toward sexual attraction to minors. We can hope that the internal controls of some and their discipline and spiritual life enable them to maintain appropriate boundaries.

Psychodynamic Predisposition

It has been so well established that clerical culture is a climate of psychosexual immaturity that I hesitate to raise the issue again. But it is central to the crisis. The commission that the bishops themselves set up to study the psychological dimensions of the priesthood in the United States is classic and will stand until one can supersede it.

Eugene Kennedy and Victor Heckler determined through a random sample and a sophisticated psychological testing set, that 66 percent of priests were psychosexually *underdeveloped*. Another 13 percent were *developing*, while 8 percent were *mal-developed*. Only 8 percent were considered *developed*—that is, psychosexually stable or mature.

This cultural of immaturity does not exclude bishops. Nor are bishops exempt from personal histories that include having experienced childhood sexual stimulation (sometimes by older priests) and other experiences that form a psychic foundation for sexual attraction to minors.

I have interviewed victims of Bishop Anthony O'Connell of Palm Beach, Florida. He resigned (1998) after admitting that he had abused a minor—a seminary student who came to him for counseling. The counseling problem was that another priest had already abused that student. Even in this tiny vignette an investigator gets one clue as to how a network of abusing priests gets established. Other students have come forward with allegations. Now there are dozens of allegations awaiting evaluation. Although there may be additional ways to understand the bishop's behavior, in his case what appears to be a strong impulse acted on with a number of minors over a long time period led me to select this category for understanding.

I have interviewed scores of priests who give this categorization meaning. Most have been abused themselves. Frequently they have had only a limited number of victims and these events occurred early in their ministry. Some struggle for a more mature orientation; of these priests, some do make it, others limp along for a lifetime, bouncing around in different modes of experimentation. Some seek comfort in alcohol along with their addicted brothers.

I had the opportunity to analyze four generations of abuse, revolving around an auxiliary bishop of a large Eastern archdiocese. A young man had approached therapy when the effects of abuse by an uncle, who had also abused his older brother, became intolerable. Each young man responded differently to abuse that was similar in behavior and duration. The older brother dismissed the activity as so much sexual play, but he supported his younger brother in seeking relief and help. At the time of confrontation the uncle was already under court-ordered probation for recently sexually abusing his own son. He attended sessions with his nephews to plead his case about his former behavior.

An orphan at the age of 4, he was sent to a Catholic institution. The priest chaplain, who was later to become a bishop, took great interest in him. Psychologically and informally he "adopted" the boy and kept him under his tutelage until he reached adulthood. He had sexual activity with him from the time he was 6 years old into his adulthood.

In recounting his association with his abuser he said, "I thought that it was all natural. The bishop told me that he had that kind of friendship with a priest when he was growing up."

Where will it stop? Only legal and psychiatric intervention, in this instance, questioned a pattern of abuse that came from the center of a system that tolerated and fostered it.

Dozens of similar—and more dramatic—cases reveal the genealogy of abuse within the clerical culture. Men who are not genetically determined to abuse minors are, often as children and young adults, actively cultivated to a degree that stamps them psychodynamically and determines their object of sexual attraction.

Situational Predisposition

Vatican spokesmen in 2002 suggested that homosexually oriented men could not be admitted to seminary training for the priesthood. That thinking is not new. Even in the early 1960s a dictum was put in writing by the bishops that said that homosexually oriented men were not acceptable candidates for ordination. The new dimension to the prohibition was a claim that even the ordinations of gay-oriented priests may be invalid. This is part of an erroneous-judgement grid that misunderstands homosexuality and blames gays for sexual misbehavior among priests, including abuse of minors.

All of this is proposed without any awareness of the power of culture on behavior. The elimination of homosexually oriented men in seminaries would not obviate sexual behavior of any stripe in the seminary or priesthood, anymore, as I said earlier, than heterosexual-only inmates in a prison would do away with homosexual activity.

The culture of the priesthood is *homosocial*. I resist the advice of colleagues to call the culture homosexual. Such a designation institutes unnecessary polemics. And I do not think it accurate. A designation of homosocial calls for objective examination of an all-male culture of power and reward.

There is overwhelming evidence that some priests are not swayed to abuse minors by their genetic endowment or by critical psychodynamic forces. Rather they respond to a social situation. Priesthood, because of its social structure, requires substantially different adjustments from other walks of life or professions. It is a culture that does not depend on progeny for generative satisfaction. Continuation of lineage depends on attracting male followers. Young men are truly valuable. The pastoral relationship to young boys and girls provides easy access and understandable bonds of trust. Appropriate association and affection can easily be sidetracked and subverted under the guise of care and mentoring.

Keith Symons, bishop of Palm Beach, Florida, resigned in 1998 after admitting he abused five minor boys 25 years earlier. If he is to be believed, his abuse would be understood as a response to the social situation of clerical culture.

Many men who under other circumstances would not express their sexual preference for men or boys do so primarily because of the situational opportunity. I knew an abbot and a novice master whose behavior of homosexual abuse could find meaning here. Although both were basically heterosexual in genetic orientation, their long association within the clerical milieu directed their affections and sexual expression toward men and later toward boys.

Lack of adequate understanding and training for celibate living contributes a great deal to the frequency of sexual activity within the clerical system.

The Category of Evil

Oddly, the category of evil seems misplaced when speaking of the behavior of men dedicated to God and religion. Evil as well as good is their business. However, the popular expectation is that bishops and priests stand on solidly good ground. Unfortunately this is not true. Not only have some clergy, by their behavior, positioned themselves in moral swamps and sewage, but the church itself uses tactics to cover sin that further contaminates the system.

Into what category can one classify the attempt to hide documents from legitimate civil authorities investigating crime? A *New York Times* (March 6, 2003) editorial commented on the Los Angeles cardinal Roger Mahony's legal maneuvers to conceal documents relating to clergy abuse, "Church leaders only compound their malfeasance by bending constitutional freedoms to make a mockery of the true obligation of church and state to protect children." The deceit is all the more appalling since the cardinal made a show of pledging full cooperation with civil authority and transparency in combating abuse. Everyone agrees that abuse is evil. What of deception?

I have already recounted the story of the young priest who was hospitalized with a severe depression. Mute for weeks, he finally confided his unbearable secret. His bishop-mentor-friend used him to procure young sexual companions from the streets. Evil, not illness, morality, psychology or situation, dominates this behavior.

John Paul II has visited the United States on several occasions during his reign as pope. The preparations for his visits take years of preparation. Even the color and type of his vestments as well as each detail of his schedule are orchestrated by a team of emissaries, mostly priests from Rome. A diocesan team headed by the local bishop or cardinal coordinates the myriad details. I have fielded complaints from local workers that they had to respond to requests for sexual companions—usually young boys—from priests based in Rome. Can there be any other word than evil for this behavior and the contamination of faith that it represents?

There is a myth that "liberalization" has caused the crisis of celibacy and sexual abuse by clergy. My experience counters that myth. Rigid and orthodox-minded priests and bishops are—and have been—abusers. Abuse of minors did not begin recently; it is not dependent on the effects of the sexual revolution or the positions taken by the Vatican Council or by liberal theologians. I have reviewed case records from throughout the 20th century. Current events are evidence of how assiduously the church has tried to bury the truth of abuse. The only difference today is that the cover-up efforts are failing.

Monsignor William Reinecke, an official of the Arlington, Virginia diocese committed suicide after a former victim of his abuse confronted him. Reinecke was well known for his conservative theology and his rigor—even harshness—in dealing with questions of doctrine and discipline. Only after death was his rich double life revealed.

Solzhenitsyn said, "Evil is not a division between groups of people, us and them. It is a line that runs through each human heart." It is with great hesitation that I relegate—anyone—to a moral category. If he does not belong here there are many who do. Priests who anoint victims with their semen, who warn children they will go to hell if they tell about the abuse, who refuse to take responsibility for their abuse, merit a place in the circle of understanding that can only be called evil.

There are many ways to categorize priest abusers. Sexual abuse of minors is multivalent. But Catholic priests, clerical culture, and celibate practice have contributions to make to the understanding of the problems of abuse generally and to their own tradition for the betterment of both if they can face the crisis in new ways.

In 2003 grand juries were empanelled in nine major cities across the United States. The report of the Suffolk County New York Supreme Court Special Grand Jury was the first to deliver a published report (Grand Jury Report CPL #190.85(1)(C), January 17, 2003). Among its conclusions:

> . . . that officials in the Diocese failed in their responsibility to protect children. They ignored credible complaints about the sexually abusive behaviors of priests. They failed to act on obvious warning signs of sexual abuse including instances where they were aware that priests had children in their private rooms in the rectory overnight, that priests were drinking alcohol with underage children and exposing them to pornography. Even where a priest disclosed sexually abusive behavior with children officials failed to act to remove him from ministry (p. 172).

> Further, the report says that the local organization demonstrates that as an institution they are incapable of properly handling issues relating to the sexual abuse of children by priests. The Grand Jury concludes that this was more than simple incompetence. The evidence before the Grand Jury clearly demonstrates that Diocesan officials agreed to en-

gage in conduct that resulted in the prevention, hindrance, and delay in the discovery of criminal conduct by priests. They conceived and agreed to a plan using deception and intimidation to prevent victims from seeking legal solutions to their problems. This included victims who were seeking compensation for their injuries in the civil courts. There, Diocesan officials pursued aggressive legal strategies to dismiss time barred claims and improperly named parties. They insisted upon confidentiality agreements in cases that were settled. This policy put children at risk inasmuch as victims were prohibited by law from speaking out about the criminal conduct of sexually abusive priests. Absent the adoption of these recommendations, the Grand Jury does not believe that the Diocese of Rockville Centre has the demonstrated capability to properly handle the issues of clergy sexual abuse (p. 173).

There is little hope that any of the grand juries in Boston, Philadelphia, Los Angeles, Phoenix, etc., will deliver a more favorable report of their jurisdictions. The incompetence noted is not merely criminal or individual, it is evil and systemic. The civil system cannot remedy the evil of a religious system, but it can intervene in criminal activity. Already two American bishops have been threatened with criminal indictments but in Suffolk County, "The Grand Jury concludes that the conduct of certain Diocesan officials would have warranted criminal prosecution but for the fact that the existing statutes are inadequate" (p. 174). An American bishop may well have to experience a criminal trial before the current phase of the crisis ends.

The crisis of celibacy has not been precipitated by public exposure. It has not been caused by litigation. These exposures are but manifestations of the reality that has long existed in secret—indeed, in a world where great good exists, but never in sufficient abundance to cover all the sickness and sin that sexual betrayal achieves. Every act of abuse by a priest or bishop is noncelibate behavior, and criminal. These celibate failures can sometimes, with difficulty, be traced. But these are but the tips of icebergs that exist only because a cultural system supports, preserves, and even, engenders them and at the same time conspires to keep them secret. Other celibate violations of every stripe, on every level of ministry stabilize the pattern and practice of abuse. Abuse is the symptom of the crisis that has been brewing for a long time and will not go away until it is adequately addressed.

11

CAN CLERGY SEXUAL ABUSE
BE PREVENTED?

*Celibate piety [can] hide the many sexual problems and unhappy ad-
justments that are the result of what can be understood . . . as an exercise of power by men over other men.*

—Eugene Kennedy

The now legendary Doyle-Mouton-Peterson Report—usually referred
to as THE REPORT—on the problems of sexual abuse of minors by
Catholic clergy was presented to all the American bishops in 1985.
In numerous depositions bishops have sworn they *knew nothing*
about the problem prior to that date. However, the then president of
the Bishops' Conference, Archbishop Daniel Pilarczyk, wrote to Fr.
Doyle in 1992: ". . . the fact remains that your report presented no
new issue (of which the NCCB was unaware) or presented information that required some materially different response."

Denial and defensiveness is still alive and well in the halls of
church power. It embraces a widespread, protean pattern that includes rationalization, avoidance, and shifting of blame. This ingrained response of the secret world impedes the development of an
adequate program for prevention. More than that, it resists the reality
that sexual corruption in the clergy proceeds from the *top down*.
Bishops claim that better screening of candidates will eliminate the
problem of abuse. This is false. The defenses that can be seen so
clearly in reaction to child sexual abuse are operative across the board
in keeping all sexual activity of priests covered.

The system of secrecy fails to examine the ecclesiogenic factors
of sexual abuse. Those are elements of church *teaching and practice*
that contribute to the development, preservation, and protection of

abusing clergy. As a result the priesthood lacks a set of adequate, professional ethical standards regarding sexual behavior and recognition of informed consent.

SCREENING

Screening of candidates for the priesthood and religious life has long been an established method of testing a boy's/man's aptness for clerical life. A time of testing during and apprenticeship to a senior clergy or in a novitiate is a centuries-old tradition. After the Council of Trent (1545–63), seminaries were established to educate secular priests. The seminary horarium copied a monastic structure of designated times for communal prayers, meals, study, recreation, silence, and sleep. Each seminarian was required to have spiritual director—a senior priest designated to mentor the candidate in his spiritual progress.

Each training system counted on itself to eliminate the inept and to form the suitable into observant priests. In every case the novice master and the senior community members or the seminary rector and faculty—ultimately the ordaining bishop—had the responsibility to attest to the candidate's fitness for ordination and ministry. These structures are still operative (Kauffman, 1988).

In the last half of the 20th century, psychological testing along with in-depth personal interviews became popular adjuncts to the traditional system in the attempt to screen out unsuitable candidates even before they enter the seminary or religious life. Already in 1936 Thomas Verner Moore, a priest-psychiatrist, registered his concern about insanity in priests and religious. He concluded: "pre-psychotic personalities may be attracted to the (priesthood) and religious life." He found that alcoholism was diagnosed about three times more frequently among priest-patients than in the general population of men (1936a). Moore proposed a screening protocol to detect psychologically questionable candidates who apply for admission to the priesthood or religious life (1936b).

Father William Bier, S. J., championed the use of psychological testing (especially the Minnesota Multiphasic Personality Inventory [MMPI]) to screen priest candidates (1954). He revised the MMPI to make it more compatible with the realities of clerical lifestyle—

more precisely directed toward those who would prove apt candidates—and to ferret out those who might be ill adapted for clerical life. His thesis was that psychology makes its best contribution in measuring the *natural* side of vocations.

He claimed that information garnered from psychological tests is useful because psychological problems are characteristic of our age. Disturbed individuals are attracted to religious life. Psychological demands are greater in religious than in lay life (1960). The MMPI remains the most frequently used psychological tool in assessing possible pathologies of candidates in both Protestant and Catholic seminaries.

But none of the tests commonly administered to clerical candidates is specifically directed to the detection of sexual attraction to minors. Dr. Gene Abel (1994) has developed two tools that are constructed to test sexual paraphilic interest: the *Able Assessment* and *Plethesmography* (measurement of penis response to visual stimulation). Neither is administered to clerical candidates, but rather, each is reserved for priests who admit or are accused of abuse. Even these measures are not *predictive* of behavior nor do they measure ego control. Interest and fantasy do not predict future performance.

Some priests who abuse children enter seminary training with a history of, or a known proclivity for, sex with minors. But a number of priests develop or discover their sexual preference for children during training. Others have a fantasy life that does not disappear, but they never act on their fantasies or desires (temptations). This burden forms the substance of their ascetical life. These men can be self-disciplined and compassionate.

The Limitations of Testing

All testing, however sophisticated, has not eliminated instances of mental breakdown, alcoholism, or sexual abuse by priests. Screening has helped save some men who would have been unhappy, inept, or mal-suited for priestly life from the pain of unnecessary failure. The great and consistent failure of psychological testing is in its failure to *predict* future behavior within the homosocial structure and celibate demands of the priesthood.

Abuse is contrary to the stated purpose of the church (that of service, healing, and integrity), but it is indigenous to the system. Some churchmen maintain that abusive behavior comes from outside the system. This is not true because the problems of abuse are not from outside the system.

Few studies have been conducted that compare a man's qualities before he enters the seminary and after he completes training. A modest early study concluded that seminarians became more introverted as seminary training progressed (Caplin, 1939). A survey of seminary faculty evaluating seminarians—*Readiness for Theological Studies*—is not encouraging. Forty-five percent of faculty viewed seminarians as academically lower than comparable lay students, and a majority of faculty agreed that the number of seminarians with dysfunctional backgrounds had increased from that of a decade ago (Hemrick & Wister, 1993).

A *Survey of Priests Ordained Five to Nine Years* (Hemrick & Hoge, 2002) recorded some differences between the responses of seminarians in 1986 and those of ordained priests in 1990. Seventy-seven percent of seminarians reported that "living celibacy as a sign of devotion to the coming of God's Kingdom," was a strong ideal. Only 57 percent of priests ordained 5 to 9 years thought so. Of course, 25 percent of ordained priests resign from the ministry during the first 5 years after ordination.

Adequate screening of candidates must focus on the real world beneath the superficial appearance of a candidate and discover his hidden treasures, potential, internal torture chambers, or skeletons. A Vatican document on vocations promulgated by the Congregation for Catholic Education, acknowledged the need to pay special attention to the "affective-sexual area" of development. The document states that "in present day culture (or subculture) . . . it is not rare that the young person exhibit certain weaknesses in this area." And that it is correct to welcome young people "with this kind of problem" *provided* he knows the root of his problem; that it is ego dystonic and that he is able to "control these weaknesses" (Laghi, 1998).

A screening process must take into account the real world *within* the system that evaluates, selects, and trains each candidate for the priesthood. To combat abuse, ecclesiastical authority must explore *itself* and face the sexual reality beneath each training program's external image. What are its spiritual treasures? What are its weaknesses and secrets?

DENIAL

Denial is an unconscious mental mechanism that allows one to reject facts that are experienced as overwhelming or a threat to one's integrity or homeostasis. By analogy, the concept can be applied to an organization. It is understandable that the Catholic Church, troubled by allegations of malfeasance, lawsuits, and a barrage of media exposure of sexual abuse by clergy, would instinctively protect itself. No problem, however, can be adequately dealt with, let alone prevented, until one recognizes that it exists.

Nine levels of denial employed in response to the problem of sexual abuse of minors by clergy are distinguishable from reports recorded in courtrooms, the media, or psychiatric treatment settings.

There Is No Problem; It Can't Be True

Bishops and superiors and even Vatican officials have made this pronouncement in the defense of priests, bishops, and cardinals who have either later admitted or have been proven to violate sexual boundaries. This form of denial is almost a knee-jerk reaction. Complete public denial of the problem is no longer politically correct. However, it exists. Denial can be highly organized and institutionalized. The pattern becomes clear in court documents or settlements with victims. Institutional cover-up, conspiracy, and fraud are prevalent.

Abuse by Priests May Exist, But It Is Very Rare

A Church spokesman responded to media coverage of a violating priest by pointing out that "only a small percentage of pedophiles who abuse children are *celibate* priests." Obviously, he was unaware of his oxymoron; no *celibate* priest can abuse.

The public admission of abuse by a priest or bishop perpetrator, (or judicial proceedings) sometimes penetrates the first level of denial. Father Gilbert Gauthe was convicted of child sexual abuse in

Lafayette, Louisiana, and sentenced to prison. This case came to media attention in 1984 and focused national attention on clergy abuse. Father James Porter, who allegedly abused more than 100 victims in at least four dioceses, and was sentenced to 18 years in prison, gained international notoriety. Several hundred court cases and more than 1,000 legal settlements by dioceses and religious orders have become a part of record.

Three hundred diocesan priests were relieved of their ministry between February and August 2002. Long before this, 10 percent of active priests in Belleville, Illinois, were alleged abusers. Santa Fe, New Mexico, dismissed 21 priests from its ranks for sexual offenses, and so on.

An independent board of inquiry was convened in 1992 at Santa Barbara, California, to investigate sexual abuse reported by former students at St. Anthony's Minor Seminary. The final report concluded that between 1964 and 1987, one-fourth (12 of 44) of the faculty members sexually abused students at one time or another. In one province of religious, four of the six major administrators have been treated for sexual abuse. Some religious communities have scores of victims abused by teachers, pastors, professors, and major superiors.

The documented cases of priest abusers in the United States alone fill volumes. One file has a registry of 2,100 priests who are alleged or convicted abusers. Psychiatric treatment facilities dedicated largely to the treatment of priest sexual abusers have treated many of this number. In court documents one psychiatrist testified that the institution in which he was employed treated 1,000 abusers in a period of 25 years.

There are disputes about the number of priests who involve themselves sexually with minors and about the number of victims. One thing is certain—abuse among the priesthood is not a rare occurrence by any definition.

The Media Distorts Everything

Since *The Boston Globe* printed its series beginning in January 2002, denial relegating the problem of priest sexual abuse to media hype has lost power. Nevertheless some Vatican officials still voice it. Ironically, it was Cardinal Bernard Law of Boston who voiced his notable public attack against the press in 1992 when he called down the wrath of God on the *Boston Globe* for printing stories about Father James Porter and his victims. But the Boston saga gives the lie to this line of defense.

Reports in the media, understandably, have been a continuing concern for bishops and the public relations office of the United States Conference of Catholic Bishops. This agency developed national media policies to handle cases of abuse, namely: *separate, settle, and seal.*

The church's first preference was to keep all cases secret—out of the press, out of the courts. Rarely was this in the best interest of the victims. But if publicity was inevitable, they tried to restrict coverage to the local media. Reporters and news sources who gave space to the problem were countered with charges of "church bashing, priest bashing and Catholic bashing" (Jichat, 1996). This line of defense made abuse a public relations challenge.

Separate referred to isolating cases in the legal forum: keep cases separate so that the scope of the problem would appear to be limited. This focused the responsibility away from the system and onto the individuals involved. The institution did not want priest sexual abuse labeled a *church* crisis.

If cases could not be settled out of court, lawyers were given the charge to settle in the courtroom *by any means necessary.* Court cases have been disastrous for the image of the church, which is revealed as heartless and indifferent to victims of abuse. Victims were ignored if possible. Statutes of limitations have saved hundreds of priests from serving prison time. Legal settlements give the appearance of high-stakes poker games. Damage control and financial advantage are prized above ecclesial integrity.

To *seal* meant that any financial settlements and in some cases all documents related to the case were sealed by the court. In some instances compensated victims were sworn to secrecy and the financial settlement they received could be revoked if they revealed its amount or circumstances. This policy relegated even proven claims to a secret system inaccessible to analysis.

These maneuvers have been seriously disrupted.

American bishops welcomed a study by historian Philip Jenkins (1996), a media expert. He wrote his book on priests and pedophiles

from the vantage of communication. Bishops used the text as a vindi-
cation of their position that abuse by priests was a media-driven phenomenon and a distortion. The media, the argument goes, exploited
"minor events" and blew the problem out of all reasonable proportion
(p. 133). Jenkins alleged that the crusade against Catholic priests was
led by anti-Catholic, anti-priest, and anti-celibacy factions, most of
whom are within the church (Clegg, 1996). Dr. Paul McHugh, head
of the department of psychiatry at Johns Hopkins University Medical School, called the atmosphere regarding child abuse a modem
"witch hunt."

The Problem Is No Worse Than in Other Religious Groups or in the General Population

Any argument with church authorities over the numbers of priests
and bishops who abuse minors is really facetious. Were the American
church eager about tabulating the number of priests who are alleged
abusers, it could have reliable figures within a few weeks. Most bishops and religious superiors know the number of alleged abusers in
their own ranks and have records. They also know the amount of
funds paid by themselves or by insurance carriers for the treatment of
offending priests and victims. The bishops do not want to know.

All experts agree that abuse is an underreported event (Abel &
Osborn, 1992). No one knows the exact number of sexually abused or
abusers, but there are some thoughtful estimates by dedicated researchers.

The Report of the Archdiocesan Commission of Inquiry into Sexual
Abuse of Children by Members of the Clergy (1990), is the best example to
date of an adequate study of the problem in a local church. The various
documents presented by the Canadian (1992), Irish (1996), English
(1994), and American Bishops (1995) talk about appropriate moral
ideals. None has been eager to open the way for in depth studies.

They Wanted It—They Liked It

The victim is blamed. This directs blame for abuse away from the
priest. A Canadian bishop provided a classic example when he said
that abuse was the result of streetwise youngsters seducing naïve clergy.

It is still not uncommon to hear the accusations for responsibility directed at victims.

After a jury found the archdiocese of Dallas grossly negligent for allowing a priest access to children after he clearly demonstrated signs of pedophilic behavior, a chancery official suggested that the boys involved had to assume their measure of responsibility for the activity. He also said that parents shared blame for not being more vigilant for their children's welfare. This was said in spite of the fact that court documents demonstrated that church authorities had sufficient knowledge to question the priest's suitability for the celibate life because of behavior even prior to and during his seminary training.

Abusers Are Sick

Refinement of the psychology of sexual abuse is an ongoing process. Before 1995 the diagnostic code of the American Psychiatric Association acknowledged situational issues such as sexual deprivation that could lead some otherwise sexually adapted men to seek sex with a minor. At that time, this behavior, although illegal, was not recognized as meriting a psychiatric diagnosis (cf. *DSM-III*, 1980, versus *DSM-IV*, 1994).

Later the APA concluded that any sexual involvement of an adult with a child is diagnosable, because it is a problem that has clinical significance of impairment in social, occupational, or other important areas (American Psychiatric Association, December, 1995). Now, once sexual abuse becomes public or threatens to, priests are invariably sent for psychiatric evaluation or treatment. In itself, this course of action seems reasonable.

Research is needed to better understand the factors that contribute to child sexual abuse by priests. In many ways, sexual abusive clergy are a distinct population and so the extensive literature concerning other sexual offenders may be of limited value in understanding factors associated with sexual abuse by clergy (Plante, 1995; Plante, Manuel, & Bryant, 1996).

Serious consideration must be given to the research on neuropsychological aspects of abuse. Psychology and psychiatry are wise to investigate any and all links between brain abnormalities and the paraphilias. But psychiatry and psychology cannot obviate evil. Some clergy choose sex with a minor as a way of satisfying themselves sexually, simultaneously maintaining their clerical status. They choose to abuse. These priests are neither demented nor uncontrollably driven to the sexual behavior by some mental aberration.

Psychiatry and psychology have been enlisted to defend a clerical system. The church will not flourish by enlisting professions to help it avoid basic systemic issues that tolerate and perpetuate abuse. Some superiors send a priest for treatment long after his activities became known but were ignored. When the threat of public exposure and legal consequence motivate referral of previously known abusers, neither psychiatry nor psychology aid in prevention if they allow themselves to be co-opted and refuse to hold the system accountable.

The Consequences Are Not Dire and the Victim Was Sick Anyway

The church has minimized the effects of abuse. They claim that sexual abuse of minors is common ([20 to 50 percent of female victims; 6 to 19 percent of male victims] Hopper, 1997). Not all of these people suffer catastrophic and irreparable harm.

Psychological studies and court proceedings demonstrate that victims who are psychically vulnerable suffer irreparable harm (Finkelhor, Hotaling, & Lewis, 1990). A study at Johns Hopkins showed that 20 percent of 1,900 women abused as children were more likely to have chronic health problems including chest pain, back pain, or drug or alcohol abuse than women who did not report sexual abuse as a child (*Journal of the American Medical Association*, May 7, 1997). Finkelhor developed a model that lists the long-term effects of abuse on child victims (1979).

Some abusing priests are attracted to needy, vulnerable, and psychically impaired youths. Vulnerability actually increases the responsibility for sexual control. The emotional, physical, and spiritual consequences of abuse by a trusted person can be and often are monumental. Minimizing the effects of abuse reinforces denial and inhibits honest exploration of the problem and the means of preventing it.

Abusing priests tend to be impulsive, immature, and narcissistic. Rather than minimize the harm to victims from clergy abuse, church authorities serve the cause of prevention better by addressing the question: How can men with that characterological profile exist and even flourish within the church structure?

Father Is Only Human

A priest entered the room of a rectory where another priest was having anal sex with a schoolchild. He closed the door quickly, retreated, and did not report the incident or speak to the offending priest about it. Years later the victim confronted the priest to determine why he had not intervened to protect him from the assault. Why did he neglect to report the abuser? The priest replied, "Father is only human" (Burkett & Bruni, 1993).

An appeal to fallen human nature is no more an excuse for sexual abuse than for robbing a bank, stealing from the Church coffers, or killing someone. The core issue is not merely one of sin or even the act of breaking a law. It is one of the violations of fiduciary responsibility—behavior essentially incompatible with one's identity, mission, and responsibilities.

How and in what way are clergy sexual abusers the same or different from other abusers? Haywood and colleagues studied 69 men who were alleged to have engaged in sexual misconduct with minors (30 Roman Catholic priests, 39 nonclerics, and 38 normal control subjects). The priests claimed fewer total victims, more older and more male victims, than nonclergy alleged child sexual abusers. Priest abusers also recorded a more rigid and conservative attitude toward sex (Haywood, Kravitz, Wasyliw, Goldberg, & Cavanaugh, 1996).

The socialization experience of priests is not the same as others. The minimization of abuse and its relationship to a more conservative-than-average attitude toward sex need more study. Excessive prohibition of early sexual expression may put a person at risk for developing pedophilic sexual desires (Berlin & Krout, 1996).

Forgive and Forget

Hot controversy surrounds the question of what to do with a priest offender after he has been treated psychiatrically. Some victims cry for blood and banishment, while some priest clinicians argue for prolonged supervision and reassignment in pastoral positions that do not involve contact with minors (Rosetti, 1997). Sexual abuse of a minor by a priest, however horrendous, is not unforgivable (Rosetti, 1995).

Forgiveness is a venerable religious ideal that can, however, be used as a defense against accepting the reality, accountability, and etiology of abuse. Reconciliation is operative only when one accepts full responsibility for transgressions, establishes reforms, and makes restitution. This is true for an abuser, a diocese, or community.

Herein is the paradox. The church and the judicial system at times disavows its own responsibility for abuse. It can perpetuate a refusal to reform by striking a compassionate pose and substituting apologies for action.

"Forgiveness" can be a public relations maneuver as a response to public outcry or legal reversals. Forgiveness, like rehabilitation, follows the acknowledgment of the scope, nature, and etiology of a problem and reformation of those elements in teaching and systemic practice that produce, *foster,* perpetuate, and protect abusers. Nothing less deserves confidence.

Victims cannot forget their abuse, even when they forgive their abuser. Neither should responsible church authorities do so.

We Are Not Responsible for Abuse; It's a Few Bad Apples

A refined level of denial does not rebut the existence of sexual abuse by priests nor its deleterious effects. It does not argue specific numbers or the need for some compensation and apologies from the church. But this level of denial does reject any responsibility beyond that of the perpetrator. Over and over again, in and out of court, one can hear this institutional disclaimer of responsibility.

This *bad apple* argument reinforces the assumption that contamination of abusiveness comes entirely from outside the ecclesial system. The argument presumes that priests who abuse minors have invaded the church and penetrated its protective ramparts—its history of good works and the corps of dedicated honest priests. But problems of abuse and malfeasance have deep historical and institutional roots.

ECCLESIOGENIC FACTORS

The idea of *ecclesiogenic pathology* was introduced in 1955. The term *ecclesiogenic neurosis* is defined as: "the syndrome caused by the widespread tabooizing education in which the sexual and erotic areas of life are banned from open discussion and are considered to be immoral, forbidden, or even threatened with punishment." The syndrome is not limited to Catholic clergy. But the largest professional group suffering from ecclesiogenic neurosis are clergy and other church employees. Sexual symptoms are a frequent element in this syndrome.

Perversions and compulsions are the main symptoms that result "whenever healthy sexuality is repressed and denied instead of being recognized and practiced or joyfully and voluntarily renounced." Quite simply stated, ecclesiogenic pathologies are those mental and emotional aberrations that are induced or fostered by church teaching or practice (Thomas, 1965).

Dr. Gelolo McHugh of Duke claimed, "the most serious problem of the clergymen or the church worker is in the sexual field." In this area the pastor's knowledge is below the average and absolutely inadequate for proper counseling of others and for himself (Thomas, 1965). These statements still apply to Catholic seminarians and priests.

Bernard Haering reflected incisively on the reality of ecclesiogenic pathology in his book on *Priesthood Imperiled* (1996). The idea that church teaching or practice can make people ill has not become popular. But the church is *dysfunctional* (Crosby, 1996). The crimes and crisis of priest sexual abuse of children are complex, distasteful, and difficult to unravel. The church focuses on an individual priest as a sinner, a culprit, or a neurotic. It is daunting to address a system as pathogenic or dysfunctional—the generator-participant in abuse. Nonetheless, these terms *do* apply to the church.

SYSTEMIC ELEMENTS

Two elements constitute the core of the systemic genesis of sexual abuse among the clergy. The first is its moral teaching: *every sexual thought, word, desire, and action outside marriage is gravely sinful.* This seamless garment of sin applies to all sexual activity outside marriage. Furthermore, each and every marital act must remain ordered *per se* in the procreation of human life. All else is mortally sinful.

The Vatican revised its stance on masturbation in 1997 to allow for "factors that can lessen, if not reduce to a minimum, moral culpability." Despite this compassionate concession to reality the underlying foundation of church reasoning about sexuality remains unaltered. But that foundation rests on an inadequate and false understanding of the nature of sexuality. Many clergy and laity consider the church teaching on sex flawed. Sexual teachings simply are not considered credible or reasonable by a large number of lay people and many clergy. Many laws (e.g., contraception, premarital sex) are not observed.

Sexual activity is clearly not so dire that any and every transgression merits Hell or separation from God's love. Sexuality is not the focal point of Christ's teaching. Refusal to discuss reasonably all the human and spiritual issues that surround the sexual agenda facing the world today forms an impediment to the prevention of abuse.

Widespread knowledge of sexual abuse by priests has magnified the loss of credibility in bishops and priests as sources of moral guidance. In addition, the crisis of sexual abuse by priests, like the often repeated papal teaching on contraception, has weakened or destroyed the faith and practice of countless thousands.

Sexual activity by priests has been known and recorded for centuries. A French priest wrote "the transgressions (of priests) are so numerous, so public and so spectacular that the world, even the Christian world, no longer believes in the chastity of priests" (Hermand, 1965, p. 17). The modern priest faces a visceral and intellectual conundrum as he tries to exist and minister within the confines of an *unbelievable* and *unlivable* teaching for the normal Christian. One of the basic problems underlying sexual abuse by priests is this fact: The church lacks a credible theology of sexuality. The minister is left foundering to make sense of his life and his ministry.

The confessional exposes a priest to the rich inner landscape of people's sexual life. That topography is traced by rugged and often untamed terrain of thoughts, desires, behaviors, and endless unnecessary worries. After a time in the ministry the average priest hearing confessions becomes privy to a wide variety of sexual practices and concerns of the laity and other priests. A priest can cease to be surprised at the frequency of masturbation, homosexuality, infidelity, and incest. He becomes familiar with varieties of sexual practice he did not previously even read about or imagine, such as necrophilia or zoophilia.

The priest learns compassion as he listens to the complexity of people's lives and the tension between their religious ideals, education, and practical realities of daily existence. He empathizes with their loneliness. If the priest is attentive to the spirit of grace, he even learns wisdom and ways to help people suffer less, be more autonomous, just, accountable, and loving.

But the priest is also burdened with his new knowledge. Sex becomes pedestrian. It is pervasive. How does he refine his celibate dedication at the same time he develops ministerial wisdom and integrity in helping his people to develop loving relationships and full sexual maturity?

It is *because* church teaching is not convincing or real that no seminary yet effectively succeeded in teaching celibacy or sexuality. The structure of the seminary institution is meant to be the seminarian's instruction in celibacy (Kauffman, 1988). This traditional method can and frequently does fail to sustain a priest in his celibate striving in his ministry. The priest is, in a very real sense, abusive if he responds to his own celibate/sexual development and the demands of ministry by simply discarding the church's teaching on sex as impossible. Or worse, he is abusive if he holds others to a standard he does not live. He is abusive if he enters the network of sexually active priests under the guise of comradeship. Finally, he is monumentally abusive if he imposes his own sexual needs on the suffering or vulnerable whom he is supposed to serve. Duplicity translates into a pathology. Sex becomes the ecclesial means of splitting—betraying integrity. In the words of Father Hermand, "Let us be frank and lucid and realistic. Strict selection will not ensure the elimination of all unsuitable candidates, and in any case how many would be left in the end?" (p. 82).

The second systemic element that generates abuse is *sexual practice within the celibate system.* Quite simply, some priests, novice masters, superiors, confessors, and so on, develop affective relationships with students, seminarians, or younger priests that violate celibate boundaries. Dr. Barry M. Coldrey, an Australian historian, describes the dynamic that results from priest sexual activity among themselves or with others as the development of a "sexual underworld" (1997). Some of the building blocks of this world become obvious as a sexual partner rises in church administration and remains beholden to his former sexual associates as they are to him—bound by an alliance of mutual memory (Sipe, 1995). These alliances are responsible for a number of ecclesiastical promotions.

Mutual sexual activity among clerics is not the only link in the ecclesiastical underworld: Attendance at gay bars or knowledge of heterosexual liaisons can be used as sets of checks and balances, one priest (bishop) against another. Sexual knowledge becomes an unholy alliance by which each priest justifies his own behavior. Institutionally, the network of this underworld can and does evolve into *blackmail.* Clerics hold knowledge against their bishop or vice versa to establish or maintain their position. Dozens of firsthand reports—some horrendous and byzantine—exist.

Bishops know a great deal about each other's sexual history. It is not uncommon for authorities to use knowledge of hidden scandalous behavior to keep each other or a religious institution in line with the threat of public exposure of secret violations if they do not conform. The power of the underworld is tremendous and destroys accountability.

This system of celibate violation gives permission for a priest to be sexually active while maintaining a celibate aura. There is no doubt that a certain number of priests who involve themselves with a minor rather than another priest or adult, repeat the pattern of sexual involvement, acceptance, and love they experienced earlier at the hands of a priest or bishop.

Some bishops and religious superiors are extremely tolerant of extracurricular sexual activities of their priests because the subject is potentially dangerous and explosive. The cover that protects the sexual underworld and its child abusers is tightly woven and intermeshed with other forms of sexual activity, which, although noncelibate, are not in themselves illegal. The network involves too many productive, highly placed, and, in other regards, exemplary men who would be exposed or jeopardized by reform.

In spite of sincere public apologies by some hierarchy, the great threat to church authorities by the child abuse crisis is not the suffering of victims or the loss of manpower or money. Many abusers continued in the priesthood until the 2002 meeting of bishops in Dallas. Sometimes known abusers received promotions. The loose thread of exposed clergy sexual abuse of minors threatens to unravel the whole protective cover of the secret sexual system. The exposed and barren sexual landscape of the church looks starkly like a wasteland of clerical corruption. This *exposure* is the greatest threat.

Scandal—that most dreaded clerical reality—is fear of exposure and truth. The church practices what Machiavelli taught: "It is not essential . . . that a prince [bishop, priest] have all the good qualities I have listed . . . but it is most essential that he should appear to have them."

MANDATORY CELIBACY

Church authorities are adamant that (the rule of mandatory) celibacy has nothing to do with sexual abuse of children. Of course it does. Sexual abuse is always noncelibate activity. Noncelibate behavior by those who profess celibacy is the main ingredient of the stew in which the Catholic clergy find themselves today. The "Winter" report recommended "that the archbishop [St. John's Newfoundland] join with other bishops across Canada to address fully, directly, honestly and without reservation questions relating to the problematic link between celibacy and the ministerial priesthood" (vol. 3, p. 35–54).

There is a strong clerical and lay movement abroad to end mandatory celibacy for diocesan priests and to legitimize optional celibacy for the clergy and ordain women to the deaconate and priesthood. These proposals are worthy of close examination, prayerful rational study, and discussion. But it would be foolhardy to expect that any mere legal adjustment would in itself bring sexual responsibility and integrity to the ministry. The great Protestant experiment has not been entirely successful in this regard although it encourages its ministers to marry and many churches have begun to ordain women. Rejection of discussion on the relationship of celibacy, priesthood, and abuse is crippling to efforts to prevent abuse by clergy.

Bishop Geoffrey Robinson, Auxiliary Bishop of Sydney, asserted that celibacy has to be examined when considering sex offenses of priests and religious: "I've suggested that there are certainly two matters that ought to be put on the table out there. One is celibacy, the other is power and how it is used within the Catholic Church, and they must both be looked at" (Robinson, 1997).

The problem of sexual abuse by the clergy is far more complex than can be resolved by a change in one custom or another. Any effective reform must be based on a reevaluation of the nature of sexuality and the separation of ecclesial power from sex, gender, and money. Only a thoroughgoing reform of the whole sexual system of the church, teaching, and practice will restore credibility to the ministry. Bernard Haring eloquently articulates the quest:

> Since the role of the priest is preeminently that of a credible witness, it is the utmost importance that all church structures, all basic relationships within the church, and the whole moral formation promote and encourage absolute sincerity and transparency. This endeavor also coincides with the critical need to prevent the development of all ecclesiogenic pathologies. Anything that could damage the absolute requirement for priestly sincerity and reliability can never be offered as an acceptable sacrifice to God." (1996, p. 94)

What will it take for the American church to engage seriously in the discussion of sexual abuse by clergy? Father Stephen Rosetti told a group of Father James Porter's victims in a Massachusetts TV studio in 1992, "the Church will not change until it is threatened with bankruptcy." He may be correct.

ETHICAL CODE

A priest's roles are multiple and daunting, involving both public and private interactions with an identical population; for instance, saying mass, preaching, and fostering social administration versus hearing confessions and giving counsel. The complexities of ministry render the boundaries of interaction questionable and in some mixtures even unethical.

The Catholic Church does not have a code of sexual ethical conduct for its priests and bishops. Even canon law does not supply a sexual ethical code. In regard to celibacy/sexuality, the canons deal with ideals, regulation of training for clergy, and prescribed punishments "for external sins against the sixth commandment of the Decalogue (the canons do not use the word sex) *that causes scandal*" (emphasis added).

Little research has been directed to priestly celibacy. It is evident that this dearth of serious consideration on the subject is not because there is little to examine—quite the contrary, as we have seen. Priestly sex and celibacy form a core reality that, if examined, would have immense consequences within the power system of the church (Sipe, 1995). Dr. Carol Ann Breyer said "the movement for optional celibacy in the priesthood is clearly about much more than allowing priests to marry. It strikes at the heart of clerical superiority and gender exclusivity."

This sexual activity, although so common among priests, has been handled secretly by ecclesiastical tolerance, cautions, reprimands, forgiveness, reassignments, or ignoring the behavior with the presumption that it is a phase. The church passes it over as unimportant because everybody in the lay world does it. These attitudes, in spite of any law, are reflected in the church's traditional reaction to sexual abuse of minors. A statement by Philip Jenkins (1994) echoes this mind-set. "It is far from obvious that a given sexual act between individuals of widely different ages constitutes immoral or criminal behavior, still less than it causes grave harm to either participant" (p. 83). It is clear that priest sex has not been a major ecclesiastical concern prior to public scandal.

The church in the United States has spent far more time, effort, and money in pursuing damage control and public relations than on proactive projects for prevention. The dichotomy between the church's public pronouncements and private behavior has spawned extreme criticism from dedicated priests and lay people.

Investigation has made it clear that superiors have known about the nature and extent of clergy sexual activity. They have not dealt with it. Their suggested remedies have so far been defensive and favor getting rid of offenders. Any religion that depends only on external controls for its ministers rather than internalized integrity is certainly in grave crisis. Such a church has failed in its fundamental mission of selecting, educating, commissioning, and monitoring trustworthy ministers.

Physicians and other professions do have sexual codes of ethics and definitions of the appropriate boundaries between doctor and patient. The American Medical Association (1997) makes explicit what is already stated in the Hippocratic oath: "sexual activity with a patient is unethical." In April 1994 the American Psychiatric Association further clarified the duty of a psychiatrist by stating that "sexual activity with a current or former patient is unethical." The therapeutic bond is sacred and eternal. What are the ethics of the pastoral bond?

IMPEDIMENTS TO
ETHICAL DEFINITIONS

The great value of the practice of celibacy is not in question (Sipe, 1996). Bishop Reinhold Stecher of Innsbruck, Austria, wrote in 1997: "For celibacy to be lived with integrity it is essential that the individual affected not suppress the loss of sexual intimacy and companionship but transform it into a healthy, spiritual, pastoral, social, intellectual, service oriented, and creative unfolding." Cardinals, bishops, and priests impede the formation and declaration of the sexual code of ethics when they deny the reality of their sexual activity.

The word *celibacy* is not always a reflection of the actual practice. "Celibacy" should not be a moniker to hide sexual activity or abuse. Fights to maintain denial, to absolve the institution from practical responsibility, and to protect the material resources of the church seldom serve the cause of prevention, or the clarification of an ethical code.

Second, the teaching of the church makes all sexual activity a sin, *omnia peccata causa finita*. If all is a sin, there is nothing to talk about—no chance to foster a sense of growth and development of celibacy or sexual identity. Currently, without a more explicit ethical code, it is impossible to address adequately and effectively the real issues that involve celibacy and sexuality. The achievement of celibacy demands truth and involves the process of internalization.

Prohibitions against discussing priestly sexuality, including masturbation, affairs, homosexuality (also contraception, abortion, sex prior to marriage or after divorce) in any perspective other than the current teachings of the Catholic catechism leave the priest without enlightenment for his pastoral duties or his own growth and guidance. Consequently, he can have compassion for the sinner but the situation actually invites him to sin sexually because of ignorance and isolation.

The delineation of an ethical code must surmount these impediments if the church expects professional status. It must develop a code of ethics no less precise, credible, and demanding than that of other professions.

ELEMENTS OF A CODE OF SEXUAL ETHICS

What would a code of sexual ethics for a priest entail? It would delineate *standards* of conduct that define the appropriate professional behavior of a priest. It would define *accountability* and recognize all the principles of *informed consent*. A code would define the responsibility to ensure competent pastoral care and to deal honestly with those served. It would define the obligation (to use the phraseology of the medical code of ethics) to *expose* those clergy, "deficient in character or competence or who engage in fraud or deception" (AMA, 1997, p. xiv). It would define the responsibility of the bishops and priests to *respect the law*.

Bishops and superiors in effect constitute licensing boards with the obligation to verify the competence of the men they commission, and to protect the public with the sure knowledge that the priests under their jurisdiction are safe. In short, since the church is a hierarchical structure, any ethical code would define the accountability of individuals and the church for the selection, education, commission, and supervision of clergy and the prevention of abuse.

All of the issues surrounding sexual boundaries that apply to therapists are relevant to the education and the practice of the pastoral ministry (Gabbard, 1994). Priests do get lovesick, and are faced with countertransference reactions. They are subject to their own emotional inadequacies caused by the unfinished business of the psychic and spiritual work involved in establishing celibate/sexual identity and maturity. Priests are faced with the daunting commitment to a lifestyle involving sexual deprivation and to creating something positive from it. Some priests must struggle periodically or constitutionally with their own psychopathy—depression, anxiety, obsessions, and personality tendencies including paranoia, borderline states, or narcissism, and the paraphilias.

Priests frequently do get sexually involved. The ideals of celibacy and the physical restrictions of seminary training are not adequate to prevent distortions and abuse. Denial that priests, superiors, and bishops are sometimes sexually active leaves the problems in place. This abandons clergy struggling to become celibate and responsible sexual beings. Lack of a sexual code of ethics endangers lay people and clergy. Priest sexual activity must be openly discussed. The effort to conceal breeds multiple negative consequences for the credibility and integrity of priests and the church.

Informed Consent

Priests must realize their responsibility *when* they become sexually involved. Abel, Becker, and Cunningham-Rathner define the problems of informed consent for a child (1984). Because of the priest's social standing and public claim of celibacy, these criteria can be applied to a priest's interaction with children and adults.

> Informed consent presents four major problems: (1) Does the child [person] understand what he or she consents to? (2) Is the child [person] aware of the accepted sexual standards of his or her community [including the expectation of celibacy for the priest]? (3) Does the child [person] appreciate the eventual possible consequences of the decision? (4) Are the child [person] and the adult [priest] equally powerful *so* that no coercion influences the child's [person's] decision? (p. 94)

A priest's sexual activity with anyone often lacks informed consent. The priesthood is in a position of power. A priest is a person who represents God and presides at religious rituals. He holds the "keys to heaven and hell" in the confessional. He is also in the employ of the church. The requirement of celibacy for his priesthood is not limited to his sacramental or teaching functions.

Denial of priest sexual activity has taken a huge toll on the image of priests and the credibility of the church. Suitable candidates for the ministry cannot be attracted or selected in an atmosphere of denial and untruthfulness. Candidates for the priesthood cannot be adequately educated without frank discussions of their sexuality, the real process and meaning of celibacy, the meaning of sexual accountability for themselves, and their superiors. These involve clear ethical guidelines about sexual activity. Priests must also respect the boundaries and constraints of informed consent *if* they do choose to be sexually active.

Prevention of sexual abuse by priests is a daunting task. The burden transcends the capacities and limits of law and psychiatry and rests squarely on the very core of religion. Haering's moral demand is, "absolute sincerity and transparency." Prevention will not occur without discussion of the *realities* of sexuality and the development of explicit honest norms for sexual responsibility and accountability on every level of the church.

Obstacles to the prevention of abuse by clergy can begin with a sincere personal and institutional examination of conscience. An old formulation is useful.

We have been silent witnesses of evil deeds—, we have been drenched by many storms; we have learnt the arts of equivocation and pretense; experience has made us suspicious of others and kept us from being truthful and open, intolerable conflicts have worn us down and even made us cynical. Are we still of any use? What we shall need is not geniuses, or cynics, or misanthropes, or clever tacticians, but plain, honest, straight-forward men. Will our inward power of resistance be strong enough, and our honesty with ourselves remorseless enough, for us to find our way back to simplicity and straightforwardness?

PART IV

PROCESS AND ATTAINMENT

12

LIVING WITH CELIBACY

The celibate has only one true friend—Jesus Christ
—Fr. Thomas Verner Moore, M.D.

If one dismisses celibacy as unnatural or abnormal, one is restricted to categories of mystery or pathology to explain its structure and process. To be sure, the goal of celibacy is not usual, but that in itself does not render it ipso facto pathological. Spiritual literature customarily clothes celibacy in garments of religious idealism. Conversely, polemical exposés rip off its religious vesture and exploit its naked historical imperfections. Neither reveal celibacy's essential dynamic. Regardless of one's limited comprehension or understanding of an ideal, there is an instinctive admiration for another's undivided dedication. Profound sacrifice in the pursuit of altruism is heroic and admirable even if not imitable.

Those who confuse celibacy with simple sexual abstinence fail to realize that celibacy involves a complex process of development. Even if one cannot define it or trace it accurately, the serious student of celibacy soon becomes aware that there must be an inner dynamic to the practice of this discipline and the pursuit of this ideal.

WHAT IS THE PROCESS
OF CELIBACY?

Two puzzling questions precede the pursuit of the dynamic of process. How does one achieve sexual identity *without* sexual experience? How does one integrate celibate practice *after* sexual experience?

In other words, how does one come to the solid awareness, conviction, and reality that "I am a celibate person"? Clearly, celibacy as I have defined it in chapter 2 is a process that involves the whole person because it involves essential elements of identity.

Since celibacy is the redirection of sexual energy from its original goal of direct discharge to both delayed and derivative gratification, it cannot be attained by a simple act of the will. The achievement of celibacy involves a series of developmental tasks that are ongoing, overlapping, and interactive. Also, since priestly celibacy is a lifelong process, it involves stages of refinement toward completion and integration.

After analyzing the celibate search from hundreds of priests' stories, I have come to formulate the process in a tripartite interactive model.

1. It involves developmental relationships and patterns, many of which precede any celibate intention but which vitally influence the celibate/sexual pattern.
2. There is a process of internalization of the celibate ideal from intention to achievement.
3. There is a sequential process that involves the refinement of the forces from awareness to integration.

In presenting these dynamics—one centrifugal, one centripetal, and one linear—I warn the reader to avoid thinking of this unfolding process as a neatly segmented reality that a schematic presentation might imply. The model represents a perspective on sexual reality from a celibate vantage in the tradition of William James's view of the phenomenal world as "one big buzzing blooming confusion."

DEVELOPMENTAL RELATIONSHIPS

At the core of the celibate search and process is the achievement of a relationship rather than the absence of one. The operative dynamic is centrifugal. The true celibate is able to forge a real and durable relationship with the transcendent. Having done so, he will develop the capacity to realize expanding potential, which, when the relationship is of sufficient satisfaction and meaning, will produce a firmness of identity in the face of the deprivation of direct sexual satisfaction.

Naturally, this developed capacity for a relationship of such depth and magnitude is preceded and conditioned by the parent-child and especially the mother-child bond. No voice has been stronger or clearer in the past half-century in delineating the steps of ego development than that of Margaret Mahler (1979). Her work forms a paradigm for psychological insight into the process of spiritual development.

Just as psychological development does not occur simultaneously with physical birth, spiritual birth is not concomitant with either physical or psychological birth. Spiritual "rebirth" is a traditional biblical concept: "Unless a man be born again he cannot enter the kingdom" (John 3:3). This transformation to a new phase of awareness or existence is mediated by a transcendent power—nonphysical and all-encompassing. Spiritual re-birth puts the believer in an essential and personal relationship of enduring meaning and significance through which he reacts with all other beings in his path.

Celibacy is possible only to the degree that this relationship becomes effective. One life story after another in our case histories of men searching for celibacy verified this core reality: the process and possibility of celibacy are essentially entwined with the capacity for a refined relationship with the unseen of ample force and measure to organize one's existence and energies. As one priest wrote, "Only those who see the invisible can do the impossible." It is the connection with the Ultimate Other that undergirds, infuses, and crowns the celibate quest. In the tradition of Erik Erikson, this conceptualization sees the life cycle as a journey from the Primary Other through and with Significant Others to the Ultimate Other.

1. The Primary Relationship

I can not overemphasize the importance of the first 3 years of life for the development of personality and character in later life. The roots of self-image are firmly established in the first 2 years of life. It is then that the awareness of identity "is maintained by comparison and contrast." It is in this period of time that the predictability of the rhythm of gratification/frustration associated with the loved and loving mother lays the foundations for object constancy and therefore meaningful and satisfying relatedness (Mahler, 1979, pp. 5–6). "The wordless appeal" of the toddler—the expressions of longing, the search for meaning in the newly discovered and expanding world—is directed to the mother for love and praise. These appeals include the wishes for sharing and expansion. How the mother responds to these early needs will forever mark the person who seeks and *must find* all of these same elements in spiritual and celibate relationships (p. 11).

An ongoing loving and supportive bond with an adequate mother, living or dead, seems to be a factor in many celibates' lives. It is not, however, invariable or essential. Some celibates report exactly the opposite: an inadequate or rejecting mother. Whereas for the former, the positive experience is enhanced, continued, generalized, and reproduced in the context of the church and the world, for the latter, deprivation is compensated for, and equilibrium and constancy are found in Mother Church. The institution of the church provides the possibility of compensation, restoration, and regeneration.

One priest who practiced celibacy for years traced the roots of his continuing struggle to an inadequate early relationship with his mother:

> As far back as I can remember, I've never gotten a word of encouragement from her. If I displeased her in any way, she would accuse me of deliberately harassing her. She was constantly disappointed in me—except my priesthood. I think she found her own self-image and worth as the mother-of-the-priest. She would not understand if I were anything else. If I were to leave the priesthood, she would have a serious depression. I see her rarely but call her every couple of weeks or so. But I'm loaded with resentment toward her—confused feelings like I let her down, like she let me down; why the hell didn't she see that I needed love and why do I feel this way about a poor old lady?

This man goes on to report how his priesthood (his "crusade") and sense of well being and righteousness, which comes with serving a cause, have sustained him. He is, as he says, "relaxed and happy" in his ministry. Community and Mother Church have been nourishing and supportive. The frustrations of celibacy were partially compensated for by these rewarding relationships that he could not hope for or duplicate in any other forum.

Not all early deficits can be rehabilitated by celibate alliance, but I have been amazed by the mystery of celibate healing which many priests report. I have been, however, equally moved by the tragic, torturous, and futile efforts some priests have to make attempting to compensate for early developmental deficiencies. The limits of nature are stretched beyond endurance in their celibate search. Grace has too little to build on.

Object constancy is most significant for later spiritual growth, especially for establishing what traditionally is called the "presence of God." The awareness of this *presence* is both necessary and fundamental for celibate development. It is obvious how directly this presence parallels a child's need to retain the mental image of his primary relationships and to be able to recall them for equilibrium as he ventures out into the world.

One thing is absolutely predictable: The quality of all subsequent bonds will be marked by the core primary relationships of the would-be celibate. Those who select candidates for ministry and who train men for celibate dedication are well advised to help them appreciate fully the importance of this endowment for their future growth and interactions.

2. Familial/Developmental

The family can provide the lifelong model for warm, close sharing and for emotionally satisfying relationships that do not involve sexual exchange. It is not accidental that "brother" and "sister," as well as "father" are appellations and paradigms of celibate functioning.

During preadolescence, home and family form the base of a boy's "intellectual and affective life. . . . He uses his friends and companions in the secret pursuit of knowledge about the body and its sexual functions, as partners in sexual games, and in the enactment of sexual fantasies" (Harley, 1975). The histories of many celibates confirm how very significant this early period is in the formation of their sexuality and impulse toward celibacy. Sexual arousal is indiscriminate, and infantile sexuality is a kind of defense against genitality and growing up sexually. The preadolescent boy can have greater fear of the mother than of the father. He can therefore more easily turn away from girls (his mother) and turn toward his father (or other idealized men like priests) for reinforcement of his budding masculinity. Many priests trace their impulse to study for the priesthood from this time in grade school. For this reason a great deal of effort was expended during the 1940s through the 1960s to encourage priestly vocations from this age group.

Many celibates find themselves years later trying to bridge the gap between the prepubertal sexual experience and growth and their adult intellectual and spiritual values. For some men, adolescent asceticism sealed their sexual development at this stage. This explains—but only in part—the relatively higher rate of sexually nondifferentiated, bisexually and homosexually oriented men among the clergy. Some years after the completion of their studies, the thread of development re-emerges to be woven into the fabric of the celibate garment. Celibate identity that is grounded in an avoidance or delay of adolescent sexual conflict will invariably be ambiguous.

Psychiatrists and others have written about the *"prepuberty trauma"* that is utilized to explain a boy's inability to enter into heterosexual activities in adolescence. "This prepuberty trauma of the boy consists of an unconscious provocation of an overt homosexual experience with an older boy or man. When he reaches adolescence, the boy then uses the fact that he had been 'homosexually assaulted' as the rationalization for his homosexual proclivities and concomitant heterosexual difficulties" (Harley, 1975).

There is no question that this is one of the factors attracting a larger number of homosexually oriented men to the priesthood than are in the general population. The atmosphere of tolerance in the church for sexual activity of priests with children also has some relation to this phenomenon.

Several priests who served on seminary faculties in widely separated geographical areas report the frequency of this phenomenon among their students. The exact nature of the sexual experience is important. But more significant is the familial context in which it occurred and the degree to which it is psychically available to the adult for incorporation into his value system, celibate lifestyle, and discipline. For some few celibates, early sexual play is the fountainhead of their process of sexual differentiation and identity.

One priest who later became an American citizen entered training for the priesthood in his home country at 5 years of age—a custom with a centuries-old tradition and very common in his homeland. It is clear from his account that the priests fulfilled maternal and paternal roles. They performed all of the educational, health care, and homemaking services for their charges. Even from this skewed and unusual environment, firm sexual identity and heterosexual orientation are clearly possible.

3. Educational/Formative

Prior to 1975, many priests began their studies for the priesthood during their high school years; others began seminary training in college; and fewer still started after graduating from a college or even after a period of time in the working world or after training in another profession. The shift toward later rather than earlier entry into seminary training is clearly progressive. Earlier entry into studies took advantage of the natural idealism of adolescence about which Anna Freud (1944) and others have spoken (Blos, 1962). The reasons for the semi-seclusion and protective schedules behind the seminary walls were the solidification of the clerical identity and the "preservation of chastity."

We found no celibate—except a few suspected of having Kallmann's syndrome—who denied ever having *any* sexual experience, even if it was relegated to this early period of his life. In fact, for some men early activity formed the prototype of their understanding of others and remained for them the set of calipers with which to measure their own subsequent feelings and reactions. When I observed this, I was reminded of wise mystics who can find the meaning of the universe in a blade of grass—a rare but beautiful thing to encounter.

The formation of bonds of security and emotional and economic sustenance also provided the basis of a brotherhood of lasting shared values and ideals. After more than 50 years of celibate living, one priest said, "I cannot imagine another profession that could supply such love and support."

Priests commonly report, however, that the specific challenges to their sexual identities were not confronted in their education and formation. For many, sex was not dealt with as a lived reality in the seminary. Instead, denial, rationalization, and intellectualization are fostered in the process of seminary training. The real questions surface later in the priests' 30s and even 40s.

There is no question that sexual activity during seminary years is far more restricted than among men of equal age and education elsewhere. It is not unusual for men to abstain from all sexual activity, including masturbation, during their seminary training. However, there is *no correlation* between sexual abstinence during training and later celibate achievement.

The purpose of the satisfying support in a system of both discipline and fraternal relationships is designed to foster an internalization of those two entities. Both are necessary to sustain celibate practice.

4. Ministerial/Service

If celibacy is to thrive, it must be able to withstand the rigorous demands of unrequited loving service. Great satisfaction as well as monumental frustration can accrue to the unselfish attention to the community. The ability to foster and maintain ministerial and service relationships that have enduring and comprehensive meaning for the celibate test his view of Man and God to ultimate depths. What eyes of faith it takes to see Christ in each human and to depend on the transcendent for one's vision and comfort in the face of daily challenge! Spiritual literature abounds with encouragement and warning for the celibate who has progressed to this level of development in his quest.

It is during this long period that the celibate heroes are made and the sexual compromises that threaten integrity are established. Priests whose ministerial relationships *are not* infused by celibate sublimation can provide humanitarian and institutional service. But the quality of relationship bonds are formed and tested by the daily demands that program, further, and refine pastoral interactions. The challenge is to infuse celibacy in those relationships.

Some pastoral situations provide a missionary-like challenge wherein the demands of service are extremely clear-cut and the sources of gratification global (i.e., progress of the community group rather than individual). Such situations were often reported as sustaining, even if exacting.

The degree to which ministerial relationships are satisfying is related to the quality and mastery of earlier stages of relational achievement. The isolate and the person of rigid ego adaptation—even if they have attained a record and degree of sexual control and abstinence—are not well defended against the pressures and demands of service. For them, a period of sexual experimentation tends to be destructive of general relatedness since it cannot be incorporated into their celibate identity. Instead, it is inclined to abort the celibate quest altogether or, more commonly, leaves their ministerial rigidity intact and establishes a split-off sexual life. *Inflexibility is not a good support for celibate exercise.*

Celibacy and the achievement of celibate relationships require a personality of fluid ego adaptation. The awareness of the transcendent and the creativity required of living one's life and serving in accordance with that awareness demand a man of unusual inner resourcefulness. He must possess a strong capacity for the memory of relatedness as well as for the projection of as yet unrealized relatedness and hope. This flexibility, demonstrated by many active celibates, revealed an independence of spirit and will which was not overly dependent upon institutional props.

A great deal of work must be done to understand the link between institutional alignment and celibate bonds. At best, dedication to the "community" of the church is a correlative of good celibate adjustment. At worst, it is an immature reliance on a power structure and a failure of differentiation that makes all relationships hollow. Indeed, hollow relationships do not reinforce celibacy but rather lead to sexual activity that is either problematic or unhealthy, or both. With the accumulation of priests' stories, at times I was forced to ask myself the question: "Does one have to be a little bit anticlerical to be a good celibate?"

One thing is certain: men of honesty and creative adaptability can more easily incorporate noncelibate experience without rationalization or splitting. Some priests felt that a period of noncelibacy, honestly dealt with, had enhanced their eventual celibate practice and enriched their subsequent ministerial/service relationships.

5. Expanding Awareness of Universal Interrelatedness

In our estimation, lived celibacy leads to greater similarity than dis-similarity between celibates and noncelibates in this one regard: Many men described the experience of a greater inner interrelatedness with all human beings as their celibate identities solidified. Several times this phenomenon took on the quality of a "religious experience." I first became aware of this interrelatedness around a cluster of men who de-scribed near-death experiences and how these had affected them. The keys to such an experience are its subsequent impact on one's life and its sustaining quality.

One man described a month-long "high" during which he had an acute awareness of both the presence of God and his own oneness with others. The time was vivid to his recall even after several years had passed. His subsequent productivity and accomplishment were visible, public, and remarkable.

Usually such an episode follows a period of turmoil or felt disinte-gration. It comes suddenly, unexpectedly, and in such diverse places as a busy street, at home in the middle of the night, on a beach, or in an airplane. In an instant, the one having the experience can see things in a unity that he had not previously known. Whether coupled with an incident or not, many celibates reported a sense of cognizance that could be labeled "universal interrelatedness." They were clearly able to transcend emotionally their institutional and cultural barriers. The ex-perience did not seem to be parochial or provincial and had a quality of trans-institutionalism in spite of a firm sense of clerical identity.

This feeling of relatedness appears to be the natural outcome of the process of celibacy and the refinement of one's relationships. It is the culmination of a progression whereby sincere, devoted, and highly motivated men seek the highest spiritual ideal of love and ser-vice to humankind. They arrive at this point by coming to terms with the sexual dimensions of their lives rather than by avoiding them. These men are self-aware and can recount subtle shades of "sexual" feelings that were generated in their ministries—the kind of *parental* love and *fraternal* warmth that suffused their service. The richness of their inner lives and motivations gave an analytic clarity and integra-tion to all of their relationships.

INTERNALIZATION

As priests describe their experience of celibacy/sexuality, one is challenged to comprehend the second dynamic of the process: a centripetal movement from *intention* or attraction to *goal* and integration. What motivates a man to sacrifice his sexuality? Naturally, one may say, "the love of God"; but if this is the only reason one can give in recounting the development of his celibacy, he ironically is very suspect both in his self-critical capacity as well as in his honesty. The determination to be celibate is usually adjunctive to and derivative of some perceived good or advantage. A person or the image of a persona whom one wants to imitate mediates the intention. The advantages of education, prestige, or opportunity, if not power, are commonly mentioned as early motivating factors. The first step toward the internalization of celibate identity is very significant since it prefigures all the stages to follow.

1. Celibate Image and Intention

This first step involves the formation of an image and awareness of an intention. It announces the direction of the process toward achievement and includes the separate but interrelated tasks of comprehension, conversion, self-control, and commitment.

The image of celibacy is usually formed through the family, church, or school where the celibate model was extolled or revered. Conversely, a negative image can inspire—creating opposition to wealth, prestige, power or rejection of one's own family's values. In any case, one comprehends the image in personal terms.

Comprehension is the cognizance of a meaning of life and of one's existence that is "one's own." That awareness may or may not be validated by a wide segment of social groups. It is the *sense* of vocation: One finds a place for oneself in the scheme of things. At first, it may just be a vague awareness that one "should be" a celibate. The awareness is a cornerstone because over the subsequent decades of the man's life, it will support the expanding edifice that is his place of service.

I have never ceased to be amazed at the young age at which many celibates record the first such awareness of their vocation. Many have memories dating from their 5th year of life. There are many celibates who *know* that the priesthood is a resolution of their oedipal strivings, even if they can not comprehend the full meaning of the dynamic. They recount a consciousness that they could be a "father" of commanding authority—one to whom their own fathers could give obeisance. At the same time, they identify with the loved mother and preserve a special relationship with her.

Several celibates came to an awareness of their life goal after serving in the armed forces during World War II, the Korean conflict, or Vietnam. Some were pressed by their conflict of conscience. Others tested the "hippie" culture and were disappointed. Some veterans witnessed deprivation or degradation that overwhelmed them. Some men sensed a futility in the direction of their lives and felt they could "do better." Commonly, the example of some person whose life they viewed as meaningful was the impetus for their "seeing the way." The example of a priest was a near universal element in history of a man who chose that route for himself.

Some priests spoke of the Depression of the 1930s and the economic hardships and insecurities suffered by their families as a counterpoint to the stability and advantage they perceived among their parish clergy. "Celibacy," one priest good-naturedly said, "seemed like a fair exchange at the time."

A death in a family can be a powerful force in the rearrangement of values and in the interpretation of life's meaning. The death of a parent, especially prior to their adolescence, was a factor in the lives of a number of priests who had practiced celibacy for many years or who had at last achieved it. It almost seemed that the death of the loved one reinforced the reality of the transcendent persona who loved them and was part of the unseen reality.

Even the threat of the death of a parent or loved one can be the precipitator of a comprehension of reality that invites a celibate response. One priest who had practiced celibacy for 16 years told of his initial awareness of his vocation. He was in the 5th grade of a Catholic school; his mother was hospitalized at the time. While praying for her recovery, he felt that he *should* be a priest, but he was also acutely aware that part of him was equally resistant to the idea.

The perception of the conflict seems to be an important factor in the validity of the resolution. Many celibates relate the agony of the initial formation of their celibate intent.

2. Awareness of the Capacity to Be Celibate

How does a man know if he has a capacity for celibacy and does not merely harbor an admiration for a personally unattainable ideal? First, he must know himself and his ability to enter into and sustain relationships. Second, he must have some knowledge of the process that supports that ability.

Since the Council of Trent, the seminary-training period has been meant to inculcate into the young aspirant a pattern of life, which will develop the necessary internal discipline to sustain celibate practice. Three other factors support motivation toward the priesthood: economic dependency; the position of specialness in a social setting; and a measure of power. In some way these factors do achieve a certain realization, at least temporarily. Many men report that regardless of subsequent sexual activity, the period of their seminary training was relatively free of sexual experimentation.

In the assessment of their vocation, most men experienced the call primarily to the priesthood and only secondarily to celibacy. That meant that a sense of inner change or the need for conversion was vaguely present in their initial awareness of the vocation. Somehow there was a need to be sexually restrained. With many, their capacity for celibacy was first confronted by an *experience* of conversion.

Conversion or *metanoia* is an ancient concept that involves not merely a comprehension or cognizance of life's meaning but also a change in heart or behavior that reflects that new awareness. It is, therefore, a test of capacity. In the same way, the cognizance of a transcendent reality and a "presence" that one can count on leads to the next step—the translating of that reality into behavior that reflects the relatedness. The re-evaluation of one's past life produces a sense of one's imperfections or a consciousness of one's sinfulness and unworthiness. At the same time it yields gratitude for being part of such a relationship. "Accepted," "validated," "loved," and "chosen" are the feelings, frequently expressed, that lead to the conversion or the sense that one's life has not been good enough, but it can be better.

Frequently, sexual feelings or former alliances are re-evaluated. Usually the younger, in age, when this part of the process is experienced the more vague the sexual context of the conversion. However, it is inevitably present, no matter how ill defined. Some priests relate many years later how their childhood sexual play was the chief element in their self-evaluation and conversion. Those who are older at the time of their conversion or who have had more sexual experience than others up until that point feel greater guilt, specifically for their sexual activity. At this stage, these variables all play a part in the test of one's ability for sexual control and sublimation.

A priest who had practiced celibacy for nearly 20 years explained that although he felt he had a capacity for celibate dedication, he needed a strict and structured atmosphere because he had lived a sexually free and active existence prior to his conversion. There are others who, although they have had very little sexual experience prior to their conversion, are acutely aware of their sexual desires and their potential capacity for acting on them.

3. Knowledge of the Process (How to Be Celibate)

Control or the ability to influence one's existence and environment, is part of the task of and reward for the celibate quest. The image of the athlete in training is borrowed from the Bible and St. Paul and has inspired many celibates. There is a justifiable pride in accomplishing a difficult feat—one that takes discipline, practice, sacrifice, and a willingness to engage a powerful, unrelenting opposing force. Regulating one's sexual instinct surely involves all of the above.

The question is *how?* Traditionally, the *system* has been depended upon to instill the necessary self-control and skills to achieve celibacy. Seminaries used to be finely tuned programs based on monastic tradition that fostered a sense of self-denial, order, community, and shared values. Ironically, the system has not proved to be particularly successful in inculcating lifelong celibacy. Sixty-eight percent of men religious respondents to a study of priests agreed with the following statement: "The traditional way of presenting the vow of chastity in

religious formation has often allowed for the development of imper-
sonalization and false spirituality." Eighty percent of the same group
felt they were well aware of the "implications" of their vow of chastity
(Greeley, 1972, p. 364).

According to the informants I interviewed, training programs and
the seminary system failed to educate them as to how to be celibate
in three ways: There was an avoidance of direct and open *discussion
and debate* about sexuality. A system of secrecy surrounded all personal exploration of sex and celibacy. There were only abstract assumptions, no personal, explicit witnesses of celibacy, its struggles
and achievements.

Celibacy cannot be practiced without confronting one's own sexuality as well as the whole subject in a realistic way. Sociologist Father
John L. Thomas told me, "A celibate should know everything there is
to know about sexuality short of experience." I know from years of
teaching in Catholic seminaries how difficult it is to teach human sexual development to candidates for the priesthood. Is Father Thomas's
ideal attainable?

In the seminary, when sexual tensions, temptations, or personal
questions arise, they are handled by secrecy—in the confessional or
counseling office. If sexual behavior or acting out comes to the attention of authorities, invariably it is dealt with in the most clandestine
manner possible to avoid scandal. Many an idealistic, serious, or
naïve seminarian goes through his training feeling that there is a sex-
free zone enjoyed by all his comrades and teachers. His own thoughts
or temptations can disturb him. Occasionally an exceptional story,
incident, or rumor confronts him. This was very much the character-
ization of seminary experiences recounted prior to the mid-1970s.

During the 1980s and '90s the number of candidates for the
priesthood seriously declined. According to studies conducted by
church researchers, the intellectual qualifications diminished and the
seminarians' families of origin were more conflicted than previously.
Reports of sexual acting out by students and faculty and the percep-
tions of a "gay sub-culture" grew (Cozzens, 1998, 2002; Hoge, 2002).

The presumption that the seminary faculty is celibate has been perpetuated without requiring personal witness. The faculty employs the
same system of avoidance and secrecy that protects their students.

One priest who had a position of authority said that he had presumed the celibate practice of his seminary faculty while he was a
student. Subsequently, he learned unequivocally that nine of his in-
structors had lived sexually active lives while performing their official
tasks well or admirably. Within the seminary, there is no tradition of
personal witness: "This is what celibacy means to me. This is how *I*
practice it and have achieved it." St. Augustine's penetrating *Confessions* have served generations of priests as a source of inspiration and
a convenient excuse for hiding their personal journey.

4. Practice

The sustained intention to be celibate—even with a capacity for sublimation and control and backed up by a solid knowledge of sexuality
and how it impinges on one's being and behavior—needs practice to
achieve reality. If virtue were attained merely by not perpetrating
vice, prisons would be bastions of holiness. If celibacy were merely
the absence of sexual activity, some of the ranks of the married would
have to be reclassified as celibate. The path from intention to integration is not traversed without risk. As part 2 of this volume "Practice
Versus the Profession," illustrates, not all those who profess celibacy
officially practice it. The question here is what constitutes an abandonment of the celibate goal and what constitutes part of a learning
process and a refinement of one's ideals.

Many priests spoke forthrightly about their celibate/sexual development and recounted failures or transgressions. Many of their stories revealed heroic struggles, tender, and humane reminiscences with loving
gratitude for relationships or incidents that temporarily broke their
vow but led them back to the pursuit of celibacy—chastened but wiser.
As far as I can tell, it is impossible to codify this paradox of spirit and
struggle wherein "sin" may indeed serve the ends of growth, maturity,
and finally, virtue.

Many psychiatrists who have treated priests speak of the challenging experiences they witness in a priest's sexual involvement—healthy
by standards of human sexual development, yet a violation of the man's
conscience and explicit church norms. Conscientious confessors witness the same struggle. The important thing for the person wishing to

practice and achieve celibacy is that the struggle remain an *honest* part of the celibate search—not hidden in denial, justified self-servingly by rationalization, or split from one's ministerial life. All of these maneuvers tend to derail the process of celibacy, at times irrevocably. It is one thing to ally oneself with David justifying his hypocrisy to Nathan, and quite another to sing the Miserere with him.

It takes delicate and unflinching self-assessment to distinguish between a *felix culpa*—which leads to greater spiritual awareness and dedication—and a pattern of compromise and self-indulgence. The literature on celibacy is almost exclusively inspirational and idealistic. Yet real-life witness and history will neither destroy the ideal nor lessen the inspiration. The lack of this real dimension in the literature and teaching of celibacy becomes glaring as one tries to explore the practice and process of celibacy. The Thomas Merton archives have much to contribute toward filling this gap (see Mott, 1984, pp. 435–54).

It is the duty of bishops to see that the priests they ordain are not sexually naïve. Correlatively a priest who cultivates his sexual immaturity is at a great disadvantage in pursuing the celibate process. Incredible stories about the sexual misuse/abuse of others abound in the histories of men pursuing the practice of celibacy. Some priests are quite open in admitting their former "ignorance," "arrogance," "folly," and "naiveté." A few cunning and experienced men or women deliberately set out to become sexually intimate with a priest. Clearly a few priests are victimized. Some of the people I interviewed had complex motivations. They assigned themselves the task of sexually "educating" the obviously uninitiated. I interviewed several women who felt a sense of obligation to teach a priest about sex. One took great pride in the number and high-ranking clerics for whom she had provided the first heterosexual encounter. Another woman, eager to bring priests "out of the closet," was active in setting up inexperienced priests with laymen who were comfortable in their own homosexual lifestyles.

Only on a person-by-person, case-by-case can the real meaning of sexual behavior by one dedicated to celibacy be determined. Is a period of sexual involvement merely a passage—an incident to be understood as part of the paradoxical and difficult pursuit of an ideal? Is it a temporary abandonment of the celibate search? Is it the initiation of a sexual pattern stripping celibacy of any real meaning? Is it psychological pathology, simple hypocrisy, or both?

The revelations of how bishops have handled sexually abusive priests demonstrate how unrefined and inept the discernment of the process of celibacy is on the highest levels of the church.

There are priests who also report a very rigid and obsessive-like period in which their self-absorption with the avoidance of sex was so energy consuming that they lost all freedom and fire for their life of service. Priests speak of times when it is easier to practice celibacy than to face the risks of confronting their own sexual identities.

5. Commitment

The initial stage of the celibate process is the determination that the relationship—or the vocation—is worth the sacrifice. Men find themselves invited to "come near" like the call to Moses from the burning bush (Exodus 3) or of Jesus, "Come follow me and I will make you fishers of men" (Matt. 4:19). Commitment is the thrilling alignment of one's energies in the service of *the* cause. It unifies the attention and energies of one's existence with *The One* who commands.

At base, it is the willingness to serve which validates the commitment. Those who are primarily or largely self-serving will be betrayed in the end by their sexual instincts. An excessive desire for acclaim will leave celibate striving undefended in the face of inevitable confrontation.

In his autobiography, Gandhi notes the relationship between the practice and commitment phases of celibacy:

> As I look back upon the twenty years of the vow, I am filled with pleasure and wonderment. The more or less successful practice of self-control had been going on since 1901. But the freedom and joy that came to me after taking the vow had never been experienced before 1906. Before the vow I had been open to being overcome by temptation at any moment. Now the vow was a sure shield against temptation. The great potentiality of *brahmacharya* daily became more and more patent to me. (1957, p. 209)

Commitment to a cause that is essentially beyond oneself demands a level of integrity and self-honesty of unusual magnitude. The temptation to compromise is ubiquitous, as is the tendency to rigidity—both of which ill prepare one to meet the demands of growth in service. Once a colleague commented on the healthy adaptation of a celibate of singular note as a man "possessing the quality of tempered steel—strong and flexible."

It is also this commitment that serves as the example to the community of believers. The single-minded devotion to the cause and the undivided attention to the service of religious conviction are needed and admired in the human community. It "enriches a nation," as Gandhi pointed out.

A certain level of commitment is involved even in the first stage—intention—and is refined and tested through the successive stages. However, real commitment cannot be accomplished without celibate/sexual knowledge and the risk/practice of celibate service in vivo—in real life, interacting with real people. Growing commitment inspires stability and predictability of response and behavior based on a fine-tuned and more or less accurate self-perception. It is apparent how interdependent this phase is on a model of relationships. The commitment is not to some abstract ideal but to a person. This, of course, demands that one's own personhood be clear, including one's sexuality.

6. Achievement and Integration

The achievement of celibacy is not the accidental passage of sexual feelings into the oblivion of physical senescence. One cannot be celibate by accident. One has to achieve it, since celibacy involves the integration of one's identity without the ongoing support and benefit of a sexual friendship. The person who has achieved celibacy can be said to be an integrated human being with knowledge of both self and reality. The use of his energies in the service of life is consistent, transparent, and tested by life. Many priests are reluctant to claim the "achievement" of celibacy. They are always waiting for the next temptation or period of stress that might reactivate their imagination and overpower their resolve.

However, sexual abstinence can also reinforce itself. I do not know if this is in part a physiological phenomenon or if the success of sublimation becomes so effective in some people that the sexual drive is truly disenfranchised. A number of older priest informants reported contradictory experiences of prolonged sexual abstinence. One group stated that temptation to sexual activity and sexual interest itself diminished with prolonged periods of abstinence. The other group maintained that sexual interest and enticement remained high although their discipline and commitment became easier to maintain despite increased periodic internal pressure.

Internalized celibacy is not directly apparent; its accomplishment is integrated into the man's life goals and meanings. The lifelong or prolonged discipline is not external, as is the flagellate's. The focus is not the subjection of the senses but rather the life system and productivity that reinforce the celibacy. There is no question that each man has a system of discipline, parts that were more apparent to the inquirer than to the celibate, since for the celibate the system seemed to be such a natural part of his life.

Prominent in the system was a routine of prayer. I was struck by the amount of time devoted each day to prayer and how it was placed to meet individual needs and schedules. One man made a "holy hour" each noon, during which time he could defend himself from professional demands since it was his lunch hour. He said people could better understand his being unavailable to take calls because of lunch than because he was "just praying."

Other men reserved the early hours of the day for the bulk of their prayer. Often, however, the system of prayer was woven throughout the day in short periods—times during which the men would pray the rosary or spend some moments in recollection and self-examination. Not a man among them was afraid to be alone; even the most sociable in temperament commented on his ability to be at peace by himself.

Celibate integration is marked by vital intellectual interests. Sometimes these interests are in areas quite esoteric for men of the cloth, such as mechanics, astronomy—or another avocation at least symbolically appropriate—sheep husbandry. Golf was mentioned as a common interest among priests, as it is among other professional men in the United States. However, it does not seem to correlate with the achievement of celibacy in any particular fashion the way some other activities do.

When asked what factors fostered his successful celibate dedication, one elderly priest responded tersely, "fishing." He said he trusted priests who fished. In fact, fishing and gardening were mentioned prominently by priests who considered themselves successful celibates.

Sex does not disappear entirely from consciousness even after years of celibate dedication. One 78-year-old man said that he did not watch certain things on television, citing the June Taylor dancers as an example, because he found them "unnecessarily stimulating." However, another priest of similar age and equal discipline and devotion relished an occasional visit to Radio City Music Hall with its Rockettes, not finding them sexually tantalizing. He did say, though, that he avoided certain literary productions that he thought might "distract" him.

Those priests who reported having had a good deal of sexual activity prior to their vow of celibacy or early in the process of their celibate search could admit to the availability of their memories. Nevertheless, only a few had to manufacture extraordinary or heroic means such as fasts or physical deprivation to "preserve" their achievement. As one priest said, "Life has a way of keeping me humble."

TEMPORAL STAGES

Although celibacy can become an integrated reality after a period of time, there seems to be a series of stages through which the seeker must pass. From the men we interviewed, we got a firm impression that the stages cluster around certain time periods. Therefore, this model is a linear one.

1. Initial Awareness/Depression: Gain/Loss

Every man who wanted to be celibate described an initial awareness, however vague, of a sense of loss. One mature priest who had traversed most of the stages of celibacy said that there were moments at each stage when he had experienced what he called "an instant stab of genital grief." I was tempted to characterize each stage as a kind of depression, but in the end I decided that the term carried too much of a one-dimensional mental health quality to it. However, the first inner determination to be celibate always has this depressive quality to it, no matter how positively a man perceived the benefits of the priesthood. Interestingly, this experience does not always precede one's determination to be a priest or even coincide with it. We interviewed some priests who had not experienced even this first stage—but then they were not practicing celibacy either.

Not all men conceptualized the downside of this stage as having to do with sex, but I am convinced that this sense of loss has much to do with the men's blurry anticipation of the future lack of a sexual outlet and the sacrifice of a sexual relationship. In men of unusual intuition, the perception seemed accurate regarding the direct sexual component of this stage, that is, they were aware at the time of forgoing a future sexual relationship, and their memory of this stage was quite clear.

In others, there appeared to be a good deal of secondary revision, that is, in light of subsequent experience and reflection, they realized that the sacrifice of intimate sexual relationships was required. This later awareness confirms the essential sexual component of the original experience. One priest said, "I realized that I would have to live my life like a man who was deprived of an arm or leg. I would do the best I could, but nothing would give me the use of a limb I didn't have." He and others expressed experience of the gospel meaning of being a "eunuch for Christ." With men like this, the choice was conscious. Others had to use denial to blunt for a time the awareness of what it was they were giving up.

The core depression is an inner battle—a sense that one *must* follow a certain path that is abhorrent or at least disagreeable. The *must* is not of the compulsive kind—as if one cannot help oneself or is moved by external forces. Nor is it of the nature of the loss of liberty, for the choice can be accompanied by a tremendous sense of inner freedom and determination, which unfortunately in itself will not alleviate the depression. Any celibate, when pressed, will be able to recall this depressive stage that may last from a week to several months—rarely as long as a year. A feeling of quiet peace, which can be quite memorable, usually followed resolution. "Joy," "peace," and "security," are words often used to describe the resolution of this initial sadness.

People of deep religious temperament often have an underlying personality component that can be called mildly depressive. The Greeks used the term "melancholic" to identify one of the four basic personality types. This kind of person, sensitive to the inner life and given to intellectual rumination, is well represented among devout men and women.

2. Like Me/Not Like Me

Priests report a post-training phenomenon that commonly occurs sometime between the 2nd and 5th years after ordination (i.e., postvow). For the priest, it constitutes an awareness of the degree and the manner in which people outside the clerical environment are "like me" or "not like me." Some of these clergy were relatively isolated from the secular world from 3 to 13 years prior to their ordination. Often, the ordination itself marks a dramatic shift in surroundings from the sequestered religious system to an open, semi-religious, or even frankly secular environment. The young man who was encapsulated and protected to some degree by a group of men who shared his beliefs, education, and ideals and who behaviorally marched more or less to the same officially regulated cadence now finds himself among people of widely varying education and religious practice. His chosen drumbeat is only one rhythm vying for orchestration. He must now simultaneously fit in and hold his own. Reflecting on this period of his life, one priest said, "I trained with the angels and then had to fight on the devil's own turf."

Especially since 1960, there has been a conscious effort in the church to bridge the gap between theoretical training and practical application. An interesting paradox comes to mind. Is it that priests are not prepared for the world, or is it that—closed to the mystery of celibacy—the world is not prepared for priests? My years of observation have convinced me that the apparent deficit in the transition from education to active service is not one of pastoral technique but one of sexual and *celibate identity* in light of the pastoral demands.

The period after ordination is not necessarily a conscious jolt. It all seems so natural; it is the achievement of a training goal. At least initially, most of the men feel personally well prepared. Even in circumstances where priests continue to live in a rather restricted environment, there is greater freedom and responsibility after ordination. People—even fellow priests or religious—put a new kind of demand on the priest. He is expected to sustain a demand for intimate sharing. He must respond to inner needs of others who have the expectation, "You will help."

The intimate sharing with parishioners, the self-revelations that people make to their priest, and the discovery of what people are really like, confront the young celibate with an awareness of how much he has changed or not changed since he began his training. Many priests ordained prior to 1970 tell of the hours they spent in the confessional, particularly prior to Christmas and Easter. They relate how their traditional views of sexuality and the sinfulness of certain sexual behaviors were challenged by the existence of good people whom they had come to know and respect whose sexual lives they were now privy to.

"Everyone has a sex life except me," said a young celibate in this stage of his search. "I'm not sure I want to spend my whole life sleeping alone," said another man who had vowed celibacy 3 years earlier. Both statements reflect the necessary confrontation of the celibate with the reality that most people are not like him. His own self-definition is in opposition to others. He *is* different.

The most successful negotiation of this stage of celibate internalization involves a solidification of one's celibate self by role definition and by identification with the community of celibates.

It is not infrequent that a certain amount of sexual experimentation is indulged in at this stage. Some men will use the experimentation as a period of testing their sexual identity. This activity may involve a few incidents or it may be a brief abandonment of celibate practice in some of the ways I have discussed in this book, only to return to a celibate search with renewed determination. Other men at this time assume a stance of functional adherence to their ministerial life but embark on a pattern of sexual activity that obviates any real celibacy. Still others will give up the priesthood to return to secular life and sexual practice.

3. In Control/Controlled By

Clerical celibacy exists in a framework of authority. The power structure in turn supports a man living within it. Sooner or later the ties with authority must be clarified, absorbed, and internalized. In one sense the relationship with power must be desexualized. If we take only one facet of the authority structure—the *filial*, where the church and her superiors assume the parental roles of protector, nurturer, and role model—we can see that sooner or later one must leave that mode to become his own man. By so doing, his conviction, values, goals, and behaviors fall under his control and there will be progressively less dependence on and devotion to externals. This movement is an internal one beyond authority; it is necessary for mature celibate practice.

Celibates most commonly report this stage clustering in the 13th to 16th years post-vow, although we have examples of it much earlier and much later. There is always an adolescent-like quality to this phase of celibate resolve. One realizes, as does an adolescent, that he cannot hope for all that he had expected from his "parents." With the dissolution of the mental construct of external control, the celibate is threatened with a new freedom. The extremes of response are to reject internalization and become a toady—a stance that does little to enhance celibacy and at times becomes a cover for a sexual relationship or even deviant behavior—or to rebel mindlessly, rejecting all authority and sexual restraint at the same time. Unfortunately many church officials are picked from the group who choose the former path.

Especially for men who have been truly celibate into their 30s, this is a period of severe trial. They have genuinely cast their lot with the celibate fraternity, sharing interests, fate, economy, spirituality, and often aesthetics—just like a family. Now they find themselves on their own in an emotional way they have never experienced before. It can constitute a disillusionment of major proportions.

A number of our informants reported their first conscious discovery of masturbation at this stage of their development. One priest had had an unusually successful course of studies and work into his 30s. His personality, intelligence, humor, and ability to translate policy into human terms had made him a favorite of teachers, students, and church superiors. He was the perfect organization man. The death of a powerful man in the church whom he had loved like a father and his subsequent replacement by a person who resented our informant's prestige and popularity precipitated a personal crisis leading him to experience a period of sexual confusion unlike any he had sustained previously.

Although some priests' stories record deep personal devotion and then disenchantment with a particular authority figure, many are not dependent on one person or circumstance. Rather they relate the progressive awareness of where the supports for celibacy must ultimately rest—in the self.

Humanae Vitae, a 1968 encyclical condemning artificial birth control, provided a crisis for many priests. It was the most commonly mentioned catalyst in many of the men in our study who were at this stage of celibate refinement. Questioning the credibility of the church's teaching on contraception for married people precipitated questions about celibacy also. The pope's teaching jarred one 40-year-old priest. He could not subscribe to it in good conscience. He used the occasion to re-evaluate and rededicate himself to celibacy at that same time, stating, "That church [meaning those who teach that all means of birth control are sinful] is not the church to which I belong."

Movement beyond external authority to greater internalization is the salient factor at this stage of celibate development. To navigate it well, one must reach a new level of relationship with the transcendent and with one's self-identity. One man reported that it was at this stage of his life that he really learned courage. As he said, "You can't count on anyone else if you are looking for a triumph over a biological imperative!"

The intensification of reliance on one's spiritual life increases rather than decreases as time passes. The relationship with the celibate fraternity deepens but is less dependent if this stage is mastered.

Productivity increases as the celibate retrenches. Literary accounts of priests' lives by sensitive authors like J. F. Powers, Graham Greene, and Georges Bernanos reveal the process of the struggle. There is a novel by Edwin O'Connor entitled *The Edge of Sadness* (1961) that describes beautifully the mood of this period.

St. Ignatius Loyola (1491–1556), the founder of the Society of Jesus, the largest order of religious priests, was a master of celibate psychology. He required that after 12 or 13 years in training his followers spend a year in reflection and rededication. His intuitive awareness dictated that there was something significant at this point in time and experience for the celibate that needed to be addressed. The witness of numerous priests who had no contact with his ideas validates his intuition.

4. Alone/Lonely

"Lonely" is one of the most frequent replies when one asks a celibate how he feels. Loneliness is a lifelong struggle for anyone who is serious about maintaining a deep relationship. It makes one aware of the untraversed and untraversable chasm that separates people who love one another.

Loneliness is a deeply personal privation that takes on different colorings at different times in life. Its roots are in the first relationship with mother, who ideally was neither too close nor too far from the child. A mother who can accept a child—being present to him as a partner in fulfilling his own needs—and yet be centered solidly in herself is an appropriate model of the human-transcendent interaction. A priest who enjoyed training and is pursuing a ministerial career that involves similar support from the church and her authorities will be well prepared for this stage of the celibate process.

To some degree, each of the previous stages deals with loneliness. Each stage involves a separation. Each contains a risk because it demands a shift in the way the celibate relates to himself, to other people, and to the primary object of his affection—the transcendent.

Inevitably a time comes in each celibate's search when he has to rise above loneliness—to transform it to a state of *aloneness*. This maturation is the final step in resolving the illusion that primal merging is possible.

A great deal needs to be said about the distinction between "lonely" and "alone." It is so vital to the resolution of inner conflict and the achievement of the goal. To be alone in the way that I intend means that one is able to accept the reality of one's self and destiny, and this acceptance requires a sense of the reality of the transcendent and of one's dependence on and relationship with that reality. Aloneness is not anti-community, anti-authority, or anti-work. It is a stance beyond community. It exists beyond the boundaries of external authority. It is the foundation and capstone of productivity. At this stage of celibate living the single-mindedness required "on account of the kingdom" is tested to its limit, and receives its greatest reward.

This stage is best defined by celibates who have been ordained for more than 2 decades (22 to 27 years) when they are confronted with the question: "Is it worth it?" The core of the crisis is doubt. Have the sacrifices made and the work done been of real value to anyone? Is it worth going on aware that to enter more deeply into celibacy obviates any possibility of a meaningful companionable relationship in old age? Men in the throes of this crisis report discouragement at seeing wizened old men grow cranky or dependent on alcohol as a way of combating their bitter loneliness.

By this stage, most priests have developed healthy celibate friendships and have been observant of their celibate discipline. Whereas passion needed temperance at earlier stages of development, at this stage it is the lack of companionship rather than sexual discharge that threatens the celibate commitment. "The pearl of great price" and the "heart's being where one's treasure is" are analogical attempts to describe the unswerving dedication to the service of others which is required to negotiate this stage of celibate growth.

The person who cannot tolerate true aloneness cannot move to a level of celibate integration. He therefore remains perpetually vulnerable to sexual compromises even after years of discipline. Celibate aloneness requires a level of sexual identity, resolve, and dedication to purpose that remains constant in the absence of external support. Many priests fail to make this final step. Or they are saddled with the choices they made at earlier stages when passion and loneliness interfered with negotiating earlier celibate challenges. The unfortunate term "celibate marriage" reflects the option some priests take when faced with the specter of an aloneness they cannot fathom.

The aloneness embraced by those who are able to do so is neither antisocial nor schizoid. It is rather based on sexual resolution, a deep relationship with the transcendent, and an ability to see the transcendent in other people. When I asked one man how he had grown through this stage, he smiled and quoted Gandhi: "If you can't find Christ in the person next to you, you can't find him anywhere."

5. Integration

Some special quality—call it mystic—surrounds men who have integrated celibacy firmly and unequivocally into their being and behavior. The awareness of the transcendent in themselves and others, past and future, comes together in them and in their work. At times, they do record moments that might be called ecstatic or might be classed as spiritual peak experiences, but the real test of their resolve is in their daily lives. They have a spiritual transparency—they indeed are what they seem to be. They are not without the faults or idiosyncrasies developed in pursuing a rarefied form of existence and service. But they also typify what is written about in the literature as a true eschatological witness. These men point to "life beyond" and to values not yet achieved. They have triumphed as much as humans can over a biological imperative. They exercise a freedom of service to their fellow humans unbound by any institutional restraints. They are what they set out to be: men of God.

It is easier to find men who will relate their celibate/sexual struggles than it is to find men who can talk in the first person about their achievements and integration. This in part is because integration is accompanied by a deep sense of humility; and in part it is because these men are a minority. The tendency to deal with celibacy only in idealistic and legalistic terms rather than in terms of process and personal history militates against a realistic literature that genuinely supports celibacy. These men both validate the process and approach the ideal.

We need more direct witness from these men. For me to become more biographical at this point would expose the best examples to recognition against their wishes. It is my hope that this formulation of a model of celibacy will encourage more celibates to expose the process of their own search. What I do know from the few men in the study who can unquestionably be categorized as having integrated celibacy beyond all of its stages is that they have transcended the self to a level beyond sexuality, when "male and female, and also Jew and Greek" no longer have meaning.

13

THE ACHIEVEMENT OF CELIBACY

What would happen if men remained loyal to the ideals of their youth?

—Ignazio Silone

If you had cut Andrew Pengilly to the core, you would have found him white clear through. He was a type of clergyman favored in pious fiction, yet he actually did exist.

—Sinclair Lewis

Classical literature about celibacy is fraught with presuppositions about the achievement of the ideal. The assumption that the ideal achieved is the ordinary state is the starting point of most presentations. The reality of this assumption is not so easily taken for granted by the serious practitioner of celibacy. "How is it possible?" was a question posed by many students in their last years of training for the priesthood. The majority of our informants are witness to a stretch for the ideal rather than a firm grasp on it.

This report has tried to avoid assumptions in favor of an accurate portrayal of the state of celibacy as it exists. We remain convinced that such a representation is more supportive of those who strive for the fulfillment of the ideal than are depictions that avoid the real difficulty in its attainment or that offer simple ascetic schemes for success.

I estimate that at any one time, 2 percent of vowed celibate clergy can be said to have *achieved* celibacy. By that I mean they have successfully negotiated each step of celibate development at the more or less appropriate stage and are characterologically so firmly established that their state is, for all intents and purposes, irreversible. These truly are the eunuchs of whom Christ spoke in the New Testament (Matt. 19:12). They made the decision for celibacy from the beginning. They surmounted the crisis of intimacy in favor of celibacy. They met the crisis of responsibility and resolved it by community. Through their permanent commitment they resolved the crisis of integrity (Balducelli, 1975, pp. 219–42).

Six to 8 percent of priests enjoy a refined condition in which the practice of celibacy is firmly established. This group can be said to have *consolidated* the practice of celibacy to such a degree that it approaches the ideal although their course of celibate practice has not been without its missteps, fumbling and, for some, serious reversals in the past.

This group represents those who clearly have the charism of celibacy. It also includes brave, courageous, and devoted men who say that, although they feel they lacked the charism, they have embraced—even if at times unenthusiastically—the discipline required by a church they love because of a work they truly feel is their own.

Even the reader who is accustomed to think only in terms of the ideal may be open to considering the realism of these figures if he or she recalls that these groups are added to the 40 percent estimated to be practicing celibacy.

The average person is not scandalized by the portrayal of clerics by Chaucer (1934 ed.) in *The Canterbury Tales*. The Monk has an aversion to the quiet and seclusion of his monastery, and he is consumed with his interest in material things, good food, and worldly pleasures. Chaucer's friar is frankly evil and cunning—using the confessions he hears as a ruse for financial profit. Another implication is clear—he is sexually familiar with another man's wife. The pardoner, that special envoy of Roman power, is drawn as an unattractive homosexual. The nun's priest betrays his vanity and vacuousness in his story of the cock and the fox. His yeoman exposes the canon's alchemy and duplicity.

None of these characters is unbelievable and each has his parallel in modern-day ministry. However, just as true to life is the Oxford cleric—the serious student who aspires to the ministry and church office—and the parson—the poor and devoted parish priest, of whom Chaucer says:

> This fine example to his flock he gave,
> That first he wrought and afterwards he taught;
> Out of the gospel then that text he caught,

And this figure he added thereunto—
That, if gold rust, what shall poor iron do?
For it the priest be foul, in whom we trust,
What wonder if a layman yield to lust?
And shame it is, if priest take thought for keep,
A shitty shepherd, shepherding clean sheep.
Well ought a priest example good to give,
By his own cleanness, how his flock should live. . . .
There is nowhere a better priest, I trowe.
He had no thirst for pomp or reverence,
Nor made himself a special, spiced conscience,
But Christ's own love, and His apostles' twelve,
He taught, but first he followed it himself. (pp. 16–17)

The question remains. Who are the men who succeed in celibacy? How do they approach the ideal of celibacy? What is involved in their success? Over the years, I have found them to be almost universally humble and very reticent about claiming "success" for themselves. Contrary to what might be expected, I found in them that a sense of humanness and flexibility of character were far more common than rigidity. Also remarkable was their general sense of good humor rather than the wizened anger and resentment some might expect among sexually deprived persons.

A discipline and purposefulness were evident in their lives in place of the harsh practices one imagines as ascetic. Judging from the men with whom I have spoken, I have come to agree with the Franciscan theologian, Fr. Martin Pable (1975), who recast celibate asceticism into a positive statement about life that refuses to be encapsulated by popular presuppositions. Humanness unbounded by sexuality, love beyond loneliness, sexual identity grounded in real generativity, and transcendent awareness and activity are all open to the celibate and are the reward of his discipline (pp. 266–76).

Often, the men who are the best examples of celibate achievement have the hardest time describing "how" they do it. They may mention some practice of prayer, or even a hobby or interest that has sustained them, or the example of others, but somehow celibacy becomes for them a natural consequence of who they are, what they love, and what they are devoted to.

Interviewing these men led me to look for the supports they established internally and used externally that fostered their development and made celibacy possible for them. What distinguished their lives from those of priests who did not practice or achieve celibacy? Was it merely a difference in character, opportunity, or motivation? Certainly, each of these factors does play a part.

ESSENTIAL ELEMENTS OF CELIBATE ACHIEVEMENT

Originally, I identified four elements that were universally present in all the celibate achievers I had interviewed up to that point—the early 1970s: *prayer, work, community,* and *service.* Men of diverse circumstances, from librarian to missionary, scholar to urban activist, all demonstrated a well-defined system of prayer that was an integral part of their day and existence. Each man was productive and, even if pressured by particular situations, was happily working. Each had a clear idea who he considered to be his community and family. The church was personalized—a group of specific people to whom he felt devoted. Finally, each man's life was one of meaningful service. Presuming generally good mental health and physical aptitude, I believe that it is within these four areas that the keys to understanding the successes and failures of celibate adjustment are to be found.

In order to expand my understanding of the system of celibacy within the Catholic priesthood, I began to examine early spiritual writers who mediated a celibate lifestyle for others. Surprisingly, little explicit reference to celibacy exists in the rules formulated by these writers. At first I was discouraged by the omission, only to realize later that the absence itself supported my own observations rather than dismissed them. I quite naturally turned first to the Rule of St. Benedict (1980 ed.), because it was the most familiar to me and because historically it occupied the premier place in propagating the celibate way of life within the monasteries and among the secular clergy as well. It did so especially through Popes Gregory I (590–604) and Gregory VII (1073–1085).

The Benedictine, Gregory I, called the Great, taking a page from his monastic training enforced celibacy in his diocese for all the clergy and even deposed offending prelates. His *Liber Regulae Pastoralis* (*Pastoral Care*) written in 591 (1950) proposed the norms of pastoral care to be provided by the secular clergy. For a thousand years, this book was traditionally handed to each bishop upon his consecration. The norms presumed a celibate ministry for bishops.

Gregory VII, who was also trained under the Rule of Benedict, as part of the Cluniac reforms re-asserted celibacy as a requirement for clergy in the Western church:

> With the object of rooting out moral abuses in the Church and freeing it from lay control, he first reinforced, at his Lenten synods of 1074 and 1075, his predecessors' decrees against clerical marriage and simony. This provoked great resistance, especially in France and Germany, but special legates armed with overriding powers were able to overcome most of it. (Kelly, 1986, p. 155)

His reform prepared the way for the declaration of universal celibacy for priests in the Latin Rite at the Second Lateran Council in 1139. After studying early monastic rules, I extrapolated six additional essential interrelated elements that support celibacy as a way of life. Later, I could identify them as addressing three main areas of human need: the spiritual, the psychological, and the physical. I hold that these elements are present in the lives and the codification of the experience of every celibate rule maker.

The most significant religious codifier in the past 500 years has been Ignatius of Loyola (1491–1556). His profound spiritual experience is transmitted in his *Spiritual Exercises* (1978), which do not necessarily demand a celibate response but rather form a solid base for the transforming religious experience or orientation indispensable to celibacy. Further, it is from this base that he founded his society, the Jesuits—a way of life that contains all the essential elements mentioned above.

To put the matter in a contemporary framework: These religious traditions endure and continue to draw men and become for some of them a structure within which they can successfully sublimate their sexual drives. This is because the structure demonstrates how one can supply sufficient bio-psychosocial reinforcement to make human development possible and religious aims realistically attainable. The 10 elements that support celibate achievement are: work, prayer, community, service, attention to physical needs, balance, security, order, learning, and beauty.

1. Work

"What are you going to do when you grow up?" "What are you going to be?" are the kinds of questions that plague and inspire the young. Everyone has to do something; everyone has to be someone. Everyone has to work. A man's celibacy is inextricably bound up with work. *Work* is mastery—the productive use of one's energies and time—rather than any particular task.

The variety of work that can absorb the vitality of a celibate is amazing. Many celibates, however, are not satisfied with the priestly functions of sacramental minister, teacher, or plant administrator. Their individual interests can range from the theoretical and ecclesiastical areas of their primary training to photography, fly-tying for fishing, or gardening. I include under this rubric of work some activities that others might number as hobbies because I have found that celibates seem to know the value of time and productivity and find these activities related to their work/mastery energies.

2. Prayer or Interiority

I have never interviewed a man who has attained celibacy without finding in him a rich and *active prayer* life. This is so intimately bound up with celibate practice and achievement that when making a clinical assessment of a priest I always inquire first about his prayer life. A celibate's prayer life reveals the capacity, quality, and nature of his relationships. He reveals his understanding of transcendent reality, other significant human beings, and his self-concept in his daily practice.

Most consistently I have found that men who achieve celibacy devote at least $1\frac{1}{2}$ to 2 hours daily to prayer. The danger in this comment is that it will be perceived in a mechanistic way or as some kind of litmus test of celibate practice. There are those who spend considerable time in prayer and yet are not celibate. There can also be periods of scanted prayer even in the observant; nevertheless, a regular and meaningful prayer life was invariably a component mentioned by those who had achieved celibacy.

There does not seem to be any shortcut or substitute for time devoted to interiority during which one is in touch with realities beyond self. Many of these men described how the time spent in prayer became a priority for them, increasingly so as they confronted challenges to their lives and ministries.

3. Community

The importance of interiority leads quite naturally to the third element found among men who have achieved celibacy: a sense of themselves as part of a *community*. They seemed to know the answer to the gospel question: "Who is my mother and brothers and sisters?" In some with a very highly developed religious personality, we found an awareness of the family of humanity, and in others an awareness of oneness with all creation.

Community consciousness in this group was not theoretical or ephemeral. The men had a deep sense of persons—people to whom they were committed and people on whom they could rely. One man, despite being incapacitated by physical injury and disgruntled and gruff with those around him, clearly manifested the depth of his allegiances. In short, strong object relationships with a wide variety of persons seem to support celibate achievement.

4. Service

All of these three elements—work, prayer, and community—are united in the awareness of *service* as a meaningful existence. In other words, all is "on account of the kingdom." Whatever the work, the prayer form, or the community for the particular celibate, the effort is beyond the self.

Some mentioned that it was not always easy to be conscious of this reality. They pointed out that at times they were tempted to be "served," to be the special one, receiving or directing the service of others. They were also aware that such a shift—so acceptable culturally—was a danger to the integrity that was essential to their rightful calling.

5. Physical Needs

Many adults think of sexual gratification as a primary physical need along with those of home, food, and clothing. They accordingly spend a good deal of their time and effort on taking care of these necessities. Many celibates are forced to spend more time than they would like on taking care of their *physical needs* even though they admit that they are generally well cared for. Some priests felt their living standard was reasonably commensurate with (or better than) that of the people they served.

We found a wide variety of adjustments in this area, not so much in the essentials as in the details left to taste and quality. Some priests savored exquisite food, whereas others seemed quite indifferent to its quality. Some also enjoyed an alcoholic drink, whereas others were abstinent. A few said they had had a problem with alcohol in the past, but no addictive alcoholic was represented in the group of celibate achievers. I believe that active alcoholism is incompatible with the achievement of celibacy.

Not all of the achievers were lean. Several portly gentlemen confessed that they had struggled with a weight problem all of their adult lives. Some said that food and drink remained the areas of their greatest and most persistent combat. I was left with the impression that this was a group of men who knew themselves, knew their limits and needs, and fulfilled them appropriately and with gentleness. One man stated it clearly, "If I don't assure myself enough legitimate pleasure, I'm liable to seek the illegitimate."

Indeed, there were some men for whom the word "ascetic" seemed the obvious description, but they lacked the rigidity of reaction formation that one often sees in the fanatic or youthful enthusiast.

There was a quiet discipline about their lives and I observed consistently an accompanying tolerance of others and their needs, along with an understanding of their different ways of meeting them.

I believe that for these priests the process of learning to assess their own limitations and needs and of finding appropriate ways to overcome and meet them not only bestowed self-satisfaction but also contributed to their appreciation of the human struggles of the people they loved and served. Several times I had the pleasure of observing the openness and uncritical acceptance these celibates demonstrated for the behaviors of deprived persons and underprivileged parishioners. The priests seemed to understand poverty as a condition rather than focusing on acts of thievery. They had empathy for the cold, unloving, and harsh environment that demoralizes people. They reverently served those others labeled as immoral, irresponsible, or perverted.

Several times I recalled Victor Hugo's bishop and his silver candlesticks in *Les Misérables*. I felt that a number of the men I interviewed really did look at the world's unfortunates with the attitude "There but for the grace of God go I."

6. Balance

Another element I identified not only in the codes of the spiritual writers but also in the lives of the celibate achievers was *balance*. It is the psychological and spiritual quality that probably ensures the flexibility necessary to juggle the inner and outer, daily and seasonal demands. Not only does balance moderate the physical instincts and their legitimate satisfaction, it also assures sufficient prayer and quiet to restore the consciousness of one's goals and values, and limits the tendency to overwork.

I met a few of these men fortuitously as they were struggling with a considerable amount of inner anguish. In some instances, a man needed a neutral and supportive arena in which to sort out his inner confusion. In every instance, I could describe the experience they were undergoing as "a dark night of the soul." The process outlined by St. John of the Cross is an apt comparison.

From these men, I learned to ask informants about their specific periods of special stress. All had undergone the periods I have described in the preceding chapter. Sometimes combined with one of those temporal stages of celibate development and sometimes independent of them, the periods were characterized as deep internal struggles, filled with confusion and disorganization.

Several of my psychiatric colleagues could understand these periods only in traditional psychiatric terms. However, several other colleagues, who had wide experience with religious, knew what I was talking about when I said that there was a "different" quality to the struggles of these men.

I found the concept of "positive disintegration" helpful in defining these periods. A psychiatrist outlined the process as follows: The developmental instinct destroys the existing structure of personality, but allows the possibility of reconstruction at a higher level.

Three phenomena make up the essence of the process.

1. The endeavor to *break* off the existing, more or less uniform structure which the individual sees as tiring, stereotyped, and repetitive, and which he begins to feel is restricting the possibility of his full growth and development.
2. The disruption of the existing structure of personality produces a *disintegration* of the previous internal unity. This is a preparatory period for a new, perhaps as yet fairly strange and poorly grounded value.
3. Clear *grounding* of the new value, with an appropriate change in the structure of personality and a recovery of lost unity— that is, the *unification* of the personality on a new and different level than the previously held one (Dabrowski, 1964, pp. 2–3).

This is closely aligned with the thinking of St. Augustine and other spiritual writers. I have found that many celibates must expand the bounds of traditional thinking in order to integrate their celibate practice with the reality of their lives. Meister Eckhart (1981 ed.) is a spiritual writer whose work helped me comprehend the progress toward inner balance that informants described. An abstract thinker,

Eckhart was interested in the sources of universal being and in the connection/relationship of an individual being in God and God in being. A celibate's sense of detachment and his understanding of sin as part of life and spiritual process are areas in which understanding aids the struggle to balance celibate values.

One priest related that his practice of celibacy was incomplete, split off, and uncommitted until he was 40 years old. At that time, he was hospitalized and nearly died. In his recuperative period, he experienced a self-evaluation the core of which was one whole night that he spent in his sickbed meditating on the Lord's Prayer. Not conscious of the passage of time that night, he has since maintained a sense of the meaning of every word and phrase in the prayer and he credits to that experience his enduring celibate practice and the balance he has kept in his life. He had not read the writings of St. Teresa of Avila prior to his illness; when he finally did study them, he was astonished that her description of the prayer of quiet echoed so accurately his own decisive spiritual encounter.

7. Security

Security is a universal human requisite for growth and for the development of adequate coping mechanisms. The sense of stability, enduring circumstances, rootedness in interpersonal relationships, with bonds to time, place, and practical realities, are fundamental to personal growth and development."

This is integral to the vow of celibacy. I have already quoted Gandhi's experience of celibacy before and after he took his vow. The prayer, work, community alliance, and service so essential to celibate practice are sealed by the internal commitment expressed in a vow. Commitment establishes inner security and allegiance manifest and concrete in relatedness.

Security is closely allied with the element of community mentioned earlier, but it is also an expansion of it. The core community, like the nuclear family, is the base from which one can reach out and to which one can retreat. Essential relationships confirm one's identity, but security allows one to refine and expand that identity.

The base for security is laid down in early childhood in attachment and separation—especially to and from the mother. The resolution of the process is strong object constancy and the solidification of basic identity and relationships. Early resolution then forms a model for problem solving and coping skills in the face of evolving challenges to one's security in new contexts.

There is an ebb and flow of problems and confrontations in any life cycle, and the celibate is not immune from life. His commitment provides him an overarching relatedness that sustains him through reversal and crisis. Many celibates have testified to this reality in their experience. Some felt that at some point they had been betrayed by those they believed they had had a right to count on, only to find a deeper sense of self in recovering from the betrayal.

Somewhere in struggle, the celibate discovers a mutuality of durability, one that can span his life cycle. Although mediated by others, its core is internal, secure in the commitment to the transcendent. Many men spoke of their test of "faith." When analyzed, it was not a test in the traditional sense of doubt about the existence of a God, but rather in the value and meaning of the relationship upon which they had built.

Security is both the father and the child of intimacy. As the product of intimacy, security is based on the interaction of trust, self-disclosure, and shared pleasure. In speaking with priests, I am struck by their frequent references to loneliness. Histories of those who have failed in the celibate practice are rife with accounts of backfired attempts at legitimate intimacy. Overeagerness, misplaced trust, and indiscriminate self-disclosure led to frustration or sexual acting out. Sometimes these attempts were followed by rejection of the celibate process.

All celibate achievers had someone to whom they felt they had confided the essence of themselves, and most had been the recipients of such disclosure. Above all, they all maintained self-respect and the respect of others—the great reinforcements to security. Security allows tolerance of differences and the expansion of one's circle of trusted friends, both clerical and lay.

Security also means the discovery of places to be oneself within the circle of relationships involving mutual interdependence. Difficult tasks for a celibate are to answer questions about intimacy. How can I remain celibate when recreating? How can I maintain a celibate identity that is not involved with official duties? A major hazard for a celibate is to know and live his celibate life separate and distinct from his profession of priest. Priesthood is not a cover under which to hide a secret life. How can I maintain celibate security and yet travel on an equal plane with those who are not celibate?

Many informants recounted how associations that began with the promise of mutual respect for the other's commitment ended with sexual compromise. Nonetheless, many of the achieved celibates had forged alliances and friendships that did fulfill the promises.

A wise priest told me that even the right work assignment could be most disruptive for the celibate with respect to establishing adult, secure, human relationships. As an example, he described the situations in which a young priest is assigned to a parish or to pastoral work. He enthusiastically throws all his energies into the task. Often when the young priest is transferred to a new situation, the young man invests less of his energies into relationships, anticipating a second additional set of painful separations. His inner security was not sufficiently developed to sustain the loss.

The danger is that with each new task the priest may become increasingly isolated in his official persona, and consequently, progressively more vulnerable to a sexual liaison. Celibate achievers, however, seemed to know what others did not—how to achieve relationships of broad mutual satisfaction and respect that enhanced their celibate identity without imposing on it clerical trappings.

I emphasize this element of security because it is the confirmation of the integrity of priests' celibate identity. These men functioned as celibates and felt they were consistently "themselves," regardless of circumstances or surroundings. They did not change into a different kind of private persona distinct from their public image and they did not split off their personal life from their stated values.

8. Order

I never met a celibate achiever who lacked a sense of *order* in his daily and seasonal life. I encountered a few whose system of order was so idiosyncratic that at first it appeared to be disorganization—or, in one case, chaos—but on further examination I discovered that such was not the case.

While achieving balance involves a spiritual quality regulating the inner competing needs, achieving order requires the regulation of time and energy, whether in prayer, work, study, hobbies, or recreation. If one cannot organize his time and energy, one is deprived of the satisfaction of mastery and achievement—those very elements of productivity, which make the sacrifice of sexual gratification possible.

Perhaps it is not surprising that celibates who have legislated for others arrange the days and the seasons of a celibate's life by way of systematizing an order of prayer. In houses of training, to some extent, and in some established religious communities, the official regimen of prayer sets aside specific times of day around which all other aspects of daily life, work, recreation, and meals fit.

The important lesson to be learned from this ordering is that the daily, seasonal, and annual cycles of prayer recitations measure out human life into *manageable segments* and make synchrony with vital rhythms possible. Celibacy that is insistently assailed by recurring human desire and buffeted by a hostile culture can only maintain itself a moment or a day or a season at a time. Order fosters productivity. Order is a conscious regulation of one's time and energies, which obviates unnecessary challenges to their values and intentions.

Ordering of work, hobbies, interests, associations, friendships, and prayer, is all part of the challenge for the celibate. Here, again, rigidity is less successful than is flexibility. One who can *reorganize* his life to meet changing demands is better equipped to maintain internal order than one who is wedded to an established routine that must be abandoned entirely in the face of new circumstances.

Several priests told me that they learned how to organize their lives only after a system on which they had previously relied failed. In most cases that system was externally ordered. Some of these men reminded me of the accounts of successful prisoners of war—men who, in solitary confinement, learned to segment and regulate their days, devising ways, even under severe deprivation, to find meaning and endurance by providing a makeshift structure to their lives.

9. Learning

Not all men who achieved celibacy were scholars, but the intellectually curious were over-represented in this group. I can say that this is a group of men who are interesting because they themselves were interested in many things and many people. A certain level of intellectual achievement was traditionally required for ministerial studies. Certainly, intelligence and successful celibate attainment are not correlative, but the love for learning and intellectual curiosity probably are. It is difficult to be a good celibate without continued learning. Many priests have told me that it is impossible. They rest their case on the need for both intelligent ministry and intellectual and spiritual growth—practical as well as theoretical.

One priest repeated the advice he had heard from a celibate whom he admired. "The only two things a priest needs are the Bible and the *New York Times*"—the timeless and the timely.

The denial of sexual pleasure by itself does not lead to intellectual achievement, but the dedication of one's life to the service of others does.

10. Beauty

There is a need for legitimate pleasure that takes the form of beauty in many celibates' lives. This is absolutely clear when celibates band together in stable communities. Even those confounded by the practice of celibacy can admire its artistic productions. A love for *beauty* seems to flow naturally from the conditions provided by community living. The order and balance in day-to-day existence, reverence for learning, and attention to simple human needs, form a psychological synergism easily demonstrable in religious history. Community gives rise to a number of expressions. For example, liturgical prayer led to its natural enhancement through psalmody and gesture. The practical necessity of providing permanent, stable housing allowed for architectural achievements. The task of copying manuscripts led to the art of embellishment and illumination. In short, it seems that the religious spirit cannot be indulged without a natural sublimation into beautiful as well as practical forms.

This is, of course, a derivative quality. However, learning and beauty are cultural achievements that inspire people to think about life and about values that are of immeasurable worth. Celibate achievers tend to be rather more culturally literate than not. Some had a deep love for music, others for art or drama. Some could translate their appreciation into their ministries; others could only use them for their own sustenance.

When I shared this observation with an eminent theologian, he pointed out to me that the first visual portrayal of Christ was in the form of Apollo, the god of beauty.

This then is the celibate structure that is manifest in the lives of celibate achievers. They created it and, in turn, they are created by it. The structure, rather than producing one kind of person, yields a wide variety of individuals. The refined aesthetes of profound gentleness as well as the rough-and-ready action-oriented are both represented. The quiet, unobtrusive and unassuming man as well as the much-noticed leader has likewise achieved celibacy. Some of these men said that they have always felt that they had a same-sex orientation, although they lacked experience. Others spoke at length about their periods of sexual stress and temptations toward women during the course of their celibate striving.

I have encouraged several informants to write autobiographies of their celibate/sexual achievement. Some just laughed in response, but none yet has accepted the challenge. The refusals are a loss to those who would like to understand and support the celibate ideal. They are also a great deficit in the propagation of the ideal and the education of those who are inspired to follow the celibate path. Having such limited written witness to what lived celibacy is like and how it is achieved by ordinary men makes it not only unattractive but also unbelievable.

WHO WILL FOLLOW?

Vocations to the priesthood have declined significantly in recent decades—many reports claim that legislated celibacy is a major stumbling block. The recurring question is who will follow the celibate path that is inextricably bound with religious life and, at least currently, with the Roman Catholic priesthood? I personally believe that the crisis is far deeper than that. At core, it is a spiritual dilemma of which sexuality and celibacy are important elements. Also at the vortex of the crisis are justice and the credibility of authority.

There have been official attempts to understand and renew the lagging spirit of the religious and priests in the United States. Reports indicate that there is serious concern about the life of celibates, but greater fear in addressing directly the questions that count. Pious generalities are reiterated without any original and careful analysis of the core conflicts presented. Authority and official teachings become the "saving" plank offered to a drowning people.

One problem with training young men for celibacy—and to be moral leaders in the area of human sexuality—is the enduring controversy between Augustinian thinking, which implies that all sexual pleasure is at least tinged with evil, and the view of sexuality as a part of good nature. What is the basis on which the church judges the *nature* of human sexuality? It is biblical? Is it traditional moral-social teaching? Is it set? Does the church have all the answers? Sex was the one topic not open for discussion at the second Vatican Council.

Cassian, writing from 420–426, was a celibate who preserved the wisdom of the early celibates of the desert and concluded from them that sexuality was woven into the fibers of our beings.

> When a thing exists in all persons without exception . . . we can only think that it must belong to the very substance of human nature, since the fall, as it were, "natural" to man . . . when a thing is found to be congenital . . . how can we fail to believe that it was implanted by the will of the Lord, not to injure us, but to help us. (Brown, 1988, p. 420)

"How do *you* do it?" is a fair question from any seminarian to his celibate professors or his bishop. It is an extremely difficult question to field, but unless more men who support celibacy as an important spiritual practice put their explicit example on the line, the practice will be doubted or become a hollow exercise. St. Augustine's *Confessions*, the first example of a real autobiography in Western literature, gave weight to his judgments about all sexuality precisely because of his personal and unstinting honesty.

Men will follow celibacy if they can find persons who have already done so with honesty and joy. Nothing is more powerful than example. Nothing exerts more authority than simple truth lived.

The problem of the selection of priests is not new. St. Paul lays it out well:

> A bishop must be irreproachable, married only once, of even temper, self-controlled, modest, and hospitable. He should be a good teacher. He must not be addicted to drink. He ought not to be contentious but, rather, gentle, a man of peace. Nor can he be someone who loves money. He must be a good manager of his own household, keeping his children under control without sacrificing his dignity; for if a man does not know how to manage his own house, how can he take care of the church of God? (I Tim. 3:2–5)

He wrote similarly on another occasion:

> As I instructed you, a presbyter must be irreproachable, married only once, the father of children who are believers and are known not to be wild and insubordinate. The bishop as God's steward must be blameless. He may not be self-willed or arrogant, a drunkard, a violent or greedy man. He should, on the contrary, be hospitable and a lover of goodness; steady, just, holy, and self-controlled. In his teaching he must hold fast to the authentic message, so that he will be able both to encourage men to follow sound doctrine and to refute those who contradict it. (Titus 1:5–9)

Some advocates of a married clergy will quickly point out Paul's presumption of such. This is beside the point here, which is the high moral standards required of any clergy. There is no lack of statement of ideals. There is, however, reticence to put oneself on the line, so to speak, in ways that people can hear and to which they can relate.

The crucial problem is that the church exacts high standards in theory without actually having enough effective means of supporting those who would subscribe to them. This is most certainly true of celibacy.

Many questions remain. How do spiritual leaders, whether celibate or married, integrate their sexuality with their ministries? What is the celibate/sexual capacity of a candidate? How are men helped through the various inevitable crises that face anyone in the *process of becoming* celibate? I hope that this book will aid those who are ferreting out the future leaders and educating them to deal directly, honestly, and intelligently with the areas of their prospects' sexuality and celibacy.

THE CRISIS OF ABUSE

What has come to be called the greatest crisis in the history of the American Catholic Church—the sexual abuse of minors—is really only the tip of the iceberg of unanswered questions about clerical celibacy and more importantly, about human sexuality generally. It is a symptom of the crisis to come. The door to the secret world has been opened. It can not be bolted shut again.

The questions raised about priests' sexual activity with minors are urgent because that behavior is criminal as well as noncelibate. Lay pressure, not moral leadership from bishops, brought this long-festering problem to public and ecclesiastical attention. But once the sexual activity of professed celibate clergy is questioned where is the line of inquiry to be drawn? Only at the criminal? What of masturbation? What of consensual relations between adults? What moral yardstick of celibate/sexual morality is to be used? What confidence can be placed in the public posture of bishops and priests? Once the church's reasoning about artificial birth control is discounted, what logic and moral compass becomes valid for married couples? Are unmarried young people really held to the same standard of chastity as priests? Are priests held only to the standard of the unmarried?

One thing is certain—none of the questions about the celibate/sexual agenda of the church can be settled behind closed doors and in secret. That world is no longer viable. Transparency and accountability manifested in dialogue is the only possible response to the current challenge to the Catholic Church.

Bernard Cardinal Law, around whom the abuse crisis centered in 2002, addressed the problem dramatically different after 10 months of exposure. The rules and standards of the secret world dictated his first responses, similar to that of all bishops and the pope. But in November he stood before his congregation, unprotected by his episcopal throne or pulpit and said, "No one is helped by keeping such things secret. No one is helped by keeping such things secret." My guess is that he said it twice with purpose, once for the victims of abuse and once for the church that tried so desperately to keep abuse—and so much else—secret.

The Secret World is being exposed and explored. It will be a better World.

EPILOGUE
DIMENSIONS OF THE CRISIS

The idea that defect, shadow, or other misfortune could ever cause the
church to stand in need of restoration or renewal is hereby condemned
as obviously absurd.

—Pope Gregory XVI, 1832

The real epilogue to this book is now playing out in the public forum. Grand juries are being empanelled to examine how bishops have handled sexual abuse by their priests. Reports so far have been devastating in their implications of complicity of bishops in the problem and coverup of abuse. District attorneys throughout the country are actively seeking indictments against priests who have abused minors. Victims of abuse are lining up to tell their stories, seek a hearing, and ask for redress from church officials.

Above all, people are clamoring for honesty—accountability, and transparency—from their leaders.

The process of investigation of the secret world of sex and celibacy within the church is at a beginning, not a conclusion. No one knows how long a resolution of the crisis will take. But the thrust is irrepressible. The forces for revelation and reform are inexorable. A number of issues are bound to come up for consideration. There are seven pillars of the crisis.

1. It has been irrefutably established that some priests and bishops abuse minors. Over 400 American priests resigned or were forced out of the priesthood in the year 2002 because of abusing minors. Hundreds of victims have spoken publicly about their abuse at the hands of priests. Some priests and former seminarians are revealing abusers

who are currently in positions of power. Unraveling the elements that give rise to and support that behavior naturally expands the focus of attention on the clerical system and related noncelibate practice. In what other ways are priests and bishops sexually active?

2. The church knows and has known for a long time a great deal about the sexual activity of its priests beyond the abuse of minors. It has looked the other way, tolerated, covered up, and simply lied about the broad spectrum of sexual activity of its priests, bound by the law but not the reality of celibacy. Cardinal Seper could say at the 1971 Synod of Bishops in Rome, "I am not at all optimistic that celibacy is in fact being observed." The desperation of the church defenses and the vehemence of its resistance to sexual reform in the church only highlight the need for truth and transformation. The official church structure is a bit like an alcoholic who hopes that just one last drink or binge will really make all the pain go away. It won't.

3. A *notably larger* proportion of the clergy has a homosexual orientation than is represented in the general population. This has always been the case and is due in part to natural sexual biodiversity and the high genetic correlation between homosexual orientation and the altruistic drive. By refusing to deal honestly with the reality of homosexuality in the clerical state (and in general), Catholic teaching fosters self-alienation of its clergy and encourages and enables identity confusion, sexual acting out, and moral duplicity.

4. The Catholic Church in the United States has not been able to monitor itself in regard to the abuse of minors. Committed Catholic lay people are assembling to demand accountability. Groups of victims/survivors (LINKUP, SNAP) have gained unprecedented power and acceptance. The VOICE OF THE FAITHFUL gained a significant following across the country in a matter of a few months. They are asking for financial openness and oversight of diocesan books. Trust in the hierarchy is at low ebb. The bishops collectively have set up a lay commission to oversee the church's protection of children and to examine the demographics and epidemiology of abuse within the priesthood. The support of the bishops is still in question. They may undermine the venture by underfunding, lack of cooperation, or by other means.

5. The homosocial system of the hierarchy that excludes women categorically from decision-making and power at the same time that

it glorifies exclusively the roles of virgin and mother creates a psychological structure that reinforces male psychosexual immaturity and malformation.

6. The Catholic moral teaching on sexuality is based on a patently false anthropology that renders magisterial pronouncement noncredible. ("Every sexual thought, word, desire, and action outside marriage is mortally sinful. Every sexual act within marriage not open to procreation is mortally sinful. In sexual matters there is no paucity of matter.") Catholics generally do not believe that masturbation is a mortal sin. Few accept the church's prohibition of birth control. Over fifty percent of Catholic college students believe that abortion should be legal. Seventy percent accept homosexual partnership as moral and sex between unmarried couples is generally acceptable if they have a commitment. The church is at a pre-Copernican stage of understanding regarding human sexuality. It is using scripture as a basis for explaining the science of human sexuality. That is no more valid that using the Bible to explain cosmology. The earth, in fact, is *still not* the center of the universe in spite of church pronouncements that such an opinion was anathema.

7. Clergy deprived of a moral doctrine in which they can believe are also deprived of moral guidance and leadership in their own lives and behavior. Sexually, priests and the hierarchy resort to denial, rationalization, and splitting in dealing with their own sexual behavior and with that of their colleagues. With the laity they often apply the full wrath of the "law" (including the threat of Hell). Only a thoroughgoing reform of the celibate/sexual structure of the church will really address the problem of sexual abuse. Sexual reform of the clergy is the most significant challenge that the priesthood has faced since the Protestant Reformation. Only a transformation similar to the 16th-century Reformation—a penetrating re-evaluation and reform of the celibate/sexual system—will meet the current sexual crisis.

REFERENCES

Abbott, E. (1999–2000). *A History of celibacy: From Athena to Elizabeth I, Leonardo da Vinci, Florence Nightingale, Gandhi, & Cher.* New York, NY: Scribner.

Abel, G. G. Screening Test for Pedophilia. (1994, March 1). *Criminal Justice and Behavior.* San Francisco: Sage, 115–31.

Abel, G. G., Becker, J. V., & Cunningham-Rathner, J. (1984). Complications, consent, and cognition in sex between children and adults. *International Journal of Law and Psychiatry,* 7, 89–103.

Abel, G. G., & Osborn, C. (1992, September). The paraphilias, the extent and nature of sexually deviant and criminal behavior. *Psychiatric Clinics of North America.* Vol. 15, No. 3.

Alexander, F. G., & Selesnick, Sheldon T. (1966). *The history of psychiatry: Psychiatric thought and practice from prehistoric times to the present.* New York: Harper & Row.

American Medical Association. (1997). *Code of medical ethics.* Washington, DC: American Medical Association.

American Psychiatric Association. (1994). *Diagnostic and statistical manual of mental disorders,* (4th ed.). Washington, DC: The American Psychiatric Association.

———. (1994, April). *Patient/therapist sexual conflict.* [Fact sheet]. Washington, DC.

———. (1995, December). *Pedophilia.* [Fact sheet]. Washington, DC.

Aries, Philippe, & Béjin, André. (1985). *Western sexuality: practice and precept in past and present times.* New York: Basil Blackwell.

Augustine, Father. (1988, October 1). Help and hope for the sex addict. *America.*

Baker, A. R. (2002, September 30). *Ordination and same sex attraction. America, The National Catholic Weekly.*

Balducelli, R. (1975). The decision for celibacy. *Theological Studies*, 36: 219–42.

Barbaro. (1969). *De Coelibatu, De Officio Legati.* Firenze: L. S. Olschki.

Barstow, A. L. (1982). *Married priests and the reformed papacy: The eleventh-century debates.* New York: E. Mellen Press.

Bartemeier, L. H. (1972). In P. E. Johnson (Ed.), *Healer of the mind: A psychiatrist's search for faith.* Nashville, TN: Abingdon, pp. 59–77.

Baum, G. (1974). Catholic homosexuals. *Commonweal*, 99: 479–82.

Bell, A. P., Weinberg, Martin S., & Hammersmith, S. K. (1981). *Sexual preference: Its development in men and women.* Bloomington, IN: Indiana University Press.

Bell, R. M. (1985). *Holy anorexia.* Chicago: University of Chicago Press.

Benedict, St. (1980). *The rule of St. Benedict.* T. Fry (Ed.). Collegeville, MN: The Liturgical Press.

Berlin, Fred S. (1986). Pedophilia: Diagnostic concepts, treatment, and ethical considerations. *American Journal of Forensic Psychiatry*, 7(1):13–30.

Berlin, F. S., & Coyle, G. S. (1981). Sexual deviation syndromes. *The Johns Hopkins Medical Journal*, 149: 119–25.

Bernanos, G. (1962). *Diary of a country priest.* New York: Macmillan.

Berry, J. (1985, June 7). Pedophilia. *National Catholic Reporter.*

———. (1987, February 27; March 7). Homosexuality. *National Catholic Reporter.*

———. (1989, September 16 and 17). *Washington Post.*

———. (1992). *Lead Us Not Into Temptation.* New York: Doubleday.

Bieber, I. (1962). *Homosexuality: A psychoanalytic study.* New York: Basic Books.

Bier, W. C. (1954). Practical requirements of a program for the psychological screening of candidates. *Review for Religious.* 13: 13–27.

———. (1960). Basic rationale of screening for religious vocations. *Selected papers from the American Catholic Psychological Association,* Bier & Schneider (Eds.). New York: Fordham University.

Bishops' Committee on Priestly Formation. (1981). *The program of priestly formation.* Washington, DC: National Conference of Catholic Bishops.

Bishops' Committee on Priestly Life and Ministry, National Conference of Catholic Bishops. (1985). *The health of American Catholic priests: A report and a study.* Washington, DC: United States Catholic Conference.

Black, M., & Rowley, H. (Eds.). (1975). *Peake's commentary on the Bible.* London: Thomas Nelson.

Blenkinsopp, J. (1968). *Celibacy, ministry, church: An enquiry into the possibility of reform in the present self-understanding of the Roman Catholic Church and its practice of ministry.* New York: Herder and Herder.

Blos, P. (1962). *On Adolescence.* Glencoe, IL: Free Press.

Bobrow, N. A., Money, J., & Lewis, V. G. (1971). Delayed puberty, eroticism, and sense of smell: A psychological study of hypogonadotropism, osmatic and anosmatic (Kallmann's syndrome). *Archives of Sexual Behavior*, 1:329–44.

Boston Globe, The, The investigative staff of the. (2002). *Betrayal: The crisis in the Catholic Church.* Boston: Little, Brown, and Company.

Boswell, J. (1980). *Christianity, social tolerance, and homosexuality: Gay people in Western Europe from the beginning of the Christian era to the fourteenth century.* Chicago: University of Chicago Press.

Boxer, S. (2000, July 22). Truth or lies? In sex survey, you never know. *New York Times.*

Brown, G. (1981). *The new celibacy.* New York: Ballantine.

Brown, P. (1988). *The body and society: Men, women and sexual renunciation in early Christianity.* New York: Columbia University Press.

Brown, R. F., Fitzmyer, J. A., & Murphy, R. E. (1968). *The Jerome biblical commentary, Vol. 2: The New Testament and topical articles.* Englewood Cliffs, NJ: Prentice Hall.

Burkett, E., & Bruni, F. A. (1993). *Gospel of shame: Child sexual abuse and the Catholic Church.* New York: Viking.

Buss, David M. (1994). *The Evolution of desire: Strategies of human mating.* New York, NY: Basic.

Bynum, C. W. (1982). *Jesus as mother: Studies in the spirituality of the high middle ages.* Berkeley, CA: University of California Press.

Canadian Conference of Catholic Bishops. (1992). *From pain to hope. Report of the Ad hoc committee on child sexual abuse.* Ottawa: Author.

Carnes, P. (1983). *Out of the shadows: Understanding sexual addiction.* Minneapolis, MN: CompCare.

Cass, V. C. (1985). Homosexual identity: A concept in need of definition. In J. P. DeCecco & M. G. Shively (Eds.), *Origins of sexuality and homosexuality.* New York: Harrington Park.

Chapman, J. D. (1984). Neuroendocrinologic developments in sexuality: Beta-endorphins in sexual phase disorders. *J. A. D. A.,* 84: 368–71.

Chaucer, G. (1934). *Canterbury tales.* (J. U. Nicolson, Trans.). Garden City, NY: Doubleday.

Cherfas, J., & Gribbin, J. (1984). *The Redundant male: Is sex irrelevant in the modern world?* London: The Bodley Head.

Chesterton, G. K. (1981). *The Penguin complete Father Brown.* New York: Penguin Books.

Child abuse. Pastoral and procedural guidelines. A report from the working party of Catholic Bishops' Conference of England and Wales on cases of sexual abuse of children involving priests, religious, and other church workers. (1994). London: Catholic Media Office.

Child sexual abuse: Framework for a Church response. Report of the Irish Catholic bishops' advisory committee on child sexual abuse by priests and religious. (1996). Dublin: Veritas Publications.

Chittister, J. D., & Marty, M. E. (1983). *Faith and ferment.* Minneapolis: Augsburg. p. 30.

Cholis, R, (1989). *Clerical celebacy in the East and West.* Herefordshire: .

Clark, K. (1982). *An experience of celibacy: Creative reflection on intimacy, loneliness, sexuality and commitment.* Notre Dame, IN: Ave Maria Press.

Clegg, P. (1996, May 14). Examining the roots of clergy abuse. Sacramento: *Sacramento Bee.*

Cochini, S. J., Christian. (1990). *The apostolic origins of priestly celibacy.* San Francisco: Ignatius.

Code of Canon Law. (1984). Washington, DC: Canon Law Society of America.

Coffin, E. (1977). *A refutation of M. Joseph Hall*. Ilkley, England: Scolar Press.

Colaianni, J. F. (Ed.). (1968). *Married priests and married nuns*. New York: McGraw-Hill.

Coldrey, B. M. (1997). *Religious life without integrity*. Unpublished manuscript. Como, West Australia.

Coleman, E. (1987). Assessment of sexual orientation. *Journal of Homosexuality*, 14: 9–24.

Comfort, A. (1972). *The Joy of Sex: A Gourmet Guide to Love Making*. New York: Simon and Schuster.

Cooney, J. (1984). *The American pope: The life and times of Francis Cardinal Spellman*. New York: Times Books.

CORPUS. (1988). *First national conference on a married priesthood*. Washington, DC: American University.

Cozby, P. C. (1973). Self-disclosure: A literature review. *Psychological Bulletin*, 79: 73–91.

Cozzens, D. (1998). *The Changing face of the Priesthood*. Collegeville, MN: The Liturgical Press.

Cozzens, D. (2002). *Sacred Silence: Denial and the crisis in the Church*. Collegeville, MN: The Liturgical Press.

Crosby, M. (1996). *The dysfunctional church*. South Bend, IN: The Ave Maria Press.

Cullmann, O. (1962). *Peter: Disciple, apostle, martyr: A historical and theological study* (2nd ed.). Philadelphia: Westminster.

Curran, C. E. (1986). *Faithful dissent*. Kansas City, MO: Sheed and Ward.

Curtis, H. (1979). *Biology* (3rd. ed.). New York: Worth.

D'Antonio, W., Davidson, J. D., Hoge, D. R. , & Meyer, K. (2001). *American Catholics: Gender, generation, and commitment*. Walnut Creek, CA: Alta-Mira Press, pp. 69–86.

Dabrowksi, K. (1964). *Positive disintegration*. Boston: Little, Brown.

Davis, H. J. (1938). *Moral and pastoral theology, Vol. 4*. New York: Sheed and Ward.

DeMause, L. (1974). *The history of childhood*. New York: Psychotherapy.

Duby, G. (1983). *The knight, the lady, and the priest: The making of modern marriage in medieval France*. New York: Random House.

Easwaran, E. (1972). *Gandhi, the man*. Berkeley, CA: Blue Mountain Center of Meditation.

Eckhart, M. (1981). *Meister Eckhart: The essential sermons, treatises, and defence*. (Edmund Colledge & Bernard McGinn, Trans.). New York: Paulist.

Homosexual love. (1983). [Editorial]. *Commonweal*, 110: 484–5.

Eisler, R. (1987). *The chalice and the blade: Our history, our future*. San Francisco: Harper and Row.

Erikson, E. (1969). *Gandhi's truth*. New York: Norton.

Fenichel, O. (1945). *Psychoanalytic theory of neurosis*. New York: Norton.

———. (1953). *Collected papers, first series*. New York: Norton.

———. (1954). *Collected papers, second series*. New York: Norton.

Finkelhor, D. (1979). *Sexually victimized children,* New York: Free Press.

Finkelhor, D., Hotaling, G. T., Lewis, F. T., et al. (1990). Sexual abuse in a national survey of adult men and women: Prevalence, characteristics and risk factors. *Child Abuse and Neglect*, 14, 19–28.

Foresi, P. M. (1969). *Celibacy put to the gospel test*. New York: New City.

Foriliti, J. (1984). *Early adolescents and their parents: Growing together*. Washington, DC: National Catholic Education Conference.

Fortune, M. M. (1989). *Is nothing sacred? When sex invades the pastoral relationship*. San Francisco: Harper and Row.

Foster, L. (1981). *Religion and sexuality: Three American communal experiments of the nineteenth century*. New York: Oxford University Press.

Foucault, M. (1972). *The archaeology of knowledge and the discourse on language*. New York: Harper and Row.

———. (1978). *The history of sexuality*. New York: Pantheon. 1:57.

Fox, R. L. (1987). *Pagans and Christians*. New York: Knopf.

Franklin, R. (1988, September 18). Accolades and ironies. Minneapolis *Star Tribune*.

Freedman, A. M., Kaplan, H. I., & Sadock, B. J. (1975). *Comprehensive textbook of psychiatry* (2nd ed.). Baltimore: Williams & Wilkins.

Freud, A. (1944). *The ego and the mechanisms of defense*. (Rev. ed.). New York: Grune and Stratton.

Freud, S. (1953a). *Complete psychological works, Vol. 7 (1901–1905)*. London: Hogarth.

———. (1953b). *Complete psychological works, Vol. 13 (1913–1914)*. London: Hogarth.

———. (1957). *Complete psychological works, Vol. 2 (1910)*. London: Hogarth.

———. (1958). *Complete psychological works, Vol. 12 (1911–1913)*. London: Hogarth.

———. (1961a). *Complete psychological works, Vol. 17 (1917–1919)*. London: Hogarth.

———. (1961b). *Complete psychological works, Vol. 21 (1927–1931)*. London: Hogarth.

———. (1963). *Complete psychological works, Vol. 16 (1916–1917)*. London: Hogarth.

———. (1966). Family romances. *Standard Edition, Vol 9*. London: Hogarth, pp. 235–41. (Originally published 1909.)

Friedan, B. (1967). *The feminine mystique*. New York: Dell.

Furlong, M. (1987, October 10). A sense of rejection. *The Tablet*.

Gabbard, G. O. (1994). *Psychotherapists who transgress sexual boundaries with patients*. Washington, DC: *Ethics Newsletter*, 10, The American Psychiatric Association.

Gaffney, G. R., & Berlin, F. S. (1984). Is there hypothalamic-pituitary-gonadal dysfunction in paedophilia? A pilot study. *British Journal of Psychiatry*, 145: 657–60.

Gaffney, G. R., Lurie, S. F., & Berlin, F. S. (1984). Is there a familial transmission of pedophilia? *Journal of Nervous and Mental Disease*, 172: 546–8.

Galdston, I. (Ed.). (1971). *The Interface between psychiatry and anthropology*. New York: Brunner/Mazel.

Gallagher, J. (1987). *Voices of strength and hope for a friend with AIDS*. Kansas City, MO: Sheed & Ward.

———. (1988). The sadness of being gay. In *The Business of Circumference*. Westminster, MD: Christian Classics, p. 248.

Gandhi, M. K. (1957). *An autobiography: The story of my experiments with truth*. (Mahadev Desai, Trans.). Boston: Beacon Press.

———. (1960). *All men are brothers*. Krishna Kripalani (Ed.). Ahmedabad: Navajivan.

Gay, P. (1986). *The bourgeois experience: Victoria to Freud. Vol. II: The tender passion*. New York: Oxford University Press.

———. (1988). *Freud: A life for our time*. New York: Norton.

Getty, M. A. (1982). *Collegeville Bible commentary: First Corinthians; Second Corinthians*. Collegeville, MN: Liturgical.

Gilbert, A. N. (1976). Buggery and the British Royal Navy 1700–61. *Journal of Social History*, 10: 72–6.

Goergen, D. (1974). *The sexual celibate*. New York: Seabury Press.

Goodich, M. (1979). *The unmentionable vice: Homosexuality in the later medieval period*. Santa Barbara, CA: Ross-Erikson.

Gould, S. J. (1985). *The flamingo's smile: Reflections in natural history*. New York: Norton.

Granfield, P. (1987). *The limits of the papacy*. New York: Crossroad.

Greeley, A. M. (1972). *The Catholic priest in the United States: Sociological investigations*. Washington, DC: United States Catholic Conference.

———. (1981). *Cardinal Sins*. New York: Warner.

———. (1982). *Thy Brother's Wife*. New York: Warner.

———. (1983a). *Ascent into Hell*. New York: Warner.

———. (1983b, March 26). Priests, celibacy and *The Thorn Birds*. *TV Guide* 31: 4–6.

Greene, G. (1946). *The power and the glory*. New York: Viking.

Gregory, Pope. (1950). *Pastoral care*. (Henry Davis, Trans.). Westminster, MD: Newman Press.

Groeschel, B. J. (1985). *The courage to be chaste*. New York: Paulist.

Groth, N. A. (1982). The incest offender. In S. Sgroi (Ed.), *Handbook of clinical intervention in child sexual abuse*. Lexington, MA: Lexington.

Groth, N. A., & Burgess, A. (1979). Sexual trauma in the life histories of rapists and child molesters. *Victimology: An International Journal*, 4: 10–16.

Gryson, R. (1970). *Les origines du célibat ecclésiastique du premier au septième siècle*. Gembloux: J. Duculot.

Haering, B. (1969). *Shalom: Peace: The sacrament of reconciliation*, (Rev. ed). New York: Image.

———. (1986). The Curran case. *Cross Currents*, Fall: 332–42.

Haering, B. (1996). *Priesthood imperiled*. Liguori, MO: Triumph.

Harkx, P. (1968). *The fathers on celibacy*. De Pere, WI: St. Norbert Abbey.

Harley, M. (1971). Some reflections on identity problems in prepuberty. In J. E. McDevitt & C. F. Settlage (Eds.), *Separation-individuation: Essays in honor of Margaret S. Mahler*. New York: International Universities Press, 11, pp. 385–403.

———. (1975). *Psychoanalysis of the prepubertal child*. Unpublished manuscript.

Hartmann, H. (1958). *Ego psychology and the problem of adaptation*. New York: International Universities Press.

———. (1964). *Essays on ego psychology*. New York: International Universities.

Hatcher, E. R. (1983, February 10). The Menninger Foundation. Personal communication to the author, based on a Letter to the Editor, *Community Times*. Reisterstown, MD. (Revised for inclusion, 1989.)

Hatterer, L. J. (1970). *Changing homosexuality in the male: Treatment for men troubled by homosexuality*. New York: McGraw-Hill.

Hawks, E. (1935). *William McGarvey and the open pulpit: An intimate history of a celibate movement in the Episcopal Church and of its collapse, 1870–1908*. Philadelphia: Dolphin.

Haywood, T., Kravitz, H., Wasyliw, O., Goldberg, J., & Cavanaugh, J. (1996). Psychological aspects of sexual functioning among clerical and non-cleric alleged sex offenders. *Child Abuse and Neglect*, 20, 527–36.

Hebert, Albert J. (1971). *Priestly Celibacy: Recurrent battle and lasting values*. Houston, TX: Lumen Christi.

Heid, S. (2000). *Celibacy in the early church: The beginnings of a discipline of obligatory continence for clerics in East and West*. San Francisco: Ignatius Press.

Hemrick, E., & Hoge, D. (1991). *A survey of priests ordained five to nine years*, Washington, DC: Seminary Department of the National Catholic Education Association.

Hemrick, E., & Wister, R. (1993). *Readiness for theological studies*. Washington, DC: Seminary Department of the National Catholic Education Association.

Hendrickson, P. (1983). *Seminary: A search*. New York: Summit.

Hermand, P. (1965). *The priest: Celibate or married*. Baltimore: Helicon.

Hoffman, R. J. (1985). Vices, gods, and virtues: Cosmology as a mediating factor in attitudes toward male homosexuality. In J. P. DeCecco & M. G. Shively (Eds.), *Origins of sexuality and homosexuality*. New York: Harrington Park.

Hoge, D. R. (2002). The first five years of the priesthood: A study of newly ordained Catholic priests. Collegeville, MN: The Liturgical.

———. (1987). *The future of Catholic leadership: Responses to the priest shortage*. Kansas City, MO: Sheed & Ward.

Hoge, D. R., Potvin, R. H., & Ferry, K. M. (1984). *Research on men's vocations to the priesthood and the religious life*. Washington, DC: United States Catholic Conference.

Hollender, M. H. (1983). The 51st landmark article. *Journal of the American Medical Association*, 250: 228–9.

Hopper, J. (1997). *Child abuse. Statistics, research and resources.* jim@jimhopper. com.

Howe, I. (1986). Introduction to *Bread and Wine* by Ignazio Silone. New York: Signet.

Hudson, W. W., & Ricketts, W. A. (1980). A strategy for the measurement of homophobia. *Journal of Homosexuality* 5: 357–72.

Ignatius, St. (1978). *The Spiritual Exercises* (David Fleming, Trans.). St. Louis, MO: The Institute of Jesuit Sources.

Illich, I. (1982). *Gender.* New York: Pantheon.

Instruction on respect for human life in its origin and on the dignity of procreation: Replies to Certain Questions of the Day. (1987, March 10). Vatican Paper.

Jaki, S. L. (1997). *Theology of priestly celibacy.* Front Royal, VA: Christendom.

Jenkins, P. (1996). *Pedophiles and priests.* New York: Oxford University Press.

Jenkins, R. (1984, October 6). Jerry Falwell's feelthy pictures. *Baltimore Sun* [Editorial].

Jichat, T. (1996, May 6). Priestly sex report not good journalism. Fort Lauderdale: *Sun Centinal.*

John Paul II, Pope. (1983, April 3). *Reporting on the Commission's Study of United States Seminaries.*

———. (1983, July 3). Letter to the bishops in the United States on religious orders. *Origins,* 13.

———. (1984, January 28). *The Baltimore Sun.*

———. (1989, February 22). Letter to the bishops of the United States of America.

———. (1997). *The theology of the body: Human love in the divine plan.* Boston: Pauline Books & Media.

John, Saint, of the Cross. (1973). *The collected works of St. John of the Cross* (Kieran Kavanaugh and Otilio Rodriguez, Trans.). Washington, DC: Institute of Carmelite Studies.

Jordan, M. D. (2000). *The silence of sodom: Homosexuality in modern Catholicism.* Chicago: The University of Chicago Press.

Jurgens, W. A. (1955). *The Priesthood: A translation of the* Peri Hierosynes *of St. John Chrysostom.* New York: Macmillan.

Kallmann, F. J., Schoenfeld, W. A., & Barrera, S. E. (1944). The genetic aspects of primary eunuchoidism. *American Journal of Mental Deficiency,* 48: 203–36.

Karpman, B. (1954). *The sexual offender and his offenses: Etiology, pathology, psychodynamics and treatment.* New York: Julian.

Katchadourian, H., M.D., & Lunde, D. T., M.D. (1980). *Fundamentals of human sexuality,* (3rd. ed.) New York: Holt, Rinehart.

Kauffman, C. J. (1988). Tradition and transformation in Catholic culture, New York: Macmillan.

Keane, P. (1975). Sexuality in the lives of celibates and virgins. *Review for Religious,* 34:2.

Keller, E. F. (1985). *Reflections on gender and science.* New Haven, CT: Yale University Press.

Kelly, J. N. D. (1986). *The Oxford dictionary of popes.* New York: Oxford University Press.

Kelly, T. (1988). *An indian journal (Visit to the Dalai Lama 1986).* The Scriptorium, Vol. 26. Collegeville, MN: St. John's Abbey.

Kennedy, E. C. (1981). *Father's Day.* Garden City, NY: Doubleday.

———. (1986, November 14). Asexuality. *National Catholic Reporter.*

———. (1988, April 23). The problem with no name. *America,* 158: 423–5.

————. (2001). *The unhealed wound: The Church and human sexuality.* New York: St. Martin's Press.

Kennedy, E. C., & Heckler, V. J. (1972). *The Catholic priest in the United States: Psychological investigations.* Washington, DC: United States Catholic Conference.

Keyser, L., & Keyser, B. (1984). *Hollywood and the Catholic Church: The image of Roman Catholicism in American movies.* Chicago: Loyola University Press.

Kinsey, A. C., Pomeroy, W. B., & Martin, C. E. (1948). *Sexual behavior in the human male.* Philadelphia: W. B. Saunders.

Kinsey, A. C., Pomeroy, W. B., Martin, C. E., & Gebhard, P. H. (1953). *Sexual behavior in the human female.* Philadelphia: W. B. Saunders.

Kleeman, J. A. A boy discovers his penis. (1965). *The Psychoanalytic Study of the Child,* 20: 239–66.

————. (1966). Genital discovery during a boy's second year: A follow-up. *The Psychoanalytic Study of the Child,* 21: 358–92.

Klein, F., Sepekoff, B., & Wolf, T. J. (1985). Sexual orientation: A multi-variable dynamic process. *Journal of Homosexuality,* 11: 35–49.

Knowles, D. (1970, July). *Canterbury Cathedral Chronicle,* 65.

Krafft-Ebing, R.V. *Psychopathia sexualis.* (1934). Brooklyn, NY: Physicians and Surgeons Book.

Kraft, W. F. (1979). *Sexual dimensions of the celibate life.* Kansas City, KS: Andrews and McMeel.

Kramer, H., & Sprenger, J. (1971). *Malleus maleficarum.* New York: Dover Publications.

Kuhn, T. S. (1962). *The Structure of scientific revolutions.* Chicago: University of Chicago Press.

Laghi, P. C. (1998). *Vocations to the priesthood.* Vatican City.

Landis, J. Experiences of 500 children with adult sexual deviants. *Psychiatric Quarterly Supplement,* 30: 91–109.

Langsley, D. G. (1980). Community psychiatry. In H. I. Kaplan, A. H. Freedman, & B. J. Sadock (Eds.), *Comprehensive textbook of psychiatry* (3rd ed.). Vol. 3. Baltimore: Williams and Wilkins, p. 2,860.

Lavallée, F. (1964). *Pourquoi le célibat du prêtre?* Lyon: Chronique Sociale de France.

Lea, H. C. (1884). *An historical sketch of sacerdotal celibacy* (2nd ed.). Boston: Houghton Mifflin.

Leishman, K. Heterosexuals and AIDS. (1987, February). *The Atlantic Monthly* 259: 39–48.

Lerner, H. G. (1986). *The dance of anger.* New York: Harper and Row.

Lewes, K. (1988). *The psychoanalytic theory of male homosexuality.* New York: Simon & Schuster.

Lewis, S. (1927). *Elmer Gantry.* New York: Harcourt, Brace.

Loughery, J. (1998). *The other side of silence: Men's lives and gay identities: A twentieth-century history.* New York: Holt.

Luhmann, F. J. (2002). *Call and response: Ordaining married men as Catholic priests.* Berryville, VA: Dialogue.

Luker, K. (1984). *Abortion and the politics of motherhood.* Berkeley, CA: University of California Press.

Mahler, M. S. (1979). Separation-individuation. In *Selected papers*. New York: Jason Aronson.

Mahler, M. S., Pine, F., & Bergman, A. (1975). *The psychological birth of the human infant: Symbiosis and individuation*. New York: Basic.

Males, J. L., Townsend, J. L., & Schneider, R. A. (1973). Hypogonadotropic hypogonadism with anosmia—Kallmann's syndrome: A disorder of olfactory and hypothalamic function. *Archives of Internal Medicine*, 131: 501–7.

Marcus, I. M., & Francis, J. J. (1975). *Masturbation from infancy to senescence*. New York: International Universities Press.

Marcus, S. (1973). *Father Coughlin: The tumultuous life of the priest of the Little Flower*. Boston: Little, Brown.

Marmor, J. (Ed.). (1965). *Sexual inversion: The multiple roots of homosexuality*. New York: Basic.

Marshall, D. S., & Suggs, R. C. (Eds.). (1971). *Human sexual behavior: Variations in the ethnographic spectrum*. New York: Basic.

Masters, W. H., & Johnson, V. E. (1966). *Human sexual response*. Boston: Little, Brown.

———. (1970). *Human sexual inadequacy*. Boston: Little, Brown.

———. (1979). *Homosexuality in perspective*. Boston: Little, Brown.

Masters, W. H., Johnson, V. E., & Kolodny, R. C. (1982). *Masters and Johnson on sex and human loving*. Boston: Little, Brown.

Maugham, W. Somerset. (1933). *"Rain" and other short stories*. London: Readers Library.

McAllister, R. J. (1986). *Living the vows: The emotional conflicts of celibate religious*. San Francisco: Harper & Row.

McAllister, R., & VanderVeldt, A. (1962). Psychiatric illness in hospitalized clergy: Alcoholism. *Quarterly Journal for the Study of Alcoholism*.

McAllister, R., & VanderVeldt, A. (1961). Factors in mental illness among hospitalized clergy. *Journal of Nervous and Mental Disease*.

McAllister, R., & VanderVeldt, A. (1965). Psychiatric illness in hospitalized Catholic religious. *American Journal of Psychiatry*.

McBrien, R. P. (1980). *Catholicism, Vol. 1*. Minneapolis: Winston.

———. (1987, June). Homosexuality & the priesthood: Questions we can't keep in the closet. *Commonweal*: 380–3.

———. (1994). *Catholicism*. San Francisco: HarperCollins.

McGovern, T. (1998). *Priestly celibacy today*. Chicago: Midwest Theological Forum.

McHugh, G. (1965). Ecclesiogenic neurosis linked to erroneous religious taboos. *Frontiers of Clinical Psychiatry*, Nutley, NJ: Roche Report.

McLaughlin, L. (1982). *The pill, John Rock, and the church: The biography of a revolution*. Boston: Little, Brown.

McMenamin, R. W. (1985). Clergy malpractice. *Case and comment*. 90: 3–6.

McNeill, J. J. (1976). *The church and the homosexual*. Kansas City, MO: Sheed, Andrews and McMeel.

———. (1987). Homosexuality: Challenging the church to grow. *The Christian Century*, March: 242–6.

Meiss, M., & Beatson, E. H. (1974). *The Belles heures of Jean, Duke of Berry*. New York: George Braniller.

Meissner, W. W. (1978). *The Paranoid Process.* New York: Jason Aronson, pp. 653–4.

Merton, T. (1997). *Learning to love: Exploring solitude and freedom.* New York: HarperCollins.

Miles, M. R. (1996). *Seeing and believing: Religion and values in the movies.* Boston, MA: Beacon.

Millenari, The. (2000). *Shroud of secrecy: The story of corruption within the Vatican.* Toronto, Ontario: Key Porter.

Miller, J. A. A song for the female finch. (1980). *Science News,* 117: 58–9.

Miller, J. A., et al. (1984, February 18). How to identify a future priest. *America.*

Miller, J. B. Women and power. (1982). In *Work in Progress.* Wellesley, MA: Stone Center for Developmental Services and Study, Wellesley College.

Modras, R. (1989). Father Coughlin and the Jews: A broadcast remembered. *America* 160(9):21; 9–222.

Mohr, J. W., Turner, R. E., & Jerry, M. B. (1964). *Pedophilia and exhibitionism.* Toronto: The University of Toronto Press.

Money, J. (1971). Clinical aspects of prenatal steroidal action on sexually dimorphic behavior. In C. H. Sawyer & R. A. Gorski (Eds.), *Steroid hormones and brain function.* Berkeley, CA: University of California Press, pp. 325–38.

———. (1984, February 24). Bisexuality and homosexuality. *Sexual Medicine Today.*

———. (1986). *Lovemaps: Clinical concepts of sexual/erotic health and pathology, paraphilia, and gender transposition in childhood, adolescence, and maturity.* New York: Irvington Publishers.

———. (1988). *Gay, straight, and in-between: The sexology of erotic orientation.* New York: Oxford University Press.

Money, J., & Ehrhardt, A. A. (1972). *Man and woman, boy and girl: The differentiation and dimorphism of gender identity from conception to maturity.* Baltimore: Johns Hopkins University Press.

Montini, G. B. (Pope Paul VI). (1963). *The priest.* Dublin: Helicon.

Moore, P. J. (1976, June 7). *Time.*

Moore, T. V. (1924). *Dynamic psychology: An introduction to modern psychological theory and practice* (2nd ed.). Philadelphia: Lippincott.

———. (1938). *Consciousness and the Nervous System.* Baltimore: Williams & Wilkins.

———. (1939). *Cognitive psychology.* Philadelphia: Lippincott.

———. (1936a). Insanity in priests and religious: I. The rate of insanity in priests and religious. *American Ecclesiastical Review,* 95, 485–98.

———. (1936b). Insanity in priests and religious: II. The detection of prepsychotics who apply for admission to the priesthood or religious communities. *The American Ecclesiastical Review,* 95, 601–13.

———. (1943). *Prayer.* Westminster, MD: Newman.

———. (1943a). *The nature and treatment of mental disorders.* New York: Grune and Stratton.

———. (1944). *Personal mental hygiene.* New York: Grune and Stratton.

————. (1948). *The driving forces of human nature and their adjustment: An introduction to the psychology and psychopathology of emotional behavior and volitional control.* New York: Grune and Stratton.

————. (1956). *The life of man with God.* New York: Harcourt Brace.

Mott, M. (1984). *The seven mountains of Thomas Merton.* Boston: Houghton Mifflin.

Murphy, P. I., & Arlington, R. Rene. (1985). *La popessa.* New York: Warner Books.

Myrick, F. (1974). Attitudinal differences between heterosexually and homosexually oriented males and between covert and overt male homosexuals. *Journal of Abnormal Psychology,* 83: 81–6.

Nash, J., & Hayes, F. (1965). The parental relationships of male homosexuals: Some theoretical issues and a pilot study. *Australian Journal of Psychology,* 17: 35–43.

National Catholic Reporter, (1976, April).

National Catholic Reporter. (1997, Sept. 5). Code to prevent abuse. Kansas City.

National Center for Health Statistics. (1983). *Health, United States.* Washington, DC: U.S. Government Printing Office.

National Conference of Catholic Bishops. (1982). *The Program of Priestly Formation,* (3rd ed.). Washington, DC: United States Catholic Conference.

————. (1983). *A Reflection guide on human sexuality and the Ordained Priesthood.* Washington, DC: United States Catholic Conference.

————. (1988, April 12). Partners in the mystery of redemption: A pastoral response to women's concerns for church and society, Washington, DC. *Origins,* 17(45):757–88.

————. (1995). *Walk in the light, Report of the Ad hoc committee on child sexual abuse.* Washington, DC: National Conference of Catholic Bishops.

Nickalls, J. L. (Ed.). (1985). *The Journal of George Fox,* (Rev. ed.). Philadelphia: Religious Society of Friends.

Nicoli, A., Jr. (1988). *The Harvard guide to psychiatry.* Cambridge, MA: Harvard University Press. (Originally published 1978.)

Niebuhr, G. (1989, April 15). Broken vows: When priests take lovers. *The Atlanta Journal.*

Nordeen, E. J., & Yahr, P. (1982). Hemispheric asymmetries in the behavioral and hormonal effects of sexually differentiating mammalian brain. *Science,* 218: 391.

Nugent, R. (1983). *A challenge to love: Gay and lesbian Catholics in the church.* New York: Crossroad.

O'Connor, E. (1961). *The edge of sadness.* Boston: Little, Brown.

Ostow, M. (Ed.). (1974). *Sexual deviation: Psychoanalytic insights.* New York: Quadrangle/ New York Times Book.

Otene, M. Celibacy in Africa. (1982). *Review for Religious,* 41(1): 14–21.

Ovesey, L. (1969). *Homosexuality and pseudohomosexuality.* New York: Science House.

Pable, M. W. (1975). Psychology and asceticism of celibacy. *Review for Religion,* 34:266–76.

Pagels, E. *Adam, Eve, and the serpent.* (1988). New York: Random House.

Peele, S., & Brodsky, A. (1975). *Love and Addiction.* New York: Signet.

Pfliegler, M. (1967). *Celibacy.* London: Sheed and Ward.

Plante, D. (1986). *The Catholic.* New York: Atheneum.

Plante, T. G. (1995). Catholic priests who sexually abuse minors: Why do we hear so much and know so little? *Pastoral Psychology, 44,* 505–10.

———. (1999). Bless me Father for I have sinned: Perspectives on sexual abuse committed by Roman Catholic priests. Westport, CT: Praeger.

Plante, T. G., Manual, G., & Bryant, C. (1996). Personality and cognitive functioning among hospitalized sexual offending roman Catholic priests. *Pastoral psychology, 45,* 129–39.

Priests who date: The third way. (1973, December 3). *Newsweek.*

Pruyser, P. W. The diagnostic process in pastoral care. In A. W. Richard Sipe & Clarence J. Rowe (Eds.). (1984). *Ministry and pastoral counseling* (2nd ed.). Collegeville, MN: Liturgical Press, pp. 103–16.

Quasten, J. (1950). *Patrology: Vol. 1. The Beginnings of Patristic Literature.* Westminster, MD: Newman, pp. 234–5.

———. (1953). *Patrology: Vol. 2. The ante-Nicene literature after Irenaeus.* Westminster, MD: The Newman, p. 205.

———. (1960). *Patrology: Vol. 3. The golden age of Greek patristic literature from the Council of Nicaea to the Council of Chalcedon.* Westminster, MD: Newman.

Raguin, Y. (1974). *Celibacy for our times* (M. H. Kennedy, Trans.). St. Meinrad, IN: Abbey.

Rahner, K. (Ed.). (1975). *The encyclopedia of theology.* New York: Seabury.

Redondi, P. (1987). *Galileo heretic.* Princeton, NJ: Princeton University Press.

Reid, W. H. (1988, April). *The Psychiatric Times.*

Reiss, I. (1986). *Journey into sexuality: An exploratory voyage.* New York: Prentice-Hall.

Report of the archdiocesan commission of inquiry into sexual abuse of children by members of the clergy. (1990). St. John's Newfoundland: Archdiocese of St. John.

Report of the Commission on Obscenity and Pornography. (1970). Washington, DC: U.S. Government Printing Office.

Reuben, D. (1969). *Everything you wanted to know about sex but were afraid to ask.* New York: D. McKay.

Rhinelander, D. Vatican ban sidesteps one procedure. *The New York Times.* (1987, March 21).

Ricoeur, P. (1964). Wonder, eroticism, and enigma. *Cross Currents,* 14(2):133–66.

Robinson, G. (1997, Sept 12). *TABLET.* London.

Rock, J. (1963). *The Time Has Come.* New York: Knopf.

Rodgers, J. E. (2001). *Sex: A natural history.* New York: Times Books.

Rosetti, S. (1995). The Mark of Cain. *America.*

———. (1997). *Painful Grace.* Collegeville, MN: The Liturgical Press.

Russell, D. (1983). Incidence and prevalence of intrafamilial and extrafamilial sexual abuse of female children. *Child Abuse and Neglect,* 7:133–46.

Russell, N. (1981). *The lives of the desert fathers.* Kalamazoo, MI: Cistercian.

Sacred Congregation for the Doctrine of the Faith (S.C.D.F.). (1976). *Declaration on certain questions concerning sexual ethics.* Washington, DC: U.S. Catholic Conference.

———. (1986). *Letter to the bishops of the Catholic Church on the pastoral care of homosexual persons.* Washington, DC: U.S. Catholic Conference.

Sanderson, M. H. B. (1986). *Cardinal of Scotland: David Beaton c. 1494–1546.* Edinburgh: John Donald.

Sarlin, C. N. Cultural and psychosexual development. (1975). In Irwin M. Marcus & John J. Francis (Eds.). *Masturbation from infancy to senescence.* New York: International Universities.

Schetky, D. H., & Green, A. H. (1988). *Child sexual abuse: A handbook for health care and legal professionals.* New York: Brunner/Mazel.

Schillebeeckx, E. (1968). *Celibacy.* New York: Sheed and Ward.

———. (1988). *The church with a human face.* New York: Crossroad.

Schnaper, N. (1970). The Talmud: Psychiatric relevancies in Hebrew tradition. In A. W. Richard Sipe *Hope: Psychiatry's commitment.* New York: Brunner/Mazel (Taylor & Francis).

———. (1984). Care of the critically ill and the dying. In A. W. R. Sipe & C. J. Rowe (Eds.). *Psychiatry, ministry and pastoral counseling,* (2nd ed.). Collegeville, MN: Liturgical Press.

Schuth, K. (1999). *Seminaries, theologates, and the future of church ministry: An analysis of trends and transitions.* Collegeville, MN: The Liturgical Press.

Seltzer, B., & Frazier, S. H. (1978). Organic mental disorders. In Armand M. Nicholi, Jr. (Ed.), *The Harvard guide to modern psychiatry.* Cambridge, MA: Harvard University Press, p. 308.

Sexton, S. (1997). *Celibacy as a form of perversion* (thesis): Sheffield, England: The University of Sheffield.

Shannon, J. P. (1998). *Reluctant dissenter: A Catholic bishop's journey of faith.* New York: The Crossroad Publishing Company.

Shea, W. M. (1986, November 7). The pope our brother. *Commonweal:* 586–90.

Silone, I. (1986). *Bread and wine.* New York: Signet.

Singer, I. (1984). *The nature of love. Vol. 1. Plato to Luther,* (2nd ed.). Chicago: University of Chicago Press.

Sipe, A. W. R. (1973). The sexuality of the apostles: An eisegetical exploration. Baltimore: Loyola College Lecture Series.

———. (1974). Memento mori: Memento vivere in the Rule of St. Benedict. *The American Benedictive Review,* 15(1), 96–107.

———. (1983). The psychological dimensions of the Rule of St. Benedict. *American Benedictine Review,* 34:4.

———. (1987). Sexual aspects of the human condition. In Paul W. Pruyser (Ed.). *Changing views of the human condition.* Macon, GA: Mercer University Press.

———. (1988). Outpatient response to sexual problems of Catholic religious. *Bulletin of the National Guild of Catholic Psychiatrists,* 32:42–57.

———. (1990). Pastoral care of religious. *Dictionary of pastoral care and counseling.* Nashville, TN: Abingdon.

———. (1990). *A Secret world: Sexuality and the search for celibacy.* New York: Brunner/Mazel (Taylor & Francis).

———. (1995). *Sex, priests and power—Anatomy of a crisis.* New York: Brunner/Mazel (Taylor & Francis).

———. (1996). *Celibacy. A way of loving, living and serving.* Ligouri, MO: Triumph.

———. (1998). Public and media responses to the Irish Catholic clergy sex scandal. In A. Schupe (Ed.). *Wolves among the fold.* New Brunswick, NJ: Rutgers University Press.

Smillie, W. G., & Kilbourne, E. D. (1962). *Preventive medicine and public health* (3rd ed.). New York: Macmillan, p. 205.

Sobo, E. J., Bell, S. (2001). *Celibacy, culture, and society: The anthropology of sexual abstinence.* Madison, WI: The University of Wisconsin Press.

Soble, A. (1986). *Pornography: Marxism, feminism, and the future of sexuality.* New Haven, CT: Yale University Press.

Socarides, C. W. (1968). *The overt homosexual.* New York: Grune & Stratton.

Spitz, R. A., & Wolf, K. M. (1949). Autoerotism: Some empirical findings and hypotheses on three of its manifestations in the first year of life. *The psychoanalytic study of the child*, 3(4): 85–120.

Stanford, P. (2000). *The legend of Pope Joan: In search of the truth.* New York: Berkley.

Steinmann, A., & Fox, D. J. (1974). *The male dilemma: How to survive the sexual revolution.* New York: Jason Aronson.

Sterba, R. (1968). *Introduction to the psychoanalytic theory of the libido* (3rd ed.). New York: Robert Brunner.

Stern, K. (1965). *The flight from woman.* New York: Farrar, Straus and Giroux.

Stewart, C. (1998). *Cassian the monk.* New York: Oxford University Press.

Stickler, A. M. Cardinal. (1995). The case of clerical celibacy: Its historical development & theological foundations. San Francisco: Ignatius.

Stoller, R. J. (1975). *Perversion: The erotic form of hatred.* Washington, DC: American Psychiatric.

———. (1979). *Sexual excitement: Dynamics of erotic life.* New York: Simon & Schuster.

———. (1985). *Presentations of gender.* New Haven, CT: Yale University Press.

Task Force on Gay/Lesbian Issues, San Francisco. (1986). *Homosexuality and social justice, reissued report.* San Francisco: Consultation on Homosexuality, Social Justice, and Roman Catholic Theology.

Taylor, J. (1996, April 28). Catholic bishops say sorry to Australian victim of child sex abuse. *International News.* Agence France Presse.

Teresa of Avila. (1964). *The Way of perfection* (E. Allison Peers, Trans.). New York: Image Books.

Tetlow, J. A. (1985). *Studies in the spirituality of Jesuits: A dialogue on the sexual maturing of celibates.* St. Louis, MO: American Assistancy Seminary on Jesuit Spirituality.

The Report of the Archdiocesan Commission of Inquiry into Sexual Abuse of Children by members of the clergy—A review of the literature. Vol. 2. (1990). St. Johns Newfoundland: Archdiocese of St. John.

Thomas, J. L. (1975). Review of the book *Sex and sin in the Catholic Church.* Englewood Cliffs, NJ: Prentice-Hall. In *National Catholic Reporter*, 12:11.

Thomas, J. L. (2000, January 30, 31; February 1). AIDS in the priesthood. *The Kansas City Star.*

Thomas, K. (1965). Ecclesiogenic neurosis linked to erroneous religious taboos. *Frontiers of Clinical Psychiatry.* Nutley, NJ: Roche Report.

Thompson, L. (1989, January 24). A new study of gay males supports the Kinsey report. *Washington Post.*

Tollison, C. D., & Adams, H. E. (1979). *Sexual disorders: Treatment, theory, and research.* New York: Gardner.

Traxler, M. E. (1979, October). *New directions for women.* Englewood, NJ: New Directions for Women.

Tripp, C. A. (1975). *The homosexual matrix.* New York: Signet.

Tuchman, B. (1978). *A distant mirror.* New York: Knopf.

Veyne, P. (1987). *A History of private life, Vol 1: From pagan Rome to Byzantium.* Cambridge, MA: Belknap.

Visser, J., Fr. (1976, May). *London Clergy Review.*

Von Bertalanffy, L. (1971). System, symbol and the image of man. In Iago Gladston (Ed.), *The interface between psychiatry and anthropology.* New York: Brunner/Mazel (Taylor & Francis).

Voobus, A. (1951). *Celibacy: A requirement for admission to baptism in the early Syrian Church.* Stockholm: Estonian Theological Society in Exile.

West, M. (1959). *Devil's Advocate.* London: Heinemann.

———. (1981). *The clowns of God.* New York: Bantam Books.

Wilkinson, E. K. (1994). *People, priests and pedophilia.* Makati, Metro Manila: International Research Foundation.

Williams, D. M. (1999). *Sensual celibacy: The sexy woman's guide to using abstinence for recharging your spirit, discovering your passions, achieving greater intimacy in your next relationship.* New York, NY: Fireside.

Williams, W. L. (1986). *The spirit and the flesh: Sexual diversity in American Indian culture.* Boston: Beacon.

Wills, G. (2000). *Papal sin: Structures of deceit.* New York: Doubleday, 122–149; 192–202.

Wilson, E. O. (1978). *On human nature.* Cambridge, MA: Harvard University Press.

Winnicott, D. W. (1965). *Family and individual development.* London: Tavistock.

———. (1971). *Playing and reality.* New York: Penguin.

Wittkower, E. D., & Dubreuil, G. (1971). Reflections on the interface between psychiatry and anthropology. In I. Galdston (Ed.), *The interface between psychiatry and anthropology.* New York: Brunner/Mazel (Taylor & Francis).

Wolter, D. L. (1992). *Sex and celibacy: Establishing balance in intimate relationships through temporary sexual abstinence.* Minneapolis, MN: Deaconess.

World of the desert fathers: Stories and sayings from the anonymous series of the Apophthegmata Patrum. (1986). Oxford: SLG.

Young-Bruehl, E. (1988). *Anna Freud: A biography.* New York: Summit.

Zilbergeld, B., & Ullman, J. (1978). *Male sexuality: A guide to sexual fulfillment.* New York: Bantam.

INDEX

341

in context of Catholic teachings about sex, 233
criminal charges for, 200, 206
denial in, 215–216
depersonalization in, 216–217
dimensions of crisis, 321–323
dismissals resulting from, 200, 205, 250, 321
double standard in, 208
financial accountability in, 23, 205–206, 224, 322
forgiving priest for, 255–256
frequency of, 52–53, 203–205, 227, 249–250, 321
  vs. general population or in other religious groups, 252, 255
historical perspective on, 199, 237
international scope of, 5, 237
legal ramifications of, 205–207, 236, 250
moral ramifications of, 207–208
physical force in, 214, 217
pornography and, 182
presumed safety and, 201, 212
prevention of, 225
  bishop roles in, 236–237
  ethical code in, 262–267
  overcoming denial in, 249–256
  screening in, 246–249
  secrecy system and, 245
priest personality and, 221, 254–255
priest psychological profile in, 228–229
by priest sexually abused as child, 210–212
psychological/pastoral ramifications of, 208–209
public awareness of, 5, 199–200, 204–205, 208, 223–224, 322
rationalization in, 214–215, 255
regression in, 217
sadism in, 214, 217
scandal avoidance in, 202, 207–208
secrecy about, 5, 200–202, 207–208, 222–224, 319–320, 322
sexual orientation and, 15–16, 52–53
sexually precocious minor in, 207
splitting in, 217–218
transferring clergy in, 15–16, 213
Vatican response to, 5, 200–201
victims of
  blaming of, 252–255
  consequences for, 218–220, 232, 254
  support groups for, 220, 322
Misérables, Les (Hugo), 309
Moore
  Paul, 148–149
  Thomas Verner, 246, 271
Moral corruption of church, 22–23, 208
  in priest abuse of minors, 235–237, 241–242
Mother
  Blessed Virgin Mary and, 84, 173
  church as, 85
  death of, 157–158
  in gender identity and sexual identity development, 174
  idealization of, 84, 173
  infant autoeroticism and, 58–59
  in latent homosexuality, 161–162
  priest devotion to, 173
  priest early relationships with, 273–275
  in transvestism, 187, 189
Mother dominance, among seminarians *vs.* general population, 83
Murder, of priests, 192–193

Narcissism, altruism in service of, 110
Narcissistic personality, 37
  adolescent masturbation and, 64
  homosexual behavior in, 166
  priest sexual behavior and, 109–110
    with minors, 221, 254–255
NASA study on social isolation, 155
National Conference of Catholic Bishops
  assumption of adherence to vows, 7
  on intrinsic nature of sexuality, 28
  on training for celibacy, 28–29
  on traits stronger in seminarians than general population, 83
Neurasthenia, 58
Neurosis, ecclesiogenic, 257
Nocturnal emissions, *see* Ejaculation, involuntary nocturnal
Nugent, Robert, 161
Nuns, *see also* Third way
  impregnated by priests, 117
  priest buddy relationships with, 116
  priest sexual abuse of, 218–220
  priest sexual relationships with, 92–93

Object relations, 58
Obligatory homosexuality, 155–156, 161
  immaturity in, 168
O'Connell, Anthony, 239
O'Connor, Edwin, 297
Oedipal, negative, 146–147
Opus Dei, 105
Order, sense of, in celibate achievement, 313–314
Ordination of women, 22
Origen, 62
Outsiders, priest sexual relationships with, 96–97, 125

Pable, Martin, 303
Parent, death of, 157–158, 282
Parishioners, priest sexual relationships with, 94–96
Pastoral Care (Liber Regulae Pastoralis Gregory I), 305
Pedophilia, *see also* Minors abused by priests
  adolescent *vs.* prepubertal child in, 203
  causes of, 210–212, 238–243, 255
  familial transmission of, 210
  fixated, 203
  genetic predisposition to, 229–230, 238
  guilt feelings in, 221–222
  medical definition of, 202
  moral corruption in, 235–237, 241–242, 253–254
  as prepubertal trauma, 276
  psychiatric observations in, 231–234, 253–254
  psychodynamics of, 230–231, 238–240
  recurrence of, 221–222
  regressive, 203, 217
  in seminary, 230, *see also* Seminary
  sexual orientation in, 24, 131, 202–203
  social situation and, 234–235, 240–241, 255
  treatment of, 220–223
Personality traits
  celibacy compatibility with, 37
  in celibate achievement, 303
  of priest pedophiles, 221
  stronger in seminarians than general population, 83
Peterson, Michael, 57
Pfeiffer, Sacha, 5

ABOUT THE AUTHOR

A.W. Richard Sipe has been on a mission to bring the problems surrounding clerical celibacy and sexuality to light since the publication of his groundbreaking books, *A Secret World* in 1990 and *Sex, Priests, and Power* in 1995. Spending 18 years in a Benedictine monastery with 11 of those years active in the priesthood, he was trained to deal with the mental health problems of Catholic priests and the religious. In tandem with his private practice of psychotherapy, teaching in major seminaries, and lecturing in a medical school, he conducted his 25-year ethnographic study of celibacy and sexuality in the priesthood. He has served as a consultant and expert witness on more than 150 cases of sexual abuse of minors by priests. Currently retired from his practice and living in California, he continues to write and lecture on clerical celibacy. His work with clerical sexuality has attracted worldwide attention. He has been interviewed in numerous publications including *Time, Newsweek, The New Yorker* and featured on hundreds of national and local radio programs. He is engaged with Sony pictures in preparing a film on clerical sexual abuse.